THIRD EDITION

THE
FEMALE
OFFENDER

To Ian Yonge Lind

To my sister, Laura White

THIRD EDITION

THE FEMALE OFFENDER

GIRLS, WOMEN, AND CRIME

EDITORS

MEDA CHESNEY-LIND • LISA PASKO

University of Hawaii at Manoa *University of Denver*

Los Angeles | London | New Delhi
Singapore | Washington DC

Los Angeles | London | New Delhi
Singapore | Washington DC

FOR INFORMATION:

SAGE Publications, Inc.
2455 Teller Road
Thousand Oaks, California 91320
E-mail: order@sagepub.com

SAGE Publications Ltd.
1 Oliver's Yard
55 City Road
London EC1Y 1SP
United Kingdom

SAGE Publications India Pvt. Ltd.
B 1/I 1 Mohan Cooperative Industrial Area
Mathura Road, New Delhi 110 044
India

SAGE Publications Asia-Pacific Pte. Ltd.
3 Church Street
#10-04 Samsung Hub
Singapore 049483

Acquisitions Editor: Jerry Westby
Editorial Assistant: Laura Cheung
Permissions Editor: Karen Ehrmann
Production Editor: Laureen Gleason
Copy Editor: Kim Husband
Typesetter: C&M Digitals (P) Ltd.
Proofreader: Theresa Kay
Indexer: Gloria Tierney
Cover Designer: Gail Buschman
Marketing Manager: Terra Schultz

Printed in the United States of America

Library of Congress Cataloging-in-Publication Data

Chesney-Lind, Meda.

The female offender: girls, women, and crime / Meda Chesney-Lind, Lisa Pasko. — 3rd ed.

p. cm.
Includes bibliographical references and index.

ISBN 978-1-4129-9669-3 (pbk.)

1. Female offenders—United States. 2. Female juvenile delinquents—United States. 3. Discrimination in criminal justice administration—United States. I. Pasko, Lisa. II. Title.

HV6046.C54 2013
364.3'740973—dc23   2011039710

This book is printed on acid-free paper.

SUSTAINABLE FORESTRY INITIATIVE

Certified Chain of Custody
Promoting Sustainable Forestry
www.sfiprogram.org
SFI-01268

SFI label applies to text stock

12 13 14 15 16 10 9 8 7 6 5 4 3 2 1

BRIEF CONTENTS

DETAILED CONTENTS

PREFACE

W hat is clear to scholars and practitioners of criminal justice is that the female offender has long been ignored. Indeed, until the 1970s, serious discussion about the gendered nature of offending was absent from most criminological research and from correctional programming and policies. If girls and women were considered at all, their offenses were often trivialized or they were portrayed in highly heterosexist ways. The gendered nature of abuse and victimization that impacts girls' and women's crime and affects their pathways to court and correctional involvement was also largely overlooked or misunderstood by the system and by researchers.

By keeping the female offender as the central focus, this book removes the shroud of invisibility from girls' and women's offending, their victimization histories, and their experiences with court and corrections. As in previous editions of this book, this third edition explains the historical and contemporary experiences of girls, women, and crime. It interrogates the complexities of current issues and offers critical examination of recent reports that girls and women are becoming more like male offenders in the criminal justice system.

In addition to updated statistical data and literature on risk behaviors, arrests, sentencing, and incarceration, new to this edition is the greater discussion of several key areas, such as the increases in girls' arrests for assault over the past decade, the impact of sexual abuse and survival sex on girls' and women's court involvement, the criminalization of sexual minority girls in the youth correctional system, the growth of the female drug offender population, the increase in the number of executions of women, and the struggle to develop gender-responsive programming and stronger advocacy efforts in order to improve the lives of offending girls and women in our communities.

Also new to the third edition is Chapter 7, authored by Janet T. Davidson, titled "Female Offenders, Community Supervision, and Evidence-Based Practices." Using her recent study of men and women on parole, this chapter discusses the growth in the female offender community correctional population and examines the efficacy of gender-neutral risk-assessment tools and other supervision practices used to monitor female parolees and probationers. Should the system of community corrections be gender blind or gender responsive? Can evidence-based risk-assessment tools and supervision techniques effectively use a "one size fits all" method? Data for this chapter include both qualitative (in-depth interviews with male and female parolees) and quantitative data (recidivism and risk-assessment information) in order to demonstrate the gendered needs female offenders have and the gendered risks they navigate as they try to successfully complete parole. National data are also used to highlight gender differences.

ACKNOWLEDGMENTS

———•◆•———

This book, like its second edition, took too long; fortunately, this round there are two of us to share the blame, which is only one of many reasons to collaborate. Also long is the list of folks who have made us think about things, helped us with ideas, and basically kept us honest.

For Meda—I once again have to thank my colleagues in the Department of Women's Studies and the Department of Sociology at the University of Hawaii at Manoa for their support. The freedom to write and think as I do comes from having a great workplace—one that celebrates rather than condemns work on girls and women. Special thanks this round goes to Brian Bilsky, Dick Dubanoski, Kathy Ferguson, Konia Freitas, Tonima Hadi, Susan Hippensteele, Katherine Irwin, David Johnson, and Mire Koikari for their encouragement and enthusiasm for my work over the years.

For Lisa—I would also like to add such thanks to friends, family, and colleagues who have continuously given me emotional support and always offered avid interest in this research. To name a few, my parents, Jean and Eugene Pasko, and my sister, Laura White, as well as Christopher Bondy, Marilyn Brown, Paul Colomy, Janet Davidson, Moira Denike, Felix Dover, Hava Gordon, Stephanie Hedrick, Terri Hurst, Michael Kohan, Nancy Marker, Lisa Martinez, Dave Mayeda, JD McWilliams, Don Orban, Andrew Ovenden, Laura Padden, Scott Phillips, Stephen Scheele, Tina Slivka, and Rick Vonderhaar.

Both of us are fortunate in our respective communities. Hawaii is such a rich and wonderful social environment within which to work and live. Close association with the Office of Youth Services and the many social service and public agencies with whom they work has greatly enriched our lives and work. Bernie Campbell, David Del Rosario, Rodney Goo, Carl Imakyure, Cheryl Johnson, Dee Dee Letts, Bert Matsuoka, David Nakada, Bob Nakata,

Tony Pfaltzgraff, and Suzanne Toguchi have kept us in touch with the youth of Hawaii and their issues. Marcy Brown, Jo DesMarets, Louise Robinson, Martha Torney, and Marian Tsuji and have given us much-needed help in understanding the issues for adult women offenders. All of these folks have kept us in the community and closer to the reality we want and need to write about. Likewise, Colorado is also a wonderfully cooperative environment in which to conduct applied research. Many thanks to the Division of Criminal Justice (with special thanks to Michele Lovejoy), Colorado Juvenile Justice and Delinquency Prevention Council, Colorado Coalition for Girls, Colorado Juvenile Defender Coalition, Girls Inc. of Metro Denver, and Colorado Springs Women's Resource Agency for their ongoing support of girl-centered justice issues.

No work of this scope, though, could have been considered without an equally rich national and international community of scholars with whom we shared ideas, expressed frustration, and plotted strategies. Many of these folks are scholar/activists, so their work is enriched by their commitment to seek not only the truth but also social justice. We extend deep thanks here to Christine Alder, Joanne Belknap, Barbara Bloom, Lee Bowker, Kathy Daly, Mona Danner, Walter Dekeseredy, Mickey Eliason, Kim English, Karlene Faith, Laura Fishman, John Hagedorn, Ron Huff, Tracy Huling, Russ Immarigeon, Nikki Jones, Karen Joe Laidler, Vera Lopez, Dan Macallair, Mike Males, Marc Mauer, Merry Morash, Barbara Owen, Ken Polk, Nicky Rafter, Robin Robinson, Vinnie Schiraldi, Marty Schwartz, Francine Sherman, Andrea Shorter, Brenda Smith, and last but certainly not least, Randy Shelden.

Nationally and internationally, practitioner/scholars have insisted that they be listened to as well—to understand how girls and women they work with in their communities live. Here we must thank Ilene Bergsman, Kimberly Bolding, Carol Bowar, Alethea Camp, Ellen Clarke, Sue Davis, Elaine DeConstanzo, Jane Higgins, Elaine Lord, Judy Mayer, Ann McDiarmid, Andie Moss, C'ana Petrick, and Paula Schaefer for keeping this work in touch with their reality. Also, wonderful journalists who care about girls and women have worked with me to publicize their situation while also doing important muck-raking work that criminologists should have done and would have in better days. Special thanks here to Gary Craig, Adrian Le Blanc, Elizabeth Mehren, Marie Ragghianti, Nina Siegal, and Kitsie Watterson.

Most important, our heartfelt thanks to the girls and women who found themselves in the criminal justice system for having the courage to speak the truth in the face of extraordinary pain. Many of these girls and women must remain anonymous, but fortunately not all. Thanks, most of all, to Linda Nunes for her friendship after so many years, and for giving the hope that women can make it through such systems and survive with integrity. Thanks also to Dale Gilmartin for her help with the girls' issue and her courage to write about her own experience, and to Michelle Alvey for her strength, courage, and trust. We hope that we've done justice to your insights and your experiences.

Finally, thanks to Jerry Westby for never giving up hope that this book would appear. Thanks also to Erim Sarbuland for the final push over the top.

—*Meda Chesney-Lind and Lisa Pasko*

ONE

INTRODUCTION

———•◆•———

Myself (by J., 2010)

I say I love you

But I barely love myself

I say I hate you

But I only hate myself

I say I miss my child

But I barely miss myself

I say I care about you

But I barely care about myself

I'm not saying I don't love you

I just don't love myself

I hate me. I hate my family

So I could try to love you

I want to love you forever through

thick and thin

Till death do us part.

But I have to learn to love myself first.

You say you're going to love me. But

how long will your love last?

I miss loving myself and having

myself.

I want to love myself, and cherish

myself

But where am I to go when I have just

myself.

—resident on Girls' Unit,
Waxter Children's Center in Laurel, Maryland[1]

Shirley Chisholm, the first African American woman elected to Congress, wisely observed, "The emotional, sexual, and psychological stereotyping of females begins when the doctor says, 'It's a girl'" (Hoard, 1973). This was both an important observation and a national call for a clearer focus on girls' lives and girls' problems. More recently, there has been a spate of books on problems that one might argue are unique to girls, largely focused on body issues and popular culture (see Harris, 2004; Hesse-Biber, 2007; Lamb & Brown, 2009). Why the need for a separate discussion of girls' problems? Somehow, in all the concern about the situation of women and women's issues during the second wave of feminism, the girls were forgotten.

Forgetting about girls is easy for adult women to do. After all, because the problems confronting adult women in the workplace and at home are so staggering (sexual harassment, salary inequity, and domestic violence, to name a few), it is difficult to spare energy to consider how their own childhoods shaped who they became and what choices they ultimately faced. Such lack of concern was particularly clear when reviewing the paucity of information on the lives of economically and politically marginalized girls of today's underclass. Coming into the 21st century, this lack of information has facilitated a spate of

---

[1] Reprinted with permission from Kumar (2010, p. 5).

mean-spirited initiatives to control the lives (and especially the sexuality and morality) of young girls, most notably African American and Hispanic girls, who are construed as welfare cheats and violent, drug-addicted gang members (Lopez, Chesney-Lind, & Foley, 2011; Males, 1994; Nichols & Good, 2004).

Consider the recent and racially different depictions of girls' violence and aggression and the media's fascination with "girls gone wild." As this book will document, when dramatic pictures of girls of color carrying guns, committing violent crimes, and wearing bandannas suddenly appeared in the popular media, there were very few careful studies to refute the vivid images. Additionally and without much critical thought, the current attention on "reviving Ophelias" and white girls' "mean girl" associations and deployment of violence also contribute to a characterization of girlhood as riddled with aggression, ferocity, and intragender victimizations (Chesney-Lind & Irwin, 2008). Why? Why this absence of critical thinking about girls, violence, and crime? Criminology has long suffered from what Jessie Bernard has called the "stag effect" (Bernard, 1964, as cited in Smith, 1992, p. 218). Criminology has attracted male (and some female) scholars who want to study and understand outlaw men, hoping perhaps that some of the romance and fascination of this role will rub off. As a result, among the disciplines, criminology is almost quintessentially male.

In recent times, feminist criminology has challenged the overall masculinist nature of criminology by pointing out two important conclusions. First, women's and girls' crime was virtually overlooked, and female victimization was ignored, minimized, or trivialized. Women and girls existed only in their peripheral existence to the center of study—the male world. Second, whereas historical theorizing in criminology was based on male delinquency and crime, these theories gave little awareness to the importance of gender—the network of behaviors and identities associated with the terms *masculinity* and *femininity*— that is socially constructed from relations of dominance, power, and inequality between men and women (Belknap, 2007; Chesney-Lind & Shelden, 2004; Daly & Chesney-Lind, 1988). Feminist criminology demonstrates how gender matters, not only in terms of one's trajectory into crime but also in terms of how the criminal justice system responds to the offenders under its authority.

Because of the interaction between the stag effect and the relative absence of criminological interest in gender theorizing and girls' issues, this book will show that the study of "delinquency" has long excluded girls' behavior from theory and research. To some extent, adult women offenders have also been ignored because it seemed clear that women committed less criminal behavior. The one exception to this generalization is prostitution, which probably came in for some scrutiny because the study of sexuality became both academically fashionable and easily marketed in the 1970s (Winick & Kinsie, 1971). But aside from a few titillating books on prostitution, the silence about girl and women offenders was more or less absolute for most of criminology's history. Such a situation, as this book will document, has hidden key information from public view and allowed major shifts in the treatment of women and girls—many on the economic margin—to occur without formidable public discussion and debate. Girls and women do get arrested, tried, and sentenced to prison. In fact, there have been major changes in the way that the United States has handled girls' and women's crime in recent decades that do not necessarily bode well for the girls and women who enter the criminal justice system.

First, for all that they are ignored, girls should no longer be an after-thought in the delinquency equation. In fact, girls remain slightly more than 30% of juvenile arrests in the year 2009 (Federal Bureau of Investigation [FBI], 2010a). Despite the fact that girls are nearly a third of those brought into the juvenile justice system, they have rarely claimed anywhere near that share of public attention or resources. As an example, the Office of Juvenile Justice and Delinquency Prevention (OJJDP) Girls Study Group recently completed a nationwide review of 61 girls' delinquency programs and found that many programs did not complete evaluations and that no program could be rated as effective. Indeed, by the end of their review, most of the programs had lost funding and were no longer in existence (Zahn, 2009). Although the last 15 years have seen a growth in gender-responsive programming as well as national and state conferences gathered to address women offenders' issues, the "get tough on crime" initiatives, particularly for drug offenses, and push for incarceration continue to adversely affect women and girls. In the area of women's crime and punishment, a disturbing reality persists: In 1980, there were about 12,000 women in prison; by 2000, there were more than 85,000; and by 2009, there were 113,000—a nine-fold increase in less than 30 years (Bureau of Justice Statistics, 2001, 2010a; Maquire & Pastore, 1994, p. 600). Moreover, this imprisonment rate for women continues to grow. In 1990, the incarceration rate for female offenders was 31 out of 100,000 female residents; by 2009, it was 68 out of 100,000 (Bureau of Justice Statistics, 2010b). Currently, more than 1.25 million women are under some kind of criminal justice supervision (Bureau of Justice Statistics, 2010c).

But why, you might ask, should "normal" people be concerned about the lives of girls and women who become involved with the criminal justice system and end up in prison? What do these people have to do with normal citizens and their daily lives? There are a couple of ways to answer that question. First and most important, these girls and women are not that different from normal people. Gibbons (1983), for example, points out that the majority of those in the criminal justice system are actually "ordinary individuals who, for the most part, engage in sporadic and unskilled crimes" (p. 203). As we shall see, this is especially true of the girls and women who are the focus of this book.

The role played by social control agencies—the police, the courts, the prisons—in labeling and shaping the "crime problem" is frequently underestimated. We also often overlook the important role the concept of criminal as "outsider" plays in the maintenance of the existing social order (Becker, 1963; Schur, 1984). Clearly, harsh public punishment of a few "fallen" girls and women as witches and whores has always been integral to enforcement of the boundaries of the "good" girls' and women's place in patriarchal society. Anyone seriously interested in examining women's crime or the subjugation of women, then, must carefully consider the role of the contemporary criminal justice system in the maintenance of modern patriarchy.

Another question to ponder, particularly as we begin to explore the experiences of women and girls in the criminal justice system, is why crime, particularly violent crime, is almost exclusively a male preserve, and why sexual crime and its buffer charges (such as being a juvenile "runaway" or an adult prostitute) are found so exclusively in the female realm.

As this book will demonstrate, the women whose lives are changed by these labels are often the victims of what might be called "multiple marginality" (Bloom, Owen, & Covington, 2003; Vigil, 1995) in that their gender, race, and class have placed them at the economic periphery of society. Understanding the lives and choices of girls and women who find themselves in the criminal justice system also requires a broader understanding of the contexts within which their "criminal" behavior is lodged. There are important links between girls' problems and women's crime—links that are often obscured by approaches that consider "delinquency" and "crime" to be separate and discrete topics.

Recent research, for example, on the backgrounds of adult female offenders reveals the importance of viewing them as people with life histories. A few facts about the lives of adult women in U.S. prisons make this point very powerfully. Female offenders are three times more likely than their male counterparts to have a history of abuse, with more than two-thirds of these women reporting the assault happened before they were 18 (Bloom et al., 2003; National Symposium on Female Offenders, 2000). Moreover, one-third of women in state prisons and one-quarter of those in jails report being raped at some point in their lives (Bloom et al., 2003). Other studies have shown that nearly one in five of these women inmates had spent time in the foster care system, that well over half (58%) grew up in homes without both parents present, and the adults abused alcohol and drugs in many of these homes (34%; Snell & Morton, 1994).

Research on the childhoods of adult women offenders reveals how the powerful and serious problems of childhood and adolescent victimization dramatically circumscribe girls' choices. In a number of instances, these same problems set the stage for their entry into youth homelessness, unemployment, drug use, survival sex (and sometimes prostitution), and, ultimately, other more serious criminal acts.

Acts that come to be labeled as delinquent or criminal, as this book will document, are like all other social behaviors—they take place in a world where gender still shapes the lives of young people in very powerful ways. This means that gender matters in girls' lives and that the way gender works varies by the community and the culture into which the girl is born. As we shall see, the choices of women and girls on the margin place them in situations in which they are likely to be swept up into the criminal justice system. Likewise, responses to girls' and women's offending must be placed within the social context of a world that is not fair to women, people of color, or those with low incomes. Because criminology has long been sensitive to the role played by class in crime, it is the introduction of gender and race that now poses new challenges for the field in its attempts to understand women's and men's crime.

The challenge in this book is to keep the criminological focus on the fact that girls and women of different cultures and races live in different situations and, as a result, face different choices than their white counterparts. This also means that in addition to the burdens they shoulder because of their gender (living with sexism), they must shoulder the burdens of racism. Because racism also tends to bring discrimination and poverty, the emphasis on class should not be lost, but it cannot be the only lens through which delinquency and crime are understood (as has historically been the case). Finally, though, the focus on race or culture (difference) should not lead to a "politics of difference" that stresses divisions among women to the exclusion of the commonalities of their gender or class. Ultimately, an overemphasis on difference (or race or culture), although appearing to be race sensitive, can actually excuse white women's silence about issues that affect their nonwhite counterparts (Barry, 1996).

Whatever the reason, there has certainly been no national outcry about the soaring rates of women's imprisonment—a 757% increase since 1977 (Frost, Green, & Pranis, 2006). Instead, with little or no public discussion, the correctional establishment has gone about the business of building new women's prisons and filling them. Our hope is that this book will help encourage a critical national discussion of this trend and, specifically, that it will provide the best answers we can find to the important questions that surface in discussions about women's crime and punishment. What led these women into criminal behavior? Are today's women offenders more violent than their counterparts in past decades? How could such a change in public policy toward women have happened with so little fanfare? Finally, what advocacy and policy efforts (if any) are being made to reverse this trend in women's imprisonment?

As this book will show, the answers to these questions are not simple, but many of them lie in our public discomfort with girl and woman offenders and the secrecy that accompanies modern punishment. Not only do we rarely think of girls and women who get arrested, we also tend to ignore the places where the people we detain and imprison are kept. Prisons are not places most of us look at, and even the citizens of towns that house the largest of these institutions tend to look the other way when they drive by.

Silence also shrouds those held by these institutions. As this book will document, most of the people we arrest, jail, try, and imprison are poor, and because they are poor, they are without legal resources, without advocates, without a voice. Such silence particularly attends the jailing of women because women are supposed to be "good" and not "bad." Their tragedies, their suffering, and their pain are not news, and most of us want to believe that whatever suffering they do endure is simply their due—that the "system" that processes these people is fair and just. Indeed, if the public gives any thought to crime and punishment, it is generally to complain that the system fails to protect us from crime and is too soft on vicious criminals—whom we imagine to be male, violent, and very much unlike ordinary people.

There is little in our everyday lives to challenge that construction. Every night, we are bombarded with images of egregious and senseless violence, and almost every face of those shown committing these senseless acts is young, black, and male. What are we to make of these frightening images of anger and violence out of control in our cities?

The first, extremely important point to make about these constructions is that they are grossly untrue. Crime is down, not up, in American society. Despite a recent economic recession and increased unemployment and joblessness, murder rates in 2009 were substantially lower than in 1929 or even 1939 and nearly reflected the low rates seen in the late 1940s and 1950s (FBI, 2010a).

But how can this be true when the media are so full of violence? The sad fact is that our media, particularly our entertainment media, have discovered that violence, unlike humor or drama, travels well. Movies are, first and foremost, increasingly made for an international market, and violence comes cheaper than other forms of "entertainment." The more television our children watch, the more they (and we) come to believe that the scary, mean world they see in the movies exists outside their doors. For example, Romer, Jamieson, and Aday (2003) found that viewing local television news is directly related to increased fear of and concern about crime.

The notion of a mean society is so abetted by local news media that find that "if it bleeds, it leads" journalism takes far less energy than the real work of explaining the complex sources of crime and other social problems. Finally, politicians have discovered the fear of crime and its root cause—unarticulated racism—and have had no qualms about turning this fear/racism to their advantage. *Crime* has become a code word for race, and being tough on crime has become almost a prerequisite for election, with virtually all politicians taking care not to be "out-crimed" by their opponents.

In their rush to appear tough on crime, our leaders have dramatically increased the penalties for virtually every offense in the books, particularly drug offenses. The prisons then exploded not with new, more vicious criminals but with the very same petty offenders who used to receive probation for their deeds. The least visible of these offenders are the women we are now jailing: the fastest-growing jail population (Frost et al., 2006).

So, as we complete the first decade of the 21st century, our nation has the dubious distinction of having the highest incarceration rate in the world (Sentencing Project, 2011). This incarceration frenzy particularly devastates communities of color—racial and ethnic minorities now constitute more than 60% of the prison population (Sentencing Project, 2011). Despite state and federal budget crunches, corrections is an ever-present and ballooning item in government budgets, robbing money from health, education, housing, and social services. This continuous spending is fueled not by an increase in crime but also by cynical political forces that have exploited the unresolved racial and economic inequities in U.S. society.

How do we begin to challenge the correctional-industrial complex that is rapidly emerging around and feeding on our fear of crime and criminals? First, we must meet the prisoner as a person and listen to her story. As she speaks about her life and her experience of prison, a human face is suddenly superimposed over the mind-numbing figures.

By focusing attention on the girl and woman offender, this book hopes to fuel a public discussion about the unintended victims of our nation's love affair with incarceration—women of color, whose incarceration rate is three times that of white women (Sentencing Project, 2007). By focusing specifically on girls and women who commit crimes, perhaps it will be easier to understand what brought them to prison. By understanding their lives, we will see that spending money to end violence against girls and women will go a long way toward reducing women's crime. We will also see that ending the grinding poverty that is destroying some neighborhoods and families rather than punishing the victims of these forces will do a great deal to reduce girls' and women's crime. Finally, the book will help to end the invisibility of the girl and woman offender. Our ignorance about their lives and their punishments costs us far more than dollars. In our silence, we begin to deny our own humanity and the humanity of those we imprison.

TWO

GIRLS' TROUBLES AND "FEMALE DELINQUENCY"

———————◆•◆•◆———————

Every year, girls account for nearly a third of all arrests of young people in America (FBI, 2010a, p. 239). Despite this, the young women who find themselves in the juvenile justice system either by formal arrest or referral are almost completely invisible. Our stereotype of the juvenile delinquent is so indisputably male that the general public, those experts whose careers in criminology have been built studying "delinquency," and those practitioners working with delinquent youth, rarely consider girls and their problems.

The next three chapters argue that this invisibility has worked against young women in several distinct ways. First, as this chapter shows, despite the fact that a considerable number of girls are arrested, explanations for the "causes" of delinquency explicitly or implicitly avoid addressing them. Second, major efforts to reform the way the juvenile justice system handles youth were crafted with no concern for girls and their problems within the system. Finally, although girls are no longer completely forgotten at the academic and policy levels, there still exists a paucity of information on girls' development, survival strategies, and pathways to criminality. This dearth of knowledge means that those who work with girls have little guidance in shaping programs or developing resources that can respond to the problems many girls experience.

TRENDS IN GIRLS' ARRESTS

Why are the girls we arrest unnoticed when, in 2009, they accounted for 30% of all juvenile arrests (FBI, 2010a, p. 239)? Much of this has to do with the sorts of delinquent acts girls commit. Though many may not realize it, youth can be taken into custody both for criminal acts and a wide variety of what are often called status offenses.

Status offenses, in contrast to criminal violations, permit the arrest of youth for a wide range of behaviors that violate parental authority: "running away from home"; being "a person in need of supervision," "a minor in need of supervision," "incorrigible," "beyond control," "truant," or in need of "care and protection." Although not technically crimes, these offenses can result in a youth's arrest and involvement in the criminal justice system. Juvenile delinquents, as a category, include youths arrested for either criminal or noncriminal status offenses. Finally, as this chapter shows, status offenses play a major role in girls' delinquency.

Examining the types of offenses for which youth are actually arrested makes it clear that most youth are arrested for the less serious criminal acts and status offenses. Of the 1.2 million youth arrested in 2009, for example, only 4.5% of these arrests were for such serious violent offenses as murder, rape, robbery, or aggravated assault (FBI, 2010a, p. 240). In contrast, more than four times that number of juvenile offenders were arrested for a single offense (larceny theft), much of which, particularly for girls, is shoplifting (Dohrn, 2004).

Table 2.1 presents the 10-year difference in arrests of boys and girls for selected offenses. From this, it can be seen that although less serious offenses dominate both male and female delinquency, trivial offenses, particularly status offenses and larceny theft (shoplifting), are more significant in the case of girls' arrests. For example, status offenses account for 15% of arrests for girls, and larceny accounts for 25%. Comparatively, status offenses account for only 9% of boys' arrests, while larceny accounts for only 13%.

Looking at Table 2.1, we can see several differences in boys' and girls' arrests over the past 10 years. First, larceny and status offenses continue to play a more significant role in girls' official delinquency than in boys'—a trend that has remained consistent over previous decades (see Chesney-Lind & Shelden, 2004). This stability is somewhat surprising because dramatic declines in arrests of youth for these offenses might have been expected as a result of the passage of the Juvenile Justice and Delinquency Prevention Act in 1974. This

Table 2.1   Ten-Year Arrest Rates for Persons Under 18, 2000–2009, by Sex

Offense Charged	Males			Females		
	2000	2009	% change	2000	2009	% change
Total	1,047,690	807,818	−22.9	407,526	354,012	−13.1
Index Offenses:						
Murder	576	599	+4.0	80	53	−33.8
Rape	2,652	1,792	−32.4	22	28	+27.3
Robbery	14,861	17,342	+16.7	1,532	1.994	+30.2
Aggravated assault	31,550	22,685	−28.1	9,583	7,247	−24.4
Burglary	51,950	40,897	−21.3	7,013	5,740	−18.2
Larceny	146,160	106,852	−26.9	85,599	90,011	+5.2
Motor vehicle theft	23,314	9,412	−59.6	4,802	1,942	−59.6
Arson	4,922	3,138	−36.2	662	477	−27.9
Total violent crime	49,639	42,418	−14.5	11,217	9,322	−16.9
Total property crime	226,346	160,299	−29.2	98,076	98,170	+0.1
Other Offenses:						
Other assaults	98,731	88,631	−10.2	43,968	46,494	+5.7
Forgery and counterfeiting	2,746	889	−67.6	1,398	388	−72.2
Fraud	3,871	2,637	−31.9	2,003	1,454	−27.4
Stolen property: buying, receiving, possessing	15,179	9,670	−36.3	2,812	2,320	−17.5
Offenses against family	3,029	1,701	−43.8	1,738	988	−43.2
Prostitution	332	167	−49.7	397	624	+57.2
Embezzlement	686	224	−67.3	638	169	−73.5
Vandalism	62,404	48,203	−22.8	8,863	7,554	−17.5
Weapons (carrying, etc.)	20,096	18,553	−7.7	2,287	2,143	−6.3
Drug abuse violations	102,909	86,857	−15.6	18,757	16,800	−10.4

Offense Charged	Males			Females		
	2000	*2009*	*% change*	*2000*	*2009*	*% change*
Gambling	431	304	−29.5	27	8	−70.4
Liquor law violations	66,585	41,879	−37.1	30,753	25,980	−15.5
Driving under the influence	10,500	6.033	−42.5	2,183	2,052	−6.0
Drunkenness	11,406	7,381	−35.3	2,846	2,456	−13.7
Disorderly conduct	69,814	61,616	−11.7	29,020	31,138	+7.3
Vagrancy	1,287	824	−36.0	360	223	−38.1
All other offenses	186,628	145,383	−22.1	65,789	50,653	−23.0
Suspicion	575	376	−79.3	174	33	−81.0
Curfew/loitering	67,275	50,288	−25.3	30,078	21,915	−27.1
Runaways	37,693	26,800	−28.9	53,571	32,423	−39.5

SOURCE: Federal Bureau of Investigation (2010b, p. 239).

act, among other things, encouraged jurisdictions to divert and deinstitutionalize youth charged with noncriminal offenses. Although the number of youth arrested for status offenses did drop considerably in the 1970s (arrests of girls for these offenses fell by 24% and arrests of boys fell by an even greater amount—66%; FBI, 1980, p. 191), this trend was reversed in the 1980s. Between 1985 and 1994, for example, girls' runaway arrests increased by 18%, and arrests of girls for curfew violations increased by 83.1% (FBI, 1995, p. 222). The first decade of the 21st century saw a decrease in runaway arrests for both girls and boys, with a 39.5% decrease in girls' runaway arrests and 29.8% decrease in boys' compared to 2000. However, runaway arrests (and, on a much lower scale, prostitution) remains the offense category for which girls are actually a majority of those arrested.

For many years, statistics showing large numbers of girls arrested for status offenses were taken to be representative of the different types of male and female delinquency. However, self-report studies of male and female delinquency (which ask school-age youth if they have committed delinquent acts) do not reflect the dramatic differences in misbehavior found in official statistics. Specifically, it appears that girls charged with these noncriminal status offenses have been, and continue to be, significantly overrepresented in court populations.

Teilmann and Landry (1981) compared girls' number of arrests for runaway and incorrigibility with girls' self-reports of these two activities and found a 10.4% overrepresentation of girls among those arrested as runaways and a 30.9% overrepresentation of girls arrested for incorrigibility. From these data, they concluded that girls are "arrested for status offenses at a higher rate than boys, when contrasted to their self-reported delinquency rates" (pp. 74–75). These findings were confirmed in another self-report study. Figueira-McDonough (1985) analyzed the delinquent conduct of 2,000 youths and found "no evidence of greater involvement of females in status offenses" (p. 277). Similarly, Canter (1982b) found in a National Youth Survey (NYS) that there was no evidence of greater female involvement, compared to males, in any category of delinquent behavior. In this sample, males were significantly more likely than females to report committing status offenses. Indeed, using the International Self-Report Survey, Junger-Tas and colleagues (2009) found that in every one of the 28 countries examined, boys reported incidents of delinquency more often than girls.

During the beginning of the 21st century, other disconcerting differences arose in arrest trends for boys and girls. Whereas boys' arrests have decreased by nearly 23% since 2000, girls' arrests have increased by more than 18%, with the largest increases occurring in simple assault, drug abuse, and liquor law violations. These offense categories now account for 28% of girls' total arrests. In 2009, girls accounted for 18% of overall violent crime committed by juveniles and 16% of drug abuse violations—a respective 6% and 4% increase since 1992. Most troubling for girls is the incidence of arrest for drug abuse offenses— a 200% increase since 1992 (compared to boys' 110% increase). In addition, overall female delinquency court caseloads grew by more than 80% between 1988 and 1997, with girls' drug offense case rates rising 106% (Sickmund, 2000). Although boys still account for the overwhelming majority of violent and drug-related offenses, questions remain: Why this increase for girls? Are girls closing the gender gap in violent behavior and drug and alcohol use?

Looking at risk behavior self-reported by adolescent boys and girls, the answer appears to be "no." If changes in arrests reflected changes in girls' behavior, then we might expect such dramatic variations to be reflected in self-report delinquency data. A comparison of 2001 and 2009 data from the National Youth Risk Behavior Survey contradicts this hypothesis: Girls are not reporting an increased use of violence nor has the gender gap in reported drug and alcohol abuse narrowed markedly.

The data presented in Table 2.2 demonstrate that girls (as well as boys) are less likely to employ violent behavior—they report fewer engagements in

Table 2.2   Percentage of High School Students Who Engaged in Risk
Behavior, Youth Risk Behavior Survey, Years 2001 and 2009

	Males		*Females*	
	2001	*2009*	*2001*	*2009*
In a physical fight	43.1	39.3	23.9	22.9
Injured in a physical fight	5.2	5.1	2.7	2.2
Carried a weapon	29.3	27.1	6.2	7.1
Lifetime alcohol use	78.6	70.8	77.9	74.2
Current alcohol use	49.2	40.9	45.0	42.9
Lifetime marijuana use	46.5	39.0	38.4	34.3
Current marijuana use	27.9	23.4	20.0	17.9
Lifetime cocaine use	10.3	7.3	8.4	5.3
Current cocaine use	4.7	3.5	3.7	2.0
Offered, sold, given illegal drug(s) on school property	34.6	25.9	22.7	19.3

SOURCE: Youth Risk Behavior Surveillance System (2010).

physical fights, injuries, and weapons in 2009 than in 2001. This despite the
fact that arrests of girls for simple assault have risen 5.7% while boys' arrests
for this offense have fallen by 10.2% (see Table 2.1). Additionally, boys and
girls are not reporting more episodes of drinking alcohol; both boys and girls
report slightly lower lifetime and current use of alcohol in 2009 than in 2001.
Likewise, both girls and boys report decreases in marijuana and cocaine use,
and the gender gap here remains.

The issue of girls, their arrest trends, and their involvement in violent,
drug, and gang activity is addressed at length in the next chapter. Sufficient to
note here is that the gender gap is still obvious when serious crimes of violence
are considered and that enforcement practices have probably dramatically narrowed the gap in minor assaults (which can range from schoolyard tussles to
relatively serious but not life-threatening assaults). Steffensmeier and
Steffensmeier (1980) first noted this trend in the 1970s and commented that
"evidence suggests that female arrests for 'other assaults' are relatively non-
serious in nature and tend to consist of being bystanders or companions to
males involved in skirmishes, fights, and so on" (p. 70). Analyzing girls'
arrests for assaults in the 1990s and 21st century, Feld (2009) adds to this

argument and points out that "the incarceration of larger numbers and proportions of girls for simple assaults suggests a process of relabeling other status-
like conduct, such as incorrigibility, to obtain access to secure placement
facilities" (p. 260). These figures strongly suggest that official practices and
shifts in these practices over time can dramatically affect the character of girls'
official delinquency, as opposed to the actual behaviors girls are committing.

Numbers tell only part of the story. How do we explain these patterns and,
in particular, the relative absence of serious property and violent delinquency
in girls as compared to boys? To answer this question, we must turn to the
theories of delinquency that have long speculated on causes of delinquent
behavior in young people.

BOYS' THEORIES AND GIRLS' LIVES

Although existing delinquency theories were developed to explain the behavior of boys, some contend that these theories can be adapted to explain the
behavior of girls as well (Baskin & Sommers, 1993; Canter, 1982a; Figueira-
McDonough & Selo, 1980; Hartjen & Priyadarsini, 2003; Rowe, Vazsonyi, &
Flannery, 1995; Simons, Miller, & Aigner, 1980; Smith & Paternoster, 1987).

To establish that this notion is problematic, this chapter begins with a brief
review of the androcentric bias in the major theories of delinquent behavior,
old and new. The need for a model of female delinquency that accounts for
rather than ignores gender is then explored by reviewing the available evidence on girls' lives and the relationships between girls' problems and their
official delinquency. This model of delinquency draws on the best of the
insights from traditional delinquency theory and also incorporates insights
from contemporary research on gender, adolescence, and social control. This
discussion shows that the extensive focus on disadvantaged males in public
settings has meant that girls' victimization and the relationship between that
experience and girls' official delinquency has been systematically ignored.

Also missed by all but feminist research has been the historic role played
by the juvenile justice system in the sexualization of female delinquency and
the criminalization of girls' survival strategies. A complete understanding of
girls' experiences with the juvenile justice system, it will be suggested, must
also include explanations of the official actions of the juvenile justice system.
The juvenile justice system should be understood as a major force in the social
control of women, because it has long served to reinforce the obedience of all

young women to the demands of familial authority, no matter how abusive or arbitrary. We will also establish that despite evidence that girls are now being arrested for fewer status offenses and more "violent" offenses, the actual situation is considerably more complicated, with these new offenses (like simple assault) often surrogates for status offenses of earlier decades.

The earliest academic efforts to explain delinquent behavior were clear and unapologetic efforts to study male delinquents. "The delinquent is a rogue male," declared Albert Cohen in his influential book on gang delinquency written in 1955 (p. 140). More than a decade later, Travis Hirschi (1969), in his equally important book titled *Causes of Delinquency,* relegated women to a footnote that suggested, somewhat apologetically, that "in the analysis that follows, the 'non-Negro' becomes 'white,' and the girls disappear" (pp. 35–36).

One might want to believe that such cavalier androcentrism is no longer found in academic approaches to delinquency. For this reason, two more relatively recent examples are instructive. Tracy, Wolfgang, and Figlio (1985), in *Delinquency Careers in Two Birth Cohorts,* revisit the practice of including only boys in their delinquency cohort:

> The decision was made, therefore, to study delinquency and its absence in a cohort consisting of all boys born in 1945 and residing in Philadelphia from a date no later than their tenth birthday until at least their eighteenth. Girls were excluded, partly because of their low delinquency, and partly because the presence of the boys in the city at the terminal age mentioned could be conclusively established from the record of their registration for military service. (p. 9)

In essence, they defend the exclusion of girls with arguments that would still be considered valid today rather than with an expression of regret over the dated and myopic ways of thinking about delinquency.

From the gang frenzy that has gripped the United States in the 1990s comes yet another example. Martin Sanchez Jankowski's (1991) widely cited *Islands in the Streets* has the following entries in his index under "Women":

–and codes of conduct

–individual violence over

–as "property"

–and urban gangs

One might be tempted to believe that the last entry refers to girl gangs and the emerging literature on girls in gangs (see Campbell, 1984, 1990; Harris, 1988; Miller, 2001; Quicker, 1983), but the "and" in the sentence is not a mistake. Girls are simply treated as the sexual chattel of male gang members or as an "incentive" for boys to join the gang (because "women look up to gang members"; Jankowski, 1991, p. 53).

Jankowski's work and other current discussions of "gang delinquency" (see Taylor, 1990, 1993) actually revive the sexism that characterized the earliest efforts to understand visible, lower-class male delinquency in Chicago more than half a century earlier. Early fieldwork on delinquent gangs in Chicago set the stage for decades of delinquency research. Then, too, researchers were only interested in talking to and following the boys. Thrasher (1927) studied more than 1,000 juvenile gangs in Chicago. He spends approximately one page out of 600 on the five or six female gangs he encountered in his field observations of juvenile gangs. Thrasher did mention, in passing, two factors he felt accounted for the lower number of girl gangs:

> First, the social patterns for the behavior of girls, powerfully backed by the great weight of tradition and custom, are contrary to the gang and its activities; and secondly, girls, even in urban disorganized areas, are much more closely supervised and guarded than boys and are usually well incorporated into the family groups or some other social structure. (p. 228)

During roughly the same period as Thrasher, others in Chicago were crafting another influential approach to delinquency. Beginning in 1929, Clifford R. Shaw and Henry D. McKay used an ecological approach (or "social ecology") to the study of juvenile delinquency. Their impressive work, particularly *Juvenile Delinquency in Urban Areas* (1942), and intensive biographical case studies such as Shaw's *Brothers in Crime* (1938) and *The Jack-roller* (1930), set the stage for much of the subcultural research on delinquency. Within the city of Chicago (and other major cities of the era), these researchers noticed that crime and delinquency *rates* varied by areas of the city (just as today, if one examined a map of a city and placed red dots on where most offenders live and where most crimes occur, they would be clustered in relatively few areas). The researchers found that the highest rates of crime and delinquency were also found in the same areas exhibiting high rates of multiple other social problems, such as single-parent families, unemployment, joblessness, multiple-family dwellings, welfare cases, and low levels of education (Chesney-Lind &

Shelden, 2004, pp. 81–82). Such a distribution is caused by a breakdown of institutional, community-based controls, which in turn is caused by three general factors: industrialization, urbanization, and immigration. People living within these areas lack a sense of "community" as the local institutions (e.g., schools, families, churches) are not strong enough to better provide nurturing and guidance for the area's children. Within such environments, there develops a subculture of criminal values and traditions that replace conventional values and traditions. Such criminal values and traditions persist over time, regardless of who lives in the area (Chesney-Lind & Shelden, 2004, pp. 81–82).

Although this ecological approach to crime—later to be broadened and called "social disorganization"—is an important contribution to sociological theorizing on crime, its genesis focused only on male delinquency. In their ecological work, Shaw and McKay (1942) analyzed the official arrest data on only male delinquents in Chicago and repeatedly referred to these rates as "delinquency rates" (though they occasionally make parenthetical reference to data on female delinquency; p. 356). Similarly, their biographical work traced only male experiences with the law. In Shaw's (1938) *Brothers in Crime,* for example, the delinquent and criminal careers of five brothers are followed for 15 years. In none of these works is any justification given for the equation of male delinquency with delinquency.

Other major theoretical approaches to delinquency also focus on the subculture of lower-class communities as a generating milieu for delinquent behavior. Here again, noted delinquency researchers concentrated either exclusively or nearly exclusively on male lower-class culture. For example, Cohen's (1955) work on the subculture of delinquent gangs, which was written nearly 20 years after Thrasher's, deliberately considers only boys' delinquency. His justification for the exclusion of girls is quite illuminating:

> My skin has nothing of the quality of down or silk, there is nothing limpid or flute-like about my voice, I am a total loss with needle and thread, my posture and carriage are wholly lacking in grace. These imperfections cause me no distress—if anything, they are gratifying—because I conceive myself to be a man and want people to recognize me as a full-fledged, unequivocal representative of my sex. My wife, on the other hand, is not greatly embarrassed by her inability to tinker with or talk about the internal organs of a car, by her modest attainments in arithmetic or by her inability to lift heavy objects. Indeed, I am reliably informed that many women—I do not suggest

that my wife is among them—often affect ignorance, frailty and emotional instability because to do otherwise would be out of keeping with a reputation for indubitable femininity. In short, people do not simply want to excel; they want to excel as a man or as a woman. (p. 138)

From this, Cohen concludes that the delinquent response, "however it may be condemned by others on moral grounds, has at least one virtue: it incontestably confirms, in the eyes of all concerned, his essential masculinity" (1955, p. 140). Much the same line of argument appears in Miller's (1958) influential paper on the "focal concerns" of lower-class life with its emphasis on the importance of trouble, toughness, excitement, and so forth. These, the author concludes, predispose poor youth (particularly male youth) to criminal misconduct. However, Cohen's comments are notable for their candor and capture both the allure that male delinquency has had for at least some male theorists and the fact that sexism has rendered the female delinquent irrelevant to their work.

Emphasis on blocked opportunities (sometimes referred to as "strain" or anomie theories) emerged from the work of Robert K. Merton (1938), who stressed the need to consider how some social structures exert a definite pressure on certain people in the society to engage in nonconformist rather than conformist conduct. Building on Durkheim's notion of anomie (the breakdown in moral ties, rules, customs, laws, and the like that occurs in the wake of rapid social change), Merton developed one of the most enduring criminological theories. His theory emphasized that there was a "discrepancy" between culturally defined goals of society and the institutionalized (i.e., legitimate) means to obtain them (Chesney-Lind & Shelden, 2004, pp. 83–84). He referred to the goals as "success" goals, which typically revolve around earning money, achieving status, obtaining material goods, and so on. Unfortunately, Merton declared, the opportunities to reach the goals are not evenly distributed throughout society— not everyone has equal access to legitimate means. In consequence, "strain" or pressure is placed "upon certain persons in the society to engage in nonconformist rather than conformist conduct" (Merton, 1938, p. 672).

The pressure, Merton argued, causes individuals to adapt in one of several ways. They might simply conform and accept both the goals and the means. They might become what Merton termed "innovators"; they accept the goals but seek deviant means to obtain them. They might give up and become what Merton called "retreatists," rejecting both the goals and the means. They might also blindly follow the means while rejecting the goals of becoming what Merton called "ritualists." Finally, they might become "rebels" and try to substitute different definitions of success and invent different means (Chesney-Lind & Shelden, 1998, pp. 83–84). His work influenced delinquency research largely through the efforts of Cloward and Ohlin (1960), who discussed access to "legitimate" and "illegitimate" opportunities for male youth. Female delinquency is problematic for both Merton's theory and its supporters. If women have the same goals as men but are more often blocked from legitimate means because of discrimination, then, following Merton's logic, women experience more strain and should therefore commit more crime. This, however, is not the case. Additionally, women and girls are also ignored by Cloward and Ohlin's work, except in *Delinquency and Opportunity,* where women are blamed for male delinquency. Here, the familiar notion is that boys "engulfed by a feminine world and uncertain of their own identification tend to 'protest' against femininity" (1960, p. 49).

The work of Edwin Sutherland emphasized the fact that criminal behavior was learned in intimate personal groups. The basic premise to his theory, "differential association," is that criminal behavior, like other forms of human behavior, is learned in association with close, intimate friends. More specifically, the learning of criminal behavior includes learning its techniques and developing the motives, drives, rationalizations, and attitudes pertaining thereto (Chesney-Lind & Shelden, 1998, pp. 86–87). In addition, the motives, drives, rationalizations, and attitudes are learned from definitions of legal codes as favorable or unfavorable toward violation of the law, depending upon the prevailing perspective within one's immediate environment. The key proposition of the differential association theory is that "a person becomes delinquent because of an excess of definitions favorable to violation of law over definitions unfavorable to violation of law" (Sutherland & Cressey, 1978, p. 75). Sutherland's work, particularly the notion of differential association, which also influenced Cloward and Ohlin's work, was also male oriented because much of his work was affected by the case studies he conducted of male criminals. Indeed, in describing his notion of how differential association works, Sutherland (1978) used male examples:

> In an area where the delinquency rate is high a boy who is sociable, gregarious, active, and athletic is very likely to come in contact with the other boys in the neighborhood, learn delinquent behavior from them, and become a gangster. (p. 131)

Finally, the work of Travis Hirschi (1969) on the social bonds that control delinquency ("social control theory") was, as stated earlier, derived from research on male delinquents (though he, at least, studied delinquent behavior as reported by youth themselves rather than studying only those who were arrested). According to Hirschi, those with close bonds to social groups and institutions (e.g., family, school) are the least likely to become delinquent because the bonds help keep people "in check." Four major elements constitute the social bond: (1) *attachment* refers to one's connection (mostly of an emotional kind) to conventional groups, such as one's immediate family, peers, the school, and so on; (2) *commitment* refers to the sort of "investment" one makes in conventional society or, as Toby (1957) once stated, a "stake in conformity" because one stands to lose a great deal (respect from others, the time one has spent preparing for a career, and the like) if one violates the law; (3) *involvement* refers to one's participation in traditional activities, such as going to school, working, and participating in sports, because if one is busy with such activities, presumably there is little time for deviant activities (this is related to the old saying "idleness is the devil's workshop"); and (4) *belief* refers to an acceptance of basic moral values and laws. Briefly, Hirschi found that, with some exceptions, the facts he collected tended to support his theory. Specifically, youths who had the strongest attachments were the most committed, had the strongest belief in conventional moral values and the law, and were the least delinquent. A conspicuous limitation to Hirschi's work lies in his myopic focus on social class, treating race and gender as afterthoughts.

Such a persistent focus on social class and such an absence of interest in gender with regard to delinquency is ironic for two reasons. As even the work of Hirschi demonstrated, and as later studies would validate, a clear relationship between social class position and delinquency is problematic, whereas it is clear that gender has a dramatic and consistent effect on delinquency causation (Hagan, Gillis, & Simpson, 1985).

Efforts to construct a feminist theory of delinquency, as this and the next chapter demonstrate, must first and foremost be sensitive to the life situations of girls. Feminist theories of crime and delinquency must account for the myriad ways that *gender matters*. It is more than mere insertion of gender as a variable or brief commentary on "girls' or women's issues." Feminist criminology requires a critical consideration of the impact of girls' structural positions in a gender- and racially stratified society. It requires a deep understanding of the strategies girls use to negotiate and resist patriarchy and how these strategies can determine what crimes girls commit. Failure to consider the existing empirical evidence on girls' lives and behavior can quickly lead to stereotypical thinking and theoretical dead ends. One example of this sort of flawed theory building was the notion that the movement for women's equality was causing an increase in women's crime; this "liberation" or "emancipation" theory was more or less discredited in the 1970s when no empirical support for its major features appeared (especially that women were committing more serious, violent, "masculine" offenses; Gora, 1982; Steffensmeier, 1980). As we shall see in the next chapter, this "liberation" or "emancipation" hypothesis has returned with a vengeance in recent discussions of girls and violence.

A more nuanced example of this same sort of thinking can be found in the "power-control" model of delinquency (Hagan, Simpson, & Gillis, 1987). In this model, the authors speculate that girls commit less delinquency in part because their behavior is more closely controlled by the patriarchal family. The authors' promising beginning quickly gets bogged down in a very limited definition of patriarchal control (focusing on parental supervision and variations in power within the family). Ultimately, the authors' narrow formulation of patriarchal control results in their arguing that mothers' workforce participation leads to increases in daughters' delinquency because these girls find themselves in more "egalitarian families."

This is a not-too-subtle variation on the "emancipation" hypothesis previously mentioned. Now, however, it is the mother's liberation that causes the daughter's crime. Aside from many methodological problems in the study (e.g., the authors assume that most adolescents live in families with both parents, argue that female-headed households are equivalent to upper-status "egalitarian" families in which both parents work, and in at least some papers they measure delinquency using a six-item scale that contains no status offense items), there is a more fundamental problem with the hypothesis. There is no evidence to suggest that as women's labor-force participation has increased, girls' delinquency has increased. Indeed, during the past several decades, when both women's labor-force participation and the number of female-headed households soared, aggregate female delinquency, measured by both self-report and official statistics, did not escalate. Instead marked *declines* were observed particularly in self-reports of serious female delinquency (Ageton, 1983; Chesney-Lind & Belknap, 2002; Chilton & Datesman, 1987; FBI, 2010a; Office of Juvenile Justice and Delinquency Prevention, 1992; Pasko & Chesney-Lind, 2011).

Feminist criminologists have faulted all theoretical schools of delinquency for assuming that male delinquency, even in its most violent forms, was somehow a "normal" response to their situations. Girls who shared the same social and cultural milieu as delinquent boys but who were not delinquents were considered by these theories somehow abnormal or "over-controlled"

(Cain, 1989). Essentially, law-abiding behavior on the part of at least some boys and men is taken by these theories as a sign of character, but when women avoid crime and violence, it is an expression of weakness (Naffine, 1987).

None of these traditional theories address the life situations of girls on the economic and political margins because they were not looking at or talking to these girls. So what might be another way to approach the issue of gender and delinquency? First, it is necessary to recognize that girls grow up in a different world than boys (Block, 1984; Orenstein, 1994). Girls are aware very early in life that, although both girls and boys have similar problems, girls "have it heaps worse" (Alder, 1986).

Likewise, girls of color grow up and do gender in contexts very different from those of their white counterparts. Because racism and poverty are often fellow travelers, these girls are forced by their color and their poverty to deal early and often with problems of violence, drugs, and abuse. Their strategies for coping with these problems, often clever, strong, and daring, also tend to place them outside the conventional expectations of white girls (Campbell, 1984; Jones, 2009; Miller, 2008; Ness, 2010; Orenstein, 1994; Robinson, 1990).

The remainder of this chapter and the next deal with two aspects of these gender differences. First, the situation of girls who come into the juvenile justice system charged with status offenses and other trivial offenses is considered. Next, the unique issue of girls' violence and girls' gang membership is explored. These two discussions explicate the unique ways gender, color, and class shape the choices made by girls—choices our society has often criminalized.

CRIMINALIZING GIRLS' SURVIVAL: ABUSE, VICTIMIZATION, AND GIRLS' OFFICIAL DELINQUENCY

Girls and their problems have been ignored for a long time. When gender was considered in criminological theory, it was often a "variable" in the testing of theories devised to explain boys' behavior and delinquency. As a result, few have considered that some, if not many, of the girls who are arrested and referred to court have unique and different problems than boys. Hints of these differences, though, abound.

For example, it has long been known that a major reason for the presence of many girls in the juvenile justice system was because their parents insisted on their arrest. After all, who else would report a youth as having "run away" from home? In the early years, parents were the most significant referral source; in Honolulu, 44% of the girls who appeared in court in 1929 to 1930 were referred by parents (Chesney-Lind, 1971).

Recent national data, although slightly less explicit, also show that girls are more likely to be referred to court by sources other than law enforcement agencies (such as parents). In 1997, only 15% of youth referred for delinquency offenses but 53% of youth referred for status offenses were referred to court by sources other than law enforcement entities. The pattern among youth referred for status offenses, in which girls are overrepresented, is also clear. More than half of the youth referred for running away from home (60% of whom were girls) and 89% of the youth charged with ungovernability (half of whom were girls) were referred by entities outside of law enforcement, compared to only 6% of youth charged with liquor offenses (68% of whom were boys; Poe-Yamagata & Butts, 1996; Pope & Feyerherm, 1982; Puzzanchera & Kang, 2010). Additionally, girls are more frequently committed for status offenses than are boys: 16% of girls in residential facilities were committed for status offenses compared to 4% of boys (Sickmund, Sladky, Kang, & Puzzanchera, 2008).

The fact that parents are often committed to two standards of adolescent behavior is one explanation for these disparities—one that should not be discounted as a major source of tension even in modern families. Despite expectations to the contrary, gender-specific socialization patterns have not changed very much, and this is especially true for parents' relationships with their daughters (Davis, 2007; Ianni, 1989; Kamler, 1999; Katz, 1979; Orenstein, 1994; Thorne, 1993). Even parents who oppose sexism in general feel "uncomfortable tampering with existing traditions" and "do not want to risk their children becoming misfits" (Katz, 1979, p. 24). Girls can also clash with their parents around issues of gender identity in families committed to heteronormative sexuality, a concern that is surfacing in recent research on girls on the streets in the juvenile justice system (see Davis, 2007; Irvine, 2010; Shaffner, 2006).

Thorne (1993), in her ethnography of gender in grade school, found that girls were still using "cosmetics, discussions of boyfriends, dressing sexually, and other forms of exaggerated 'teen' femininity to challenge adult, and class and race-based authority in schools" (p. 156). She also found that "the double standard persists, and girls who are overtly sexual run the risk of being labeled sluts" (p. 156).

Contemporary ethnographies of school life echo the validity of these parental perceptions. Orenstein's (1994) observations also point to the durability of the sexual double standard; at the schools she observed, "sex 'ruins' girls; it enhanced boys" (p. 57). Parents, too, according to Thorne (1993), have new reasons to enforce the time-honored sexual double standard. Perhaps correctly concerned about sexual harassment and rape, to say nothing of HIV/ AIDS, "parents in gestures that mix protection with punishment, often tighten control of girls when they become adolescents, and sexuality becomes a terrain of struggle between the generations" (Thorne, p. 156). Finally, Thorne notes that as girls use sexuality as a proxy for independence, they sadly and ironically reinforce their status as sexual objects seeking male approval— ultimately ratifying their status as the subordinate sex.

Whatever the reason, parental attempts to adhere to and enforce the sexual double standard will continue to be a source of conflict between them and their daughters. Another important explanation for girls' problems with their parents that has received attention only in more recent years is that of physical and sexual abuse. Looking specifically at the problem of childhood sexual abuse, it is increasingly clear that this form of abuse is a particular problem for girls.

Girls are, for example, much more likely to be the victims of child sexual abuse than are boys (Smith, Leve, & Chamberlain, 2006). In nearly 8 out of 10 sexual abuse cases, the victim is female (Flowers, 2001, p. 146). From a review of community studies, Finkelhor and Baron (1986) estimate that roughly 70% of the victims of sexual abuse are female (p. 45). Sexual abuse of girls tends to start earlier than that of boys (Finkelhor & Baron, 1986, p. 48). Girls are more likely than boys to be assaulted by a family member (often a stepfather; DeJong, Hervada, & Emmett, 1983; Russell, 1986), For example, in 2008, 57% of sexual assaults on females were committed by someone they knew (Catalano, Smith, Snyder, & Rand, 2009). As a consequence, their abuse tends to last longer than boys' (Bergen et al., 2004; DeJong et al., 1983), and all of these factors can cause more severe trauma and dramatic short- and long-term effects in victims (Adams-Tucker, 1982; Hennessey et al., 2004). The effects noted by researchers in this area move from the well-known "fear, anxiety, depression, anger and hostility, and inappropriate sexual behavior" (Browne & Finkelhor, 1986, p. 69) to behaviors that include running away from home, difficulty in school, truancy, drug abuse, pregnancy, and early marriage (Browne & Finkelhor, 1986; Widom & Kuhns, 1996). In addition, girls who have experienced sexual abuse in their families are at greater risk for subsequent sexual abuse later in life (Flowers, 2001).

Herman's (1981) study of incest survivors in therapy found that they were more likely to have run away from home than a matched sample of women whose fathers were "seductive" (33% vs. 5%). Another study of women patients found that 50% of the victims of child sexual abuse, but only 20% of the nonvictim group, left home before the age of 18 (Meiselman, 1978). Further, the girls may learn "that the most effective way to communicate with adults is through sex" (Campagna & Poffenberger, 1988, p. 66) and view themselves as commodities. Indeed, Boyer (2008), in her research on female prostitution in Seattle, found a direct relationship between sexual abuse of girls and their subsequent involvement in prostitution.

Research on the characteristics of girls in the juvenile justice system shows the role played in girls' delinquency by physical and sexual abuse. Pasko and Chesney-Lind's (2010) study of girls in the Hawaii juvenile justice system found that more than one out of three girls had histories of physical and/or sexual abuse, with sexual abuse as a statistically significant predictor of girls' commitment: More than two-thirds of committed girls in their study had histories of sexual abuse. According to a study of girls in juvenile correctional settings conducted by the American Correctional Association (ACA; 1990), a very large proportion of these girls—about half of whom were of minority backgrounds—had experienced physical abuse (61.2%), and nearly half said that they had experienced this abuse 11 or more times. Many had reported the abuse, but a large number said that either nothing changed (29.9%) or that reporting it just made things worse (25.3%). More than half of these girls (54.3%) had experienced sexual abuse, and for most this was not an isolated incident; a third reported that it happened 3 to 10 times, and 27.4% reported that it happened 11 times or more. Most were 9 years old or younger when the abuse began. Again, although many reported the abuse (68.1%), reporting the abuse tended to cause no change or made things worse (ACA, 1990, pp. 56–58).

Given this history, it should be no surprise that the vast majority ran away from home (80.7%) and that of those who ran, 39% had run away 10 or more times. More than half (53.8%) said they had attempted suicide, and when asked the reason why, said it was because they "felt no one cared" (ACA, 1990, p. 55). Finally, what might be called a survival or coping strategy has been criminalized; girls in correctional establishments reported that their first arrests were typically for running away from home (20.5%) or for larceny theft (25.0%; ACA, 1990, pp. 46–71).

Detailed studies of youth entering the juvenile justice system in Florida have compared the "constellations of problems" of girls and boys (Dembo, Sue, Borden, & Manning, 1995; Dembo, Williams, & Schmeidler, 1993). These researchers found that girls were more likely than boys to have abuse histories and contact with the juvenile justice system for status offenses, whereas boys had higher rates of involvement with various delinquent offenses. Further research on a larger cohort of youth ($N = 2,104$) admitted to an assessment center in Tampa concluded that "girls' problem behavior commonly relates to an abusive and traumatizing home life, whereas boys' law violating behavior reflects their involvement in a delinquent life style" (Dembo et al., 1995, p. 21).

This suggests that many young women are running away from profound sexual victimization at home and, once on the streets, are forced into crime to survive. Girls who are sexually abused are more likely than abused boys to run away from home as a direct result of their sexual victimization. As long-term runaway youth, these girls are more likely to engage in a prostitution lifestyle, which is highly correlated with other future problems and victimizations, such as AIDS, depression, and rape (Boyer, 2008; Flowers, 1987, 2001; Widom & Kuhns, 1996). It is also correlated with a larger possibility of justice involvement: An estimated 1,450 arrests/detentions were made in the United States in 2005 for crimes related to juvenile prostitution (Mitchell, Finkelhor, & Wolak, 2009, p. 21). Moreover, the average age of entry into prostitution for girls in the United States is 14; this makes sense when considering that the rate of child sexual abuse is highest for girls when they are age 12 to 17 (Flowers, 2001, p. 146; O'Toole & Schiffman, 1997).

Recent scholarship has also shown that childhood physical and sexual abuse are central risk factors for girls' commercial sexual exploitation. Wilson and Widom (2010) found that the strongest predictor for sexual exploitation was initiation of sexual behavior before age 15 but that early sexualization was particularly harmful when coupled with a history of abuse. In fact, juveniles in their study with documented cases of abuse were more than twice as likely to have been involved in commercial sexual exploitation than were juveniles who did not have such histories.

Interviews with girls who have run away from home show, very clearly, that they do not have much attachment to their delinquent activities. They are angry about being labeled as delinquent yet engage in illegal acts (Chesney-Lind & Shelden, 1998; Pasko & Dwight, 2010). A Wisconsin study found that 54% of the girls who ran away found it necessary to steal money, food, and clothing to survive. A few exchanged sexual contact for money, food, or shelter (Phelps et al., 1982, p. 67). Martin, Hearst, and Widome (2010) found that commercially sexually exploited juveniles in North Minneapolis were more likely to be engaged in "survival sex" (exchanging sex for food, shelter, clothes, and other daily needs) than adult sex workers, an indication of the juvenile samples' neglect history. Lastly, in their study of runaway youth, McCormack and his colleagues found that sexually abused female run-aways were significantly more likely than their nonabused counterparts to engage in delinquent or criminal activities, such as substance abuse, petty theft, and prostitution (McCormack, Janus, & Burgess, 1986, pp. 392–393).

The backgrounds of adult women in prison underscore the important links between women's childhood victimization and their later criminal careers (Snell & Morton, 1994). Women offenders frequently report abuse in their life histories. About half of the women in jail (48%) and 57% of women in state prisons report experiences of sexual and/or physical abuse in their lives (Bureau of Justice Statistics, 1999).

Confirmation of the consequences of childhood sexual and physical abuse on adult female criminal behavior has come from a large quantitative study of 908 individuals with substantiated and validated histories of victimization. Widom (1988) found that abused or neglected girls were twice as likely as a matched group of controls to have an adult crime record (16% vs. 7.5%). The difference was also found among men but was not as dramatic (42% vs. 33%). Men who had been abused were more likely to contribute to the "cycle of violence," having more arrests for violent offenses as adult offenders than the control group. In contrast, when women with abuse backgrounds did become involved with the criminal justice system, their arrests tended to involve property and order offenses (such as disorderly conduct, curfew, and loitering violations; Widom, 1988, p. 17).

Given this information, taking a feminist perspective on the causes of female delinquency seems an appropriate next step. First, like boys, girls are frequently the recipients of violence and sexual abuse. But unlike boys, girls' victimization and their response to that victimization is specifically shaped by their status as young women. Perhaps because of the gender and sexual scripts found in patriarchal families, girls are much more likely than boys to be the victim of family-related sexual abuse. Men, particularly men with traditional attitudes toward women, are likely to consider their daughters or stepdaughters as their sexual property and feel justified in turning their adult sexual power against them (Armstrong, 1994; Finkelhor, 1982). In a society that ideal-izes inequality in male and female relationships and that venerates youth in women, girls are easily defined as sexually attractive by older men (Bell, 1970).

In addition, girls' vulnerability to both physical and sexual abuse is heightened by norms that require that they stay at home where their victimizers have access to them.

Moreover, as we will see in a subsequent chapter, girls' victimizers (usually men) have the ability to invoke official agencies of social control in their efforts to keep young women at home and vulnerable. That is to say, abusers traditionally have been able to use the uncritical commitment of the juvenile justice system to parental authority to force girls to obey them. Girls' complaints about abuse were, until recently, routinely ignored. For this reason, statutes that were originally placed in law to "protect" young people have, in the case of some girls, criminalized their survival strategies. Although they run away from abusive homes, parents can employ agencies to enforce their return. If they persist in their refusal to stay at home, they are incarcerated.

Young women, a large number of whom are on the run from sexual abuse and parental neglect, are forced by the very statutes designed to protect them into the lives of escaped convicts. Unable to enroll in school or take jobs to support themselves because they fear detection, young female runaways are forced into the streets. Here, they engage in panhandling, petty theft, and occasional prostitution to survive. Young women in conflict with their parents (often for legitimate reasons) may actually be forced by present laws into petty criminal activity, prostitution, and drug use.

In addition, because young girls (but not necessarily young boys) are defined as sexually desirable—more desirable than their older sisters due to the double standard of aging—their lives on the streets (and their survival strategies) take a unique shape—once again shaped by patriarchal values. It is no accident that girls on the run from abusive homes or on the streets because of profound poverty get involved in criminal activities that exploit their sexual object status. American society has defined youthful, physically perfect women as desirable. This means that girls on the streets, who have little else of value to trade, are encouraged to use this "resource" (Campagna & Poffenberger, 1988). Sexuality becomes their main source of power and sexual services their main commodity. This also means that the criminal subculture views them from this perspective (Miller, 1986).

The previous description is clearly not the entire story about female delinquency, but it illustrates a theory that starts with the assumption that experiences that differentiate boys and girls might illuminate perplexing but persistent facts, such as the fact that more female than male status offenders find their way into the juvenile justice system. However, theories that are sensitive to shared aspects of girls' and boys' lives should not be entirely neglected (see Chesney-Lind & Shelden, 2003, for a discussion of how these theories might shed light on female delinquency). Many such theories, though, were crafted without considering the ways gender shapes both boys' and girls' realities and need to be rethought with gender in mind.

Two additional comments are important here. First, a recent attempt to salvage the theories crafted to explain boys' behavior argues that the theories are correct; girls and boys are raised very differently, but if girls were raised like boys and found themselves in the same situations as boys, then they would be as delinquent as boys (Rowe et al., 1995). This seems to be a regression from the insights of Hagan and his associates. Girls and boys inhabit a gendered universe and find themselves in systems (especially families and schools) that regulate their behavior in radically different ways. These differences, in turn, have significant consequences for the lives of girls (and boys). We need to think about these differences and what they mean not only for crime but, more broadly, about the life chances of girls and boys.

In general, the socialization of boys, especially of white privileged boys, prepares them for lives of power (Connell, 1987). The socialization of girls, particularly during adolescence, is very different. Even for girls of privilege, there are dramatic and negative changes in their self-perception that are reflected in lowered achievement in girls in math and science (American Association of University Women, 1992; Orenstein, 1994). Sexual abuse and harassment are just being understood as major rather than minor themes in the lives of all girls. The lives of girls of color, as we shall see in the next chapter on girls in gangs, illustrate the additional burdens that these young women face as they attempt to contend with high levels of sexual and physical victimization in the home and with other forms of neighborhood violence and institutional neglect (Joe & Chesney-Lind, 1995; Miller, 2008; Ness, 2010; Orenstein, 1994).

Not surprisingly, work focusing on the lives of girls and women, particularly the data on the extent of girls' and women's victimization, has caused a "backlash" in which some suggest the numbers are inflated and meaningless (Roiphe, 1993; Wolf, 1993). Others have argued that emphasizing victimization constructs girls and women as having no agency (Baskin & Sommers, 1993; Morrissey, 2003). Both perspectives (arguably one from the right and another from the left) seek to shift the focus away from the unique experiences of women back to a more familiar and less intellectually and politically threatening terrain of race and class. They also seek to deny to the starkest victims of the sex/gender system the ability to speak about their pain. To say that a person has had a set of experiences (even very violent ones) is not to reduce that person to a mindless pawn of personal history but, rather, to fully illuminate the context within which that person moves and makes choices.

DELINQUENCY THEORY AND GENDER: BEYOND STATUS OFFENSES

Delinquency theory has all but ignored girls and their problems. As a result, few attempts have been made to understand the meaning of girls' arrest patterns and the relationship between these arrests and the very real problems that these arrests mask.

Girls live, play, and go to school in the same neighborhoods as boys, but their lives are dramatically shaped by gender. A glance at the pattern of girls' arrests causes as many questions as answers for those theorizing about girls' defiance. Why is running away such a major part of girls' delinquency and such a minor part of boys' misbehavior? Also interesting is the relative absence of the mainstays of boys' delinquency (such as burglary) and of serious crimes of violence in both self-reported and official female delinquency.

Conventional theories of delinquency seem best situated to explain the relative absence of girls from traditional boys' delinquency. Yet in general, these theories talk about how to learn the skills and attitudes to commit male delinquency and how to get the opportunity to engage in these behaviors. This chapter has described major differences between girls' and boys' official delinquency and has offered a gender-based theory to account for these differences. Having done this, it is now appropriate to turn to a particular form of girls' delinquency—girls' involvement in violence and gangs—to see how applicable traditional and feminist theories are to explain girls' involvement in what many might feel is the most "macho" of boys' delinquent activities.

THREE

GIRLS, GANGS, AND VIOLENCE

---◆---

GIRLS GONE WILD?

Although arrest statistics still reflect the dominance of status and other trivial offenses in official female delinquency, the 1990s saw a curious resurgence of interest in girls, often girls of color, engaged in nontraditional, masculine behavior—notably joining gangs, carrying guns, and fighting with other girls. The beginning of the 21st century continued this "bad girl" discourse, with an added focus on white girls' relational aggression and bullying as an undiscovered, concealed culture.

The increase in the arrests of girls for "other assaults" added fuel to this fire. Since the mid-1980s, arrests of girls for this offense have increased by nearly 200%, and by 2009, more than one out of three juveniles arrested for "other assaults" was female (FBI, 2010a). What is going on? Are we seeing a major shift in the behavior of girls and an entry of girls into violent behaviors, including gang violence, that were once the nearly exclusive domain of young boys? As we shall see, this is the conclusion one would draw from the papers and television, but a closer look at the trends presents a more complex view.

THE MEDIA, GIRLS OF COLOR, AND GANGS

Fascination with a "new," violent female offender is not really new. In the 1970s, a notion emerged that the women's movement had "caused" a surge in women's serious crimes, but this discussion focused primarily on an imagined increase in crimes of adult women, usually white women (Chesney-Lind, 1986). The current discussion has settled on girls' commission of violent crimes. Indeed, there has been a veritable siege of news stories and online video postings with essentially the same theme: Girls are getting more violent, girls are in gangs, and their behavior in these gangs does not fit the traditional stereotype of female delinquency.

On August 2, 1993, for example, in a feature spread on teen violence, *Newsweek* printed a box titled "Girls Will Be Girls" that noted, "Some girls now carry guns. Others hide razor blades in their mouths" (Leslie, Biddle, Rosenberg, & Wayne, 1993, p. 44). Explaining this trend, the article notes that "the plague of teen violence is an equal-opportunity scourge. Crime by girls is on the rise, or so various jurisdictions report" (p. 44). Exactly a year earlier, a short-subject broadcast appeared on a CBS program titled *Street Stories*. "Girls in the Hood," which was a rebroadcast of a story that first appeared in January 1992, opened with this voiceover:

> Some of the politicians like to call this the Year of the Woman. The women you are about to meet probably aren't what they had in mind. These women are active, they're independent, and they're exercising power in a field dominated by men. In January Harold Dowe first took us to the streets of Los Angeles to meet two uncommon women who are members of street gangs. (CBS, 1992)

The beginning of the 21st century did not see an end to the panic of girls in gangs. In June 2001, ABC reported that while nationally, gang membership was down in the United States, the Justice Department was alarmed about a growing problem: girl gang membership. ABC maintained that girls are "catching up with boys in this one area," "joining gangs for the same reasons as boys," and "doing the same activities as boys: selling drugs and committing murder." The same story that opened with a proclamation of how gang membership was on the decline—as low as 20% in some areas—closed with a fear that the drug-selling, violent gang member—*girl* gang member—is "everywhere" (Gibbs, 2001).

Well into the century's first decade, such stories continued. On May 16, 2006, the *Toronto Star* reported that although no all-female gangs existed in Toronto and girls only comprised 6% of known gang members, female violence was on the rise as "more and more, girls are becoming involved in youth gangs in Canada—a trend that was virtually unheard of just five years ago" (*Toronto Star*, 2006). On August 3, 2008, *The Independent* lamented in an editorial, "Sugar and Spice . . . Why Have Our Little Girls Turned Sour?" (Street-Porter, 2008).

And on August 25, 2010, the *Las Vegas Review Journal* reported that "ten members of an all-female gang were arrested on robbery and burglary charges" (Blasky, 2010). Admitting that the young women mostly stole shoes and clothes and that no one was seriously hurt, the article nonetheless pointed out that attempted murder charges were expected against at least one of the women.

These stories are only a few examples of the many media accounts that have appeared since the second wave of the hypothesis that women's struggle for equality results in unintended consequences, such as the dramatic increase in girls' violent activities. Where did this come from? Perhaps the start was an article titled "You've Come a Long Way, Moll," which appeared in the *Wall Street Journal* January 25, 1990. This article noted that "between 1978–1988 the number of women arrested for violent crimes went up 41.5%, vs. 23.1% for men. The trend is even starker for teenagers" (Crittenden, 1990, p. A14). The trend was accelerated by the identification of a new, specific version of the liberation hypothesis. "For Gold Earrings and Protection, More Girls Take the Road to Violence," announced the front page of the *New York Times*, in an article that opened as follows:

> For Aleysha J., the road to crime has been paved with huge gold earrings and name-brand clothes. At Aleysha's high school in the Bronx, popularity comes from looking the part. Aleysha's mother has no money to buy her nice things so the diminutive 15 year old steals them, an act that she feels makes her equal parts bad girl and liberated woman. (Lee, 1991, p. A1)

This is followed by the assertion that

> there are more and more girls like Aleysha in troubled neighborhoods in the New York metropolitan areas, people who work with children say. There are more girls in gangs, more girls in the drug trade, more girls carrying guns and knives, more girls in trouble. (Lee, 1991, p. A1)

Whatever the original source, at this point, a phenomenon known as "pack journalism" took over. The *Philadelphia Inquirer*, for example, ran a story subtitled "Troubled Girls, Troubling Violence" on February 23, 1992, that asserted the following:

> Girls are committing more violent crimes than ever before. Girls used to get in trouble like this mostly as accomplices of boys, but that's no longer true. They don't need the boys. And their attitudes toward their crimes are often as hard as the weapons they wield—as shown in this account based on

documents and interviews with participants, parents, police and school officials. While boys still account for the vast majority of juvenile crime, girls
are starting to catch up. (Santiago, 1992, p. A1)

This particular story featured a single incident in which an African
American girl attacked another girl (described as "middle class" and appearing white in the picture that accompanies the story) in a subway. The
Washington Post ran a similar story titled "Delinquent Girls Achieving a
Violent Equality in D.C." on December 23, 1992 (Lewis, 1992). In March
2006, ABC's *Good Morning America* contributed to these stories with a
series titled "Why Girls Are Getting More Violent: Violence Is on the Rise
among High School Girls" (ABC, 2006). One segment was specifically
labeled "Girls Are Beating and Bullying."

In almost all of the stories on this topic, the issue was framed in a similar
fashion. Generally, a specific and egregious example of female violence is
described. This is then followed by a quick review of the FBI's arrest statistics,
showing what appear to be large increases in the number of girls arrested for
violent offenses. Finally, there are quotes from "experts," usually police officers,
teachers, or other social service workers, but occasionally criminologists,
interpreting the events.

Following suit, popular talk shows such as *The Oprah Winfrey Show*
(November 1992), *Larry King Live* (March 1993), *Ricki Lake Show* (October
1997), *The Maury Show* (November 2008), and *Tyra Banks Show* (February
2009) devoted programs to the subject. Indeed, NBC news broadcast a story
on its nightly news that opened with the same link between women's "equality"
and girls' participation in gangs:

> Gone are the days when girls were strictly sidekicks for male gang mem-
> bers, around merely to provide sex and money and run guns and drugs. Now
> girls also do shooting . . . the new members, often as young as twelve, are
> the most violent. . . . Ironic as it is, just as women are becoming more
> powerful in business and government, the same thing is happening in gangs.
> (NBC, 1993)

For many feminist criminologists, this pattern is more than a little familiar. For
example, a 1972 *New York Times* article titled "Crime Rate of Women Up
Sharply Over Men's" noted that "Women are gaining rapidly in at least
one traditional area of male supremacy—crime" (Roberts, 1971, p. 1). And in
April 2006, *Corrections Today* made similar "equality" claims, stating that the

number of girls in gangs was on the rise in America, and that girls commit crimes, such as robbery and murder, just like their male counterparts (Eghigian & Kirby, 2006, pp. 48–49).

An expanded version of what would come to be known as the emancipation hypothesis appeared in Adler's (1975b) *Sisters in Crime,* in a chapter titled "Minor Girls and Major Crimes":

> Girls are involved in more drinking, stealing, gang activity, and fighting— behavior in keeping with their adoption of male roles. We also find increases in the total number of female deviances. The departure from the safety of traditional female roles and the testing of uncertain alternative roles coincide with the turmoil of adolescence creating criminogenic risk factors which are bound to create this increase. These considerations help explain the fact that between 1969 and 1972 national arrests for major crimes show a jump for boys of 82 percent—for girls, 306 percent. (p. 95)

The women's crime wave described by Adler (1975b) and, to a lesser extent, by Simon (1975), was definitively refuted by subsequent research (see Gora, 1982; Steffensmeier & Steffensmeier, 1980), but the popularity of this perspective, at least in the public mind, is apparently undiminished. Whether in the 21st century something different was going on, particularly with reference to girls and gangs and violence, remains to be seen. This chapter now turns to that question.

TRENDS IN GIRLS' VIOLENCE AND AGGRESSION

A review of girls' arrests for violent crime in the past decade (2000–2009, 2005–2009; see Table 3.1) initially seems to provide support for the notion that girls are engaged in more violent crime. Although arrests of girls for murder and aggravated assault were both down since 2000, robbery rose 30.2% for girls, along with a slight increase in the "other assault" category (FBI, 2010a, p. 239). Note too that while recent years have shown some decrease in girls' arrests for these violent offenses, those decreases are far smaller than the decreases seen in the arrests of boys for these same offenses. Changes in arrest rates, which adjust for changes in the population of girls in certain time periods, show much the same pattern.

These increases certainly sound notable, but they are considerably less dramatic on closer inspection. First, if we compare both 10-year and 5-year

Table 3.1 Percent Change in Male and Female Juvenile Arrests for Violent Crimes

Offense Charged	Males		Females	
	2000–2009 % Change	2005–2009 % Change	2000–2009 % Change	2005–2009 % Change
Index Offenses:				
Murder	+4.0	−1.2	−33.8	−36.4
Forcible rape	−32.4	−20.5	+27.3	−32.1
Robbery	+16.7	+7.7	+30.2	+13.6
Aggravated assault	−28.1	−21.3	−24.4	−19.6
Total violent crime	−14.5	−11.1	−18.2	−10.6
Other Violent Offenses:				
Other assaults	−10.2	−14.4	+5.7	−10.6
Offenses against the family	−43.8	−18.2	−43.2	−27.8

SOURCE: Federal Bureau of Investigation (2010b, pp. 239, 241).

trends in arrests (Table 3.1), we can see that most violent Index offenses[1] for girls have decreased in the past 5 and 10 years. Additionally, "other assaults" decreased since 2005 (by −10.6%), and offenses against the family have actually" decreased as well since 2000 (−43.2%) and 2005 (−27.8%). If girls were becoming increasingly more aggressive, then violent crime arrests overall should have escalated. Indeed, the opposite is true, with most offenses only marginally increasing in the past several years or declining altogether.

Second, what is important to note is that although boys' violent crime has gone down in the past 10 and 5 years (with some exceptions), boys constitute 92% of murder and nonnegligent manslaughter arrests, 90% of robbery arrests, and 76% of aggravated assaults. Serious crimes of violence are a very small proportion of all girls' delinquency, and that figure has remained essentially unchanged historically; violent crime is overwhelmingly a male enterprise. Additionally, if we compare the overall violent crime arrests since 2000 for both boys and girls, we find that increases and decreases in girls' arrests more or less parallel fluctuations with boys' arrests. Patterns, then, reflect general changes in youth behavior rather than dramatic changes and shifts in only girls' behavior.

---

[1] Index offenses are defined by the FBI as murder, forcible rape, robbery, burglary, aggravated assault, larceny theft, auto theft, and arson (added in 1979).

GIRLS, ROBBERY, AND "OTHER" ASSAULTS

What remains to be explained, then, is the increase in girls' "other assaults" and robbery arrests. Relabeling and "up-criming" behaviors that were once categorized as status offenses into violent offenses cannot be ruled out as a cause for higher assault arrests statistics (Steffensmeier et al., 2005). For example, a review of the more than 2,000 cases of girls referred to Maryland's juvenile justice system for "person-to-person" offenses revealed that almost all of these offenses (97.9%) involved "assault." A further examination of these records revealed that about half were "family centered" and involved such activities as "a girl hitting her mother and her mother subsequently pressing charges" (Mayer, 1994, p. 1). In earlier decades, such behavior would probably have been labeled "incorrigibility" by parents and police. Other mechanisms for relabeling and up-criming status offenses as criminal offenses include police officers advising parents to block the doorways when their children threaten to run away, and then charging the youth with "assault" when they shove past their parents (R. Shelden, personal communication, 1995). Indeed, Pasko (2006) found in her in-depth case file analysis of 112 female juvenile probationers that if the girl offender pushed or threw a small object at her guardian as she ran from the home, she was more likely to be charged with simple assault rather than a status offense. Arrest for this "person offense" could then result in detention or commitment.

With specific reference to domestic violence involving female juveniles, Buzawa and Hotaling (2006) found that these youth were "often less likely to receive statutorily required police actions," with authorities often arresting them and minimizing the violence the girls experienced, even if there existed evidence the parents were also perpetrators. As examples, the researchers noted two cases in which daughters were slapped by their mothers and retaliated by slapping or pushing their mothers back. In neither case was the parent arrested. Instead, parents, as the complainants, were treated by the police as the "injured parties," and the girls were arrested (Buzawa & Hotaling, 2006, p. 29). Indeed, the authors also found that both women and juveniles (particularly daughters), if suspects, were more likely to be arrested. Whether the incident involved adult partners, daters, siblings, or parents and children, the odds of female arrest were always higher.

The relabeling of girls' arguments with parents from status to assault is a form of "bootstrapping" and has also facilitated the incarceration of girls in detention facilities and training schools—something that would not be possible if the girl were arrested for noncriminal status offenses. As Feld's analysis (2009) of girls' arrests for person offenses points out, "the incarceration of larger numbers and proportions of girls for simple assaults suggests a process of relabeling other status-like conduct, such as incorrigibility, to obtain access to secure placement facilities" (p. 260).

Pasko and Dwight's research (2010) on girls and school-based assaults confirms similar conclusions. Despite their considerable domestic, community, and emotional stressors and troubled conditions, girls in their study reported quite a bit of resistance to fighting. Of the girls arrested for an on-campus assault, only 23% had engaged in a physical fight. The remaining 10 had been arrested for throwing a pencil at a student, throwing a pencil at a teacher, throwing a lit cigarette at a security officer, throwing a book at a student, hitting a student with a locker door, and shoving a student. For those who were arrested, several sought out mediation before their assaultive exchanges. Rarely did girls in her study report spontaneous and unpremeditated fighting. If they fought, an extended history of conflict was present. They often reported seeking help from school counselors, informing teachers, or being caught in a verbal battle when problems with other peers were eminent. Such help was infrequently fruitful. One girl noted:

> I got into it with this girl who kept texting (rumors) about me and we got into it in class so the teacher sent us to the principal's office and when we both tried to explain our sides, he got tired of us and told us it was over, he was done with it, and told us to stop and leave. So we did, but it didn't stop and then the next week, she grabbed my hair in the bathroom and cut it, so I hit her and now I'm here (court-ordered program). But they knew about it. They didn't care. It's like, just catch 'em fighting so we can get kicked out.
>
> —Latina, age 15, on probation for assault

Pasko and Dwight's research demonstrates how the school response to girls' aggressive altercations may be partially responsible for the increase in girls' arrests for assault. Pasko and Dwight's research also reveals a school system that is hyperreactive to physical aggression, that applies zero-tolerance policies, and that outsources the matters to an external body (juvenile justice system). However, schools also seemed underreactive in taking girls' reports of conflicts seriously.

Similar findings can be reached when looking at girls and robbery. A 1998 Honolulu study of robbery arrests for girls suggests that no major shift in the pattern of juvenile robbery occurred over the period 1991 to 1997, which, like other jurisdictions, had seen the number of girls arrested for robbery increase substantially (Chesney-Lind & Paramore, 1998). Rather, it appears that less serious offenses, particularly those committed by girls, were being swept up into the system. Consistent with this explanation were the following observable patterns: The age of offenders shifted downward, the value of items taken decreased, weapons used were less likely to be lethal in nature, and as a result, fewer injuries to the victims occurred. Most significantly, the proportion of adult victims declined sharply while the number of juvenile victims increased. In short, the study suggested that the problem of female juvenile robbery in the City and County of Honolulu was largely characterized by slightly older youth bullying and "hi-jacking" younger youth for small amounts of cash and, occasionally, jewelry—incidents that had previously been handled informally or formally within the confines of the school system, not law enforcement.

Finally, Steffensmeier and Schwartz's (2009) examination of girls and violence also confirms that girls are not narrowing the gender gap in robbery offenses. Using a time-series analysis to determine whether the gender gap in juvenile arrest trends has been converging, diverging, or essentially stable/ trendless (no change) from 1980 to 2003, they found that no significant change had occurred for robbery, rape, and homicide. Furthermore, when the authors examined self-report data to see if notable changes had occurred, their results indicated "marked stability in the gender gap both for composite assault and for robbery" (p. 72).

Other analyses of trends in self-report data of youthful involvement in violent offenses also fail to show the dramatic changes. Specifically, a matched sample of "high-risk" youth (ages 13 to 17) surveyed in the 1977 National Youth Study and the 1989 Denver Youth Survey revealed significant decreases in girls' involvement in felony assaults, minor assaults, and hard drugs, and no change in a wide range of other delinquent behaviors—including felony theft, minor theft, and index delinquency (D. Huizinga, personal communication, 1994). Additionally, the Youth Risk Behavior Surveillance System (YRBSS) data express similar conclusions. In 1991, 34.3% of girls reported engaging in a physical fight in their lifetimes. This dropped to 23.9% in 2001 and 22.9% in 2009 (YRBSS, 2010).

Although many questions can be raised about the actual significance of differences between official and self-report data, careful analyses of these data shed doubt on the media's construction of the hyperviolent girl. However, these data are less helpful in helping us understand girls' involvement with gangs. The reason for this is simple: Changes in official crime statistics and self-report data failed to signal the rise of youth gangs of either gender. As a consequence, it might be more useful to examine other sources of information on gangs and the role of gender in gang membership.

GIRL GANG MEMBERSHIP

After years of decline, the gang problem in the United States has become more serious. The most recent police estimates put the number of gangs in the United States at 27,000 and the number of gang members at approximately 788,000. This represents a 25% increase in the number of jurisdictions reporting gang problems since the nation recorded a 12-year low in 2001 (National Gang Center, 2009). In 2007, 86% of large cities reported a gang problem; this is up from about 50% in 1983 when the gang problem in our country was just beginning to grow (Curry, Fox, Ball, & Stone, 1992; National Gang Center, 2009). But what is the role of gender in gang membership?

Are there girls in gangs? If so, how many and how does gender work in the gang environment? Let's start with some estimates of the number of girls in gangs. Despite their image as prototypically male, there are girls in gangs, and they are there in pretty substantial numbers. However, the gendered habits of both practitioners and researchers long rendered the girls "present but invisible" until the last few decades (McRobbie & Garber, 1975).

Asking the youth themselves if they have ever been in a gang (self-report) indicates that in 2006, 3% of boys (aged 12–16) and 1% of girls reported they were in a gang (Green & Pranis, 2007, p. 36); this would mean that girls are roughly one quarter of all the youth in gangs. Another national self-report study conducted a bit earlier (2001) found that girls were a third of those youth reporting "belonging to a gang" (Snyder & Sickmund, 2006, p. 70). A study done in England and Wales, with a looser definition of "gang," found that girls were roughly half of those classified as belonging to a "delinquent youth group" (Sharp, Aldridge, & Medina, 2006, p. 3). By contrast, police estimates of the number of girls in gangs are frequently very low (often considerably less than 10%; Curry, Ball, & Fox, 1994; National Gang Center, 2009). Studies of gang problems done by researchers in the field tend to line up with the self-report data and find that girls are roughly 20 to 46% of those in gangs (Miller, 2002).

One explanation for the different estimates of the number of girls in gangs is a function of the age of the sample being surveyed, since girls tend to join gangs at a younger age, and they tend to leave gangs earlier than boys (Peterson, Miller, & Esbensen, 2001; Williams, Curry, & Cohen, 2002). A study done of youth ages 11 to 15 found that nearly half the gang members were girls, but one surveying an older group (13–19) found only a fifth were girls (Esbensen & Huizinga, 1993). In the sample of young people drawn to evaluate the antigang program GREAT, girls were 38% of those reporting gang membership in the eighth-grade sample (Esbensen, Deschanes, & Winfree, 1999). This means that in addition to focusing on girls when seeking to prevent girls joining gangs, we especially need to focus on the "tweens" when crafting prevention strategies. One researcher noted that this is about the same age as girls are attracted to scouting (Quicker, 1994).

That said, it is important to remember that gang youth might not be more delinquent than nongang delinquents. One Hawaii study found women and girls labeled by police as gang members committed fewer total numbers of most offenses than men and committed fewer serious offenses. Indeed, the offense profile for the females in the gang sample bears a very close relationship to typical female delinquency. More than a third of the "most serious" arrests of girls (38.1%) were property offenses (larceny theft). This offense category was followed by status offenses (19%) and drug offenses (9.5%). For boys, the most serious offense was likely to be "other assaults" (27%), followed by larceny theft (14%). This profile indicated that although both the boys and girls in this sample of suspected gang members were chronic but not serious offenders, this was particularly true of the girls (see Chesney-Lind, Rockhill, Marker, & Reyes, 1994).

These patterns prompted further exploration of the degree to which young women labeled by police as "suspected gang members" differed from young women who had been arrested for delinquency. To carry out this exploration, a comparison group was created for those in the Oahu sample who were legally juveniles. Youth suspected of gang membership were matched on ethnicity, age, and gender with youth who were in the juvenile arrest database but who had not been labeled as gang members. A look at offense patterns of this smaller group indicates no major differences between girls suspected of gang membership and their nongang counterparts. The most serious offense for gang girls was status offenses, and for nongang girls it was other assaults (Chesney-Lind, 1993, p. 338).

This finding is not totally unexpected. Similar studies, comparing groups in Arizona with Hispanic gangs (Zatz, 1985) and in Las Vegas with African American and Hispanic gangs (Shelden, Snodgrass, & Snodgrass, 1993), although not focusing on gender, found little to differentiate gang members from other "delinquent" or criminal youth. Accordingly, the 1997 National Longitudinal Youth Survey found that the contribution of active gang members to overall delinquency may only be 20% (Snyder & Sickmund, 2006). Bowker and Klein (1983), in an examination of data on girls in gangs in Los Angeles in the 1960s, compared the etiology of delinquent behavior of gang girls and their nongang counterparts and asserted the following:

> We conclude that the overwhelming impact of racism, sexism, poverty and limited opportunity structures is likely to be so important in determining the gang membership and juvenile delinquency of women and girls in urban ghettos that personality variables, relations with parents and problems associated with heterosexual behavior play a relatively minor role in determining gang membership and juvenile delinquency. (pp. 750–751)

Recent studies of girls in gangs reveal that for girls as well as boys, gang membership increases delinquent behavior. Gangs clearly increase girls' involvement in serious delinquency when compared to nongang girls drawn from similar neighborhoods. Relative to young women who are not in a gang, young women in gangs reported higher levels of ever carrying concealed weapons (79% compared to 30%), ever being in a gang fight (90% compared to 9%), and ever "attacked someone with a weapon to cause serious injury" (69% compared to 28%). Gang-involved girls are also far more likely to both sell and use illegal drugs than nongang girls (with 56% having sold crack cocaine compared to only 7% of nongang girls;. Miller, 2002, 85; see also Deschenes & Esbensen, 1999).

However, gang girls' involvement in the most serious of gang crimes still remained nominal. Deschenes and Esbensen (1999) found that gang membership did increase girls' chances of experiencing violence (as both victims and offenders) but that the frequency of violence used by gang girls was overall relatively low. Girl gang members reported committing robberies or shooting a firearm an average of only once a year and assaulting someone with a weapon twice a year (p. 286). Moore and Hagedorn's (2001) examination of Chicago arrest records from 1993 to 1996 revealed similar findings: Only 0.1% and 2.8% of female juvenile arrestees were arrested on homicide and weapons charges, respectively (p. 5).

These quantitative data do not provide support for the rise of a "new" violent female offender and suggest that the hype surrounding the issue has more to do with racism than with crime. Focus on girls in gangs, like its early counterpart, did have one positive effect; it brought much-needed attention to the lives of girls of color. There have been a small but growing number of excellent ethnographic studies of girls in gangs that suggest a much more complex picture wherein some girls solve their problems of gender, race, and class through gang membership. As we review these studies, it will become clear that girls' experiences with gangs cannot simply be characterized as "breaking into" a male world. Girls and women have always been engaged in more violent behavior than the stereotype of women supports; girls have also been in gangs for decades. However, their participation in these gangs, even their violence, is heavily influenced by their gender.

GIRLS AND GANGS: QUALITATIVE STUDIES

Given the range of estimates of girls' involvement with gangs, one might wonder whether girls' involvement with gang life resembles the involvement of girls in other youth subcultures, where they have been described as "present but invisible" (McRobbie & Garber, 1975). The longstanding "gendered habits" of researchers have meant that girls' involvement with gangs has been neglected, sexualized, and oversimplified.[2] So, although there have been a growing number of studies investigating the connections among male gangs, violence, and other criminal activities, there has been no parallel development in research on female involvement in gang activity. As with all young women who find their way into the juvenile justice system, girls in gangs have been invisible.

As noted earlier, this pattern of invisibility was undoubtedly set by the initial efforts to understand visible lower-class, male delinquency in Chicago more than half a century ago. As an example, Jankowski's (1991) highly

---

[2]For exceptions, see Bowker and Klein (1983), Brown (1977), Campbell (1984, 1990), Fishman (1995), Giordano, Cernkovich, and Pugh (1978), Harris (1988), Moore (1991), Ostner (1986), and Quicker (1983).

regarded *Islands in the Streets* implicitly conceptualizes gangs as a distinctly male phenomenon, and girls are discussed, as noted earlier, in the context of male property:

> In every gang I studied, women were considered a form of property. Interestingly, the women I observed and interviewed told me they felt completely comfortable with certain aspects of this relationship and simply resigned themselves to accepting those aspects they dislike. The one aspect they felt most comfortable with was being treated like servants, charged with the duty of providing men with whatever they wanted. (p. 146)

Taylor's (1993) work, *Girls, Gangs, Women and Drugs*, does focus on girls, but from a distinctly masculine perspective. His work, like Thrasher's and Jankowski's, tends to minimize and distort the motivations and roles of female gang members and is the result of the gender bias of male gang researchers, who describe the female experience from the male gang members' or their own viewpoint (Campbell, 1990). Typically, male gang researchers have characterized female members as maladjusted tomboys or sexual chattel who, in either case, are no more than mere appendages to the male members of the gang.

Taylor's (1993) study provides a veneer of academic support for the media's definition of the girl gang member as a junior version of the liberated female crook of the 1970s. Exactly how many girls and women he interviewed for his book is not clear, but the introduction clearly sets the tone for his work: "We have found that females are just as capable as males of being ruthless in so far as their life opportunities are presented. This study indicates that females have moved beyond the status quo of gender repression" (p. 8). His work stresses the similarities between boys' and girls' involvement in gangs, despite the fact that when the girls and women he interviews speak, it is clear that this view is oversimplified. Listen, for example, to Pat responding to a question about "problems facing girls in gangs":

> If you got a all girls crew, um, they think you're "soft" and in the streets if you soft, it's all over. Fellas think girls is soft, like Rob, he think he got it better in his sh*t 'cause he's a fella, a man. It's wild, but fellas really hate seeing girls getting off. Now, some fellas respect the power of girls, but most just want us in the sack. (Taylor, 1993, p. 118)

Other studies of female gang delinquency stress that girls have auxiliary roles in boys' gangs (see Bowker, 1978; Brown, 1977; Bullock & Tilley, 2002;

Flowers, 1987; Hanson, 1964; Laidler & Hunt, 2001; Lauderdale & Burman, 2009; Miller, 1975, 1980; Rice, 1963). Overall, these studies portray girls who are part of gangs as either girlfriends of the male members or "little sister" subgroups of the male gang (Bowker, p. 184; Hanson, 1964). Furthermore, they suggest that the role girls play in gangs is "to conceal and carry weapons for the boys, to provide sexual favors, and sometimes to fight against girls who were connected with enemy boys' gangs" (Mann, 1984, p. 45).

Some firsthand accounts of girl gangs, although not completely challenging this image, focus more directly on the race and class issues confronting these girls. Quicker's (1983) study of Chicana gang members in East Los Angeles found that these girls, although still somewhat dependent on their male counterparts, were becoming more independent. These girls identified themselves as "homegirls" and their male counterparts as "homeboys," a common reference to relationships in the barrio. In an obvious reference to "strain theory," Quicker notes that there are few economic opportunities within the barrio to meet the needs of the family unit. As a result, families are disintegrating and cannot provide access to culturally emphasized success goals for young people about to enter adulthood. Not surprisingly, almost all their activities occur within the context of gang life, where they learn how to get along in the world and are insulated within the harsh environment of the barrio (Quicker, 1983).

Moore's (1991) ethnography of two Chicano gangs in East Los Angeles, initiated during the same period as Quicker's (1983), brought the work into the present. Her interviews establish both the multifaceted nature of girls' experiences with gangs in the barrio and the variations in male gang members' perceptions of girls in gangs. Notably, her study establishes that there is no one type of gang girl, with some of the girls in gangs, even in the 1940s, "not tightly bound to boy's cliques" and "much less bound to particular barrios than boys" (p. 27). All the girls in gangs tended to come from a "more troubled background than those of the boys" (p. 30). Significant problems with sexual victimization haunt girls but not boys. Moore documents that the sexual double standard characterized male gang members' and the neighborhood's negative view of girls in gangs (see also Moore & Hagedorn, 1995). Girl gang members were called "tramps" and "no good," despite the girls' vigorous rejection of these labels. Furthermore, some male gang members, even those who had relationships with girl gang members, felt that "square girls were their future" (Moore & Hagedorn, p. 75).

Harris's (1988) study of the Cholas, a Latina gang in the San Fernando Valley, echoes this theme. Although the Cholas resemble male gangs in many respects, the gang challenged girls' traditional destiny within the barrio in two direct ways. First, the girls rejected the traditional image of the Latina woman as "wife and mother," supporting instead a more "macho" homegirl role. Second, the gang supported the girls in their estrangement from organized religion, substituting instead a form of familialism that "provides a strong substitute for weak family and conventional school ties" (p. 172).

The same "macho themes" emerged in a study of the female "age sets" found in a large gang in Phoenix, Arizona (Moore, Vigil, & Levy, 1995). In these groups, fighting is used by girls and boys to achieve status and recognition. Even here, though, the violence is mediated by gender and culture. One girl recounts how she established her reputation by "protecting one of my girls. He [a male acquaintance] was slapping her around and he was hitting her and kicking her, and I went and jumped him and started hitting him" (p. 39). Once respect is earned, these researchers found that girls relied on their reputations and fought less.

Girls in these sets also had to negotiate a Mexican American culture that is "particularly conservative with regard to female sexuality" (Moore et al., 1995, p. 29). In their neighborhoods and in their relations with the boys in the gang, the persistence of the double standard places the more assertive and sexually active girls in an anomalous position. They must contend with a culture that venerates "pure girls" while also setting the groundwork for the sexual exploitation of girls by gang boys. One of their respondents reports that the boys sometimes try to get girls high and "pull a train" (where a number of boys have sex with one girl), something she clearly objects to, although she admits to having had sex with a boy she didn't like after the male gang members "got me drunk" (p. 32).

Further description of the sexual victimization of girls and women involved in Chicano gangs is supplied by Portillos and Zatz (1995) in their ethnography of Phoenix gangs. They noted that girls can enter gangs either by being "jumped in" or "trained in," the former involving being beaten into the gang and the latter involving having sex with a string of male gang members. Often, those who are "trained in" are later regarded as "loose" and "not really" a gang member. Portillos and Zatz also found extremely high levels of some type of family abuse among the girls they interviewed, which caused them to conclude that "her treatment by male gang members may simply replicate how she is typically treated by males" (p. 24).

Work by Cepeda and Valdez, who conducted interviews with gang-involved Latino youth (2003), adds importantly to notions of "good" and "bad" girls in the gang context. They found that male gang members tended to view Latinas in very particular ways, and that the "partying" involved with the two different groups put one group of girls particularly at risk. Girls with whom the boys had an "emotional" relationship, sometimes a live-in relationship, were invited to family parties and generally regarded as respectable (p. 96). "Hoodrats," by contrast, were perceived as "loose" and sexually available, even if they were members of the gang. Partying with one's girlfriend often meant family gatherings, with relatively little risk to young women; but the spontaneous parties with hoodrats often involve excessive drug use and drinking and can include sexual assault of "wasted" girls (Cepeda & Valdez, 2003, p. 98).

Fishman (1995) studied the Vice Queens, an African American female auxiliary gang to a boys' gang, the Vice Kings, that existed in Chicago during the early 1960s. Living in a mostly black community characterized by poverty, unemployment, deterioration, and a high crime rate, the gang of about 30 teenage girls was loosely knit (unlike the male gang) and provided each other with companionship and friends. Failing in school and unable to find work, the girls spent the bulk of their time "hanging out" on the streets with the Vice Kings, which usually included the consumption of alcohol, sexual activities, and occasional delinquency. Most of their delinquency was "traditionally female," such as prostitution, shoplifting, and running away, but some was more serious (e.g., auto theft). They also engaged in fights with other groups of girls, largely to protect their gang's reputation for toughness.

Growing up in rough neighborhoods provided the Vice Queens "with opportunities to learn such traditional male skills as fighting and taking care of themselves on the streets" (Fishman, 1995, p. 87). The girls were expected to learn to defend themselves against "abusive men" and "attacks on their integrity" (p. 87). Their relationship with the Vice Kings was primarily sexual, as sexual partners and mothers of their children, but with no hope of marriage. Fishman perceptively points out that the Vice Queens were

> socialized to be independent, assertive and to take risks with the expectations that these are characteristics that they will need to function effectively within the black low income community. . . . As a consequence, black girls demonstrate, out of necessity, a greater flexibility in roles. (p. 90)

There has been little improvement in the economic situation of the African American community since the 1960s, and today's young women undoubtedly face an even bleaker future than the Vice Queens. In this context, Fishman speculates that "black female gangs today have become more entrenched, more violent, and more oriented to 'male' crime" (p. 91). These changes, she adds, are unrelated to the women's movement but are instead the "forced 'emancipation' which stems from the economic crisis within the black community" (p. 90).

The gender oppression and structural limitations faced by girls in contemporary poverty-stricken neighborhoods have been largely confirmed by current research by Miller (2001) on girl gang members in Columbus and St. Louis—both relatively new gang cities. With the majority of her gang interviewees African American, Miller found that the segregated and economically devastated neighborhood environments—which consequently led girls to growing up around crime and gang activity—were influential determinants in whether girls joined gangs. Additionally, girl gang members reported that problems within the family, such as drug abuse, violence, and sexual victimization, led them to avoid home and join a gang (p. 35). Experiencing gender as both a protective and a risk factor, the girls in Miller's study found gang life empowering as well as victimizing in some ways; they negotiated and strategized gender devaluation within their gangs and social inequality and dangers in their communities. Miller found that girls in gangs not only performed more delinquency and violence, but "it's also the case that gang involvement itself opens up young women to additional victimization risk and exposes them to violence, even when they are not the direct victims, that is sometimes haunting and traumatic in its own right" (p. 151).

Hunt and Joe-Laidler (2001) confirm such findings of victimization and violence in their study of ethnic youth gangs in the San Francisco Bay area. The researchers conclude that "girl gang members experience an extensive amount of violence in their lives whether on the streets, in their family lives, or in their relationships with lovers and boyfriends" (p. 381). Although violence does not consume their everyday lives, girls in gangs do sometimes experience roles of victims (by both men and their own homegirls), perpetrators of, and witnesses to violence. Moreover, these experiences with violence stem from violence-prone situations and life in tension-filled, occasionally hostile neighborhoods, and not the "demonic character" of gang girls themselves (p. 366).

Furthering investigation into gang girls' lives and pathways into and out of the gang, Moloney Hunt, Joe-Laidler, and MacKenzie's (2011) study of 65 parenting/pregnant female gang members and their transition to motherhood found that girls had difficulty negotiating their identities as young mothers and gang girls—both stigmatized identities. While motherhood meant retreat from the street, girls in their study still struggled with issues of respect, respectability, and financial and economic resources. Gang life meant more autonomy for them—an aspect of their lives they craved and often did not receive as mothers (Moloney et al., 2011).

Dorais and Corriveau (2009) research also shows the complexity and negotiations gang girls face in terms of sexuality, sexual activity, and victimization. Focusing on the culture of machismo that leads gang boys to controlling prostitution rings, Dorais and Corriveau show how such street gangs maintain and perpetuate the sexual trafficking of underage girls. The authors first document how young girls become romantically involved with and attached to gang members through emotional, psychological, and financial manipulation and then eventually are sold into prostitution. Dorais and Corriveau demonstrate how techniques, such as "love bombing (showering girls with affection and gifts), are employed by gang members to initially bring young women into the fold, and how such techniques can make it difficult for women to withdraw and leave" (p. 45).

The effects of race and gender, coupled with growing up in economically and socially deprived violent areas, are further illuminated in work by Lauderback, Hansen, and Waldorf (1992) in their study of African American female gangs in San Francisco and by Moore and Hagedorn (1995) in their exploration of ethnic differences between African American and Hispanic female gang members in Milwaukee. Disputing the traditional notions of female gang members as "maladjusted, violent tomboys" and sex objects completely dependent on the favor of male gang members, Lauderback and colleagues studied an independent girl gang that engaged in crack sales and organized "boosting" to support themselves and their young children (p. 57). All under 25, abandoned by the fathers of their children, abused and controlled by other men, these young women wanted to be "doing something other than selling drugs and to leave the neighborhood," but "many felt that the circumstances which led them to sell drugs were not going to change" (Lauderback et al., p. 69). Enhancing these research findings, Moore and Hagedorn found that when they asked their interviewees if they agreed with the statement, "The way men are today, I'd rather raise my kids myself," 75% of the African American female gang members agreed, compared to only 43% of the Latina gang members. By contrast, 29% of Latinas but none of the African American women agreed that "all a woman needs to straighten out her life is to find a good man" (Moore & Hagedorn, 1995, p. 18).

Campbell's work (1984, 1990) on Hispanic gangs in the New York City area further explores the role of the gang for girls in this culture. The girls in her study joined gangs for reasons that are largely explained by their place in a society that has little to offer young women of color (1990, pp. 172–173). First, the possibility of their obtaining a decent career, outside of "domestic servant," was practically nonexistent. Many came from female-headed families subsisting on welfare and most had dropped out of school with no marketable skills. Their aspirations for the future were both sex-typed and unrealistic, with girls wanting to be rock stars or professional models. Second, they found themselves in a highly gendered community in which the men in their lives, although not traditional breadwinners, still make many decisions that circumscribe the possibilities open to young women. Third, the responsibilities of young Hispanic mothers further restrict the options available to them. Campbell cites recent data revealing a very bleak future: 94% will have children and 84% will raise their children without a husband. Most will be dependent on some form of welfare (1990, p. 182). Fourth, these young women face a future of isolation as single mothers in the projects. Finally, they share with their male counterparts a future of powerlessness as members of the urban underclass. Their lives, in effect, reflect all the burdens of their triple handicaps of race, class, and gender.

For these girls, Campbell (1990) observes, the gang represents "an idealized collective solution to the bleak future that awaits" them. The girls portray to themselves and the outside world a very idealized and romantic life (p. 173). They develop an exaggerated sense of belonging to the gang. Many were loners prior to joining the gang, only loosely connected to schoolmates and neighborhood peer groups. Yet the gangs' closeness and the excitement of gang life is more fiction than reality. Their daily "street talk" is filled with exaggerated stories of parties, drugs, alcohol, and other varieties of "fun." However, as Campbell notes,

> These events stand as a bulwark against the loneliness and drudgery of their future lives. They also belie the day to day reality of gang life. The lack of recreational opportunities, the long days unfilled by work or school and the absence of money mean that the hours and days are whiled away on street corners. "Doing nothing" means hang out on the stoop; the hours of "bull***t" punctuated by trips to the store to buy one can of beer at a time. When an unexpected windfall arrives, marijuana and rum are purchased in bulk and the partying begins. The next day, life returns to normal. (1990, p. 176)

Joe and Chesney-Lind's (1995) interviews with youth gang members in Hawaii further describe the social role of the gang. Everyday life in marginalized and chaotic neighborhoods sets the stage for group solidarity in two distinct ways. First, the boredom, lack of resources, and high visibility of crime in their neglected communities create the conditions for youth to turn to others who are similarly situated. The group offers a social outlet. At another level, the stress on the family from living in marginalized areas, combined with financial struggles, creates heated tension and, in many cases, violence in the home. Joe and Chesney-Lind found, like Moore, high levels of sexual and physical abuse in the girls' lives: 62% of the girls had been either sexually abused or assaulted. Three fourths of the girls and more than half of the boys reported suffering physical abuse.

The group provides both girls and boys with a safe refuge and a surrogate family. Although the theme of marginality cuts across gender and ethnicity, there were critical differences in how girls and boys, and Samoans, Filipinos, and Hawaiians, express and respond to the problems of everyday life. For example, there are differences in boys' and girls' strategies for coping with these pressures—particularly the boredom of poverty. For boys, fighting—even looking for fights—is a major activity within the gang. If anything, the presence of girls around gang members depresses violence. As one 14-year-old Filipino put it, "If we not with the girls, we fighting. If we not fighting, we with the girls" (Joe & Chesney-Lind, 1995, p. 424). Many of the boys' activities involved drinking, cruising, and looking for trouble. This "looking for trouble" also meant being prepared for trouble. Although guns are somewhat available, most of the boys interviewed used bats or their hands to fight, largely but not exclusively because of cultural norms that suggest that fighting with guns is for the weak.

For girls, fighting and violence are part of their lives in the gang but not something they necessarily seek out. Instead, protection from neighborhood and family violence was a consistent and major theme in the girls' interviews. One girl simply stated that she belongs to the gang to provide "some protection from her father" (Joe & Chesney-Lind, 1995, p. 425). Through the group she has learned ways to defend herself physically and emotionally: "He used to beat me up, but now I hit back and he doesn't beat me much now." Another 14-year-old Samoan put it, "You gotta be part of the gang or else you're the one who's gonna get beat up." Although this young woman said that members of her gang had to "have total attitude and can fight," she went on to say, "We want to be a friendly gang. I don't know why people are afraid of us. We're not that violent." Fights do come up in these girls' lives: "We only wen mob this girl 'cause she was getting wise, she was saying 'what, slut' so I wen crack her and all my friends wen jump in" (Joe & Chesney-Lind, pp. 425–426).

Gangs also produce opportunities for involvement in criminal activity, but these are affected by gender as well. Especially for boys from poor families, stealing and small-time drug dealing make up for their lack of money. These activities are not nearly as common among the female respondents. Instead, their problems with the law originate with more traditional forms of female delinquency, such as running away from home. Their families still attempt to hold them to a double standard that results in tensions and disputes with parents that have no parallel among the boys.

LABELING GIRLS VIOLENT?

Historically, those activities that did not fit the official stereotype of "girls' delinquency" have been ignored by authorities (Fishman, 1995; Quicker, 1983; Shacklady-Smith, 1978). Taken together, assessments of gang delinquency in girls, whether quantitative or qualitative, suggest there is little evidence to support the notion of a new, violent female offender. A close reading of ethnographies of gang girls indicates that girls have often been involved in violent behavior as a part of gang life. During earlier periods, however, this occasional violence was ignored by law enforcement officers, who were far more concerned with girls' sexual behavior or morality.

As noted earlier, traditional schools of criminology have assumed that male delinquency, even in its most violent forms, was somehow an understandable if not "normal" response to their situations. This same assumption is not, however, extended to girls who live in violent neighborhoods. If they engage in even minor violence, they are perceived as being more vicious than their male counterparts. In this fashion, the construction of an artificial, passive femininity lays the foundation for the demonization of young girls of color, as shown by the media treatment of girl gang members. Media portrayal of girls and gangs creates a political climate in which the victims of racism and sexism can be blamed for their own problems (Chesney-Lind & Hagedorn, 1999). This demonization can then be used as justification for inattention to these marginalized girls' genuine problems or their harsh treatment in the juvenile justice system.

At best, these ethnographic accounts suggest that girls in gangs are doing far more than seeking "equality" with their male counterparts (Daly & Chesney-Lind, 1988). Girls' involvement in gangs is more than simple rebellion against traditional, white, middle-class notions of girlhood. Girls' gang membership is shaped by the array of economic, educational, familial, and social conditions and constraints that exist in their families and neighborhoods. Indeed, the very structure of the gang and its social life are dependent upon the myriad ways boys and girls manage and construct their gender.

Curry (1995) argues that the discussion of girls' involvement with gangs has tended to go to one extreme or the other. Either girls in gangs are portrayed as victims of injury or they are portrayed as "liberated," degendered gangbangers. The truth is that both perspectives are partially correct and incomplete without the other. Careful inquiry into the lives of these girls shows the ways in which the gang facilitates survival in their world. In addition, focusing on the social role of the gang in girls' lives illuminates the ways in which girls' and boys' experiences of neighborhood, family, and violence converge and diverge.

GIRLS, GANGS, AND MEDIA HYPE: A FINAL NOTE

A quick comparison of the articles that appeared in each surge of media interest in the "crime wave" committed by girls and women shows many similarities. Most important, those who tout these "crime waves" use a crude form of equity feminism to explain the trends observed and, in the process, contribute to the "backlash" against the women's movement (Faludi, 1991).

There are also crucial differences between the two women's "crime waves." In the stories that announced the first crime wave during the 1970s, the "liberated female crook" was a white political activist, a "terrorist," and a drug-using hippie. For example, one story syndicated by the *New York Times* service included pictures of both Patty Hearst and Friederike Krabbe (Klemesrud, 1978). Today's demonized woman is often a violent African American or Hispanic teenager.

In both instances, there was some small amount of truth in the articles. As this chapter has shown, girls and women have always engaged in more violent behavior than the stereotype of women supports; girls have also been in gangs for decades. The periodic media rediscovery of these facts, then, must be serving other political purposes.

In the past, the goal may have been to discredit young white women and their invisible but central African American counterparts (Barnett, 1993) who were challenging the racism, sexism, and militarism of that day. Today, as the research on girls and gangs has indicated, young minority youth of both genders face a bleak present and a grim future. Today, it is clear that *gang* has become a code word for race. A review of the media portrayal of girls in gangs suggests that, beyond this, media stories on the youth gang problem can create a political climate in which the victims of racism and sexism are held accountable for their own problems and deserving of punishment.

In short, this most recent women's "crime wave" appears to be a cultural attempt to reframe the problems of racism and sexism in society. As young women are demonized by the media, their genuine problems can be marginalized and ignored. Indeed, the girls have become the problem. The challenge to those concerned about girls is, then, twofold. First, responsible work on girls in gangs must make the dynamics of this victim blaming clear. Second, it must continue to develop an understanding of girls' gangs that is sensitive to the contexts within which they arise. In an era that is increasingly concerned about the intersections of class, race, and gender, such work seems long overdue.

FOUR

THE JUVENILE JUSTICE SYSTEM AND GIRLS

——•◦•——

Juvenile Justice Counselor Is Guilty of Sexually Assaulting Two Girls

—*New York Times,* January 22, 2011

Girls Alleges Sex Abuse in Prison

—*Chicago Tribune,* October 9, 2007

Sex Abuse Alleged at 2nd Youth Jail—Agency Denies Cover-up after Guard Accused of Luring Girls with Drugs

—*Dallas Morning News*, March 2, 2007

I ronically, although the fathers of criminology had little interest in female delinquents during the early part of the 20th century, the same could not be said for the juvenile justice system. Indeed, the early history of the system reveals that concerns about girls' immoral conduct was at the center of what some have called the "childsaving movement" (Platt, 1969) that set up the juvenile justice system.

Half a century later, reforms in the juvenile justice system, particularly in the way that the system handles noncriminal status offenses (running away from home, curfew violation, incorrigibility, etc.), would be crafted. Despite the fact that these offenses, as we saw in Chapter 2, play a major role in girls' experiences with the juvenile justice system, concern about girls would be absent from these discussions as well. Finally, a century after the establishment of the juvenile court, the voices of women's and girls' organizations would force the U.S. Congress to begin asking hard questions about the lives of girls who become labeled delinquents.

This chapter briefly reviews the often invisible experiences of the girls who enter the juvenile justice system (including problems such as those captured in the previous headlines). This chapter also offers some suggestions about how the 21st century might better respond to girls' needs.

"THE BEST PLACE TO CONQUER GIRLS"[1]

The movement to establish separate institutions for youthful offenders was part of the larger Progressive movement that, among other things, was keenly concerned about prostitution and other "social evils" (e.g., white slavery; Knupfer, 2001; McDermott & Blackstone, 1994; Rafter, 1990, p. 54; Schlossman & Wallach, 1978). Childsaving was also a celebration of women's domesticity, although, ironically, women were influential in the movement (Platt, 1969; Rafter, 1990).

In a sense, privileged women found, in the moral purity crusades and the establishment of family courts, a safe outlet for their energies. As the legitimate guardians of the moral sphere, women were seen as uniquely suited to patrol the normative boundaries of the social order. Embracing rather than challenging this stereotype, women carved out for themselves a role in the policing of women and girls (Alexander, 1995; Feinman, 1980; Freedman, 1981; Kunzel, 1993; Messerschmidt, 1987). Ultimately, many of the activities of the early childsavers revolved around monitoring the behavior of young girls, particularly immigrant girls, to prevent their straying from the right path.

This state of affairs was the direct consequence of a disturbing coalition between some feminists and the more conservative social purity movement. Concerned about female victimization and suspicious of male (and, to some degree, female) sexuality, notable women leaders, including Susan B.

---

[1]This phrase is taken from an inmate file by Rafter (1990) in her review of the establishment of New York's Albion Reformatory.

Anthony, found common cause with the social purists around such issues as opposing the regulation of prostitution and raising the age of consent (Messerschmidt, 1987). The consequences of this partnership teach an important lesson to contemporary feminist movements that are, to some extent, faced with the same possible coalitions.

Girls, particularly working-class girls, were the clear losers in this reform effort. Studies of early family court activity reveal that virtually all the girls who appeared in these courts were charged for "immorality" or "waywardness" (Chesney-Lind, 1971; Pasko, 2010a; Schlossman & Wallach, 1978; Shelden, 1981). More to the point, the sanctions for such misbehavior were extremely severe. For example, in Chicago (where the first family court was founded), half of the girl delinquents but only a fifth of the boy delinquents were sent to reformatories between 1899 and 1909. In Milwaukee, twice as many girls as boys were committed to training schools (Schlossman & Wallach, 1978, p. 72), and in Memphis, girls were twice as likely as boys to be committed to training schools (Shelden, 1981, p. 70).

Similarly, Knupfer found in her analysis of the early juvenile court in Chicago that between 1904 and 1927, 60 to 70% of delinquent girls placed on probation or in institutions were charged with incorrigibility (2001, p. 91). Judges more frequently institutionalized girls than boys for sexual delinquency or immorality, considering it a "more dangerous" sex offense. Embedded in these deliberations was a dichotomous image of girls—one, a victim, an errant yet essentially good girl and two, a "sexualized demon" who was a danger not just to herself but to the larger society (Knupfer, 2001, p. 94). Consequently, nearly all girls who had sex with more than one partner were institutionalized. Additionally, nearly 70% of the girls who were institutionalized were victims of incest, although this "discovery" was noted mostly as fact and not as a mitigating circumstance.

In Honolulu during 1929 to 1930, more than half of the girls referred to court were charged with "immorality," which meant evidence of sexual intercourse. In addition, another 30% were charged with "waywardness." Evidence of "immorality" was vigorously pursued by both arresting officers and social workers by questioning the girl and, if possible, the boys with whom she was suspected of having sex. Other evidence of "exposure" was provided by the gynecological examinations that were routinely ordered in virtually all girls' cases. Doctors, who understood the purpose of such examinations, would routinely note the condition of the hymen: "admits intercourse, hymen ruptured," "no laceration," and "hymen ruptured" are typical notations on the forms. Girls were also twice as likely as boys to be detained during this period, and they spent, on average, five times as long in detention as their male counterparts. They were also nearly three times more likely than boys to be sentenced to the training school (Chesney-Lind, 1971). Indeed, girls comprised half of those committed to training schools in Honolulu well into the 1950s (Chesney-Lind, 1973).

Not surprisingly, large numbers of reformatories and training schools for girls were established during this period, in addition to places of "rescue and reform." For example, Schlossman and Wallach (1978) note that 23 facilities for girls were opened during the decade 1910 to 1920, in contrast to the period from 1850 to 1910, in which the average was five reformatories per decade (p. 70). These institutions did much to set the tone of official response to female delinquency. Obsessed with precocious female sexuality, these institutions isolated the girls from all contact with men while housing them in bucolic settings. The intention was to hold the girls until marriageable age and to occupy them in domestic pursuits during their sometimes lengthy incarceration.

So clear was the bias that a few decades into the court's history, astute observers became concerned about the abandonment of minors' rights in the name of treatment, rescue, and protection. One of the most insightful of these critical works, and one that has been unduly neglected, was Paul Tappan's (1947) *Delinquent Girls in Court.* Stating that he was going to look at "what the courts do rather than what they say they do" (p. 2), Tappan evaluated several hundred cases in the Wayward Minor Court in New York City during the late 1930s and early 1940s. These cases caused Tappan to conclude that there were serious problems with a statute that brought young women into court simply for disobedience of parental commands or because they were in "danger of becoming morally depraved" (p. 33). Tappan was particularly concerned that "the need to interpret the 'danger of becoming morally depraved' imposes upon the court a legislative function of a moralizing character" (p. 33). Noting that many young women were being charged simply with sexual activity, he asked, "What is sexual misbehavior—in a legal sense—of the non-prostitute of 16, or 18, or 20 when fornication is no offense under criminal law?" (p. 33).

Tappan (1947) observed that the structure of the Wayward Minor Court "entrusted unlimited discretion to the judge, reformer or clinician and his personal views of expedience" and cautioned that, as a consequence, "the fate of the defendant, the interest of society, the social objectives themselves, must hang by the tenuous thread of the wisdom and personality of the particular administrator" (p. 33). Such an arrangement deeply disturbed Tappan, who noted that "the implications of judicial totalitarianism are written in history" (p. 33).

A more recent historical work on the Los Angeles Juvenile Court during the first half of the 20th century (Odem & Schlossman, 1991) supplies additional evidence of the court's historical preoccupation with girls' sexual morality, along with evidence that the concern clearly colored court activity into the 1950s. Odem and Schlossman reviewed the characteristics of the girls who found their way into this system at two different periods of time during the first half of this century: 1920 and 1950. In 1920, 93% of the girls accused of delinquency were charged with status offenses. Of these, 65% were charged with immoral sexual activity (though the majority of these— 56%—had engaged in sex with only one partner, usually a boyfriend). Odem and Schlossman found that 51% of the referrals had originally come from the girls' parents, a situation they explain as caused by working-class parents' fears about their daughters' exposure to the omnipresent temptations to which working-class daughters in particular were exposed in the modern ecology of urban work and leisure (pp. 197–198). Although working-class girls were encouraged by their families to work (in fact, 52% were currently working or had been working within the past year), their parents were extremely ambivalent about changing community morals and some were not hesitant about involving the court in their arguments with their daughters.

Odem and Schlossman (1991) also found that the Los Angeles Juvenile Court did not shirk its perceived duty. Seventy-seven percent of the girls were detained prior to their hearing. Both pre- and posthearing detention was common in this court and "clearly linked" to the presence of venereal disease in this population. Data reveal that 35% of all delinquent girls during this period and more than half of the alleged sex offenders had gonorrhea, syphilis, or other venereal infections. Odem and Schlossman further note that the presence of disease and the desire to force treatment (which during this period was quite a lengthy and painful proceeding) accounted for the large numbers of girls held in detention centers. Analysis of court actions revealed that although assigning probation was the most common court response (with 61% receiving this outcome), only 27% of girls were released on probation immediately following the hearing. Many girls, it appears, were held in detention centers for weeks or months after their initial hearings.

Girls not placed on probation were often placed in private homes to work as domestics or in a wide range of private institutions, such as the Convent of the Good Shepherd or homes for unmarried mothers. Ultimately, according to this analysis, about 33% of the "problem girls" during this period received a sentence of institutional confinement (Odem & Schlossman, 1991, pp. 198–199).

Between 1920 and 1950, Odem and Schlossman (1991) found that "the make-up of the court's female clientele changed very little" (p. 200). Although the number of black girls brought to court doubled (from 5% to 9%) during this time, the group was still predominantly white (69% compared to 73.5% in 1920), working class, and from disrupted families. Girls were, however, more likely to be in school and less likely to be working in 1950 than in 1920 (p. 200).

Girls referred to court in Los Angeles in 1950 were also overwhelmingly referred for status offenses (78%), though the charges had changed. Now, 31% of the girls were being charged for running away from home, truancy, curfew violations, or "general unruliness at home." Nearly half of the status offenders were charged directly with sexual misconduct, although this was "usually with a single partner; virtually none had engaged in prostitution" (Odem & Schlossman, 1991, p. 200). All these girls were also given physical exams, although the rate of venereal disease had plummeted, with only 4.5% of all girls testing positive. Despite this, the concern for female sexual conduct "remained determinative in shaping social policy" in the 1950s (p. 200).

Referral sources changed within the intervening decades, however, as did sanctions. Parents referred 26% of the girls at mid-decade, school officials about the same percentage in 1950 as 1920 (21% compared to 27%), and police officers referred a greater number in 1950 (54% compared to 29% in 1920). Sanctions shifted slightly, with fewer girls detained prior to hearing in 1950 (56% compared to 77% in 1920), but ultimately, the courts ended up placing about the same proportion of girls referred to them in custodial institutions (26% in 1950 compared to 33% in 1920; Odem & Schlossman, 1991).

GIRLS AND JUVENILE JUSTICE REFORM

Problems with the vague nature of status offenses and their sinister meaning for girls continued to haunt the juvenile justice system of the 1960s and 1970s. Status offense categories, students of the court during this period noted, were essentially "buffer charges" for suspected sexuality when applied to girls.

Consider the observations of Vedder and Somerville (1970) in their 1960s study of girls in training schools. They found that although girls in their study were incarcerated for the "big five" (running away from home, incorrigibility, sexual offenses, probation violation, and truancy), "the underlying vein in many of these cases is sexual misconduct by the girl delinquent" (p. 147).

Such attitudes were also present in other parts of the world. Naffine (1989) found that, in Australia, official reports noted that, "Most of those charged [with status offenses] were girls who had acquired habits of immorality and freely admitted sexual intercourse with a number of boys" (p. 13). Another study conducted in the early 1970s in a New Jersey training school revealed large numbers of girls incarcerated "for their own protection." When asked about this pattern, one judge explained, "Why most of the girls I commit are for status offenses. I figure if a girl is about to get pregnant, we'll keep her until she's sixteen and then ADC (Aid to Dependent Children) will pick her up" (Rogers, 1972, p. 227).

Andrews and Cohn's (1974) systematic review of the judicial handling of cases of ungovernability in New York in 1972 concluded with the comment that judges were acting "upon personal feelings and predilections in making decisions" (p. 1404). As evidence for this statement, they offer courtroom lectures recorded during the course of their study, such as the following: "She thinks she's a pretty hot number; I'd be worried about leaving my kid with her in a room alone. She needs to get her mind off boys" (p. 1403).

Similar attitudes expressing concern about premature female sexuality and the proper parental response are evident throughout the comments. Another judge remarked that at the age of 14, some girls "get some crazy ideas. They want to fool around with men, and that's sure as hell trouble" (Andrews & Cohn, 1974, p. 1404). Another judge admonished a girl,

> I want you to promise me to obey your mother, to have perfect school attendance and not miss a day of school, to give up these people who are trying to lead you to do wrong, not to hang out in candy stores or tobacco shops or street corners where these people are, and to be in when your mother says. (p. 1404)

As to where the young woman can go, the judge concluded, in rather telling terms: "I don't want to see you on the streets of this city except with your parents or with your clergyman or to get a doctor. Do you understand?" (p. 1404).

Empirical studies of the processing of girls' and boys' cases that came before the courts between the 1950s and the 1970s clearly documented the effect of these sorts of judicial attitudes. That is, girls charged with status offenses were often more harshly treated than their male or female counterparts charged with crimes (Chesney-Lind, 1973; Cohn, 1970; Datesman & Scarpitti, 1977; Gibbons & Griswold, 1957; Kratcoski, 1974; Mann, 1979; Pope & Feyerherm, 1982; Schlossman & Wallach, 1978; Shelden, 1981). Gibbons and Griswold, for example, found in a study of court dispositions in Washington state between 1953 and 1955 that although girls were far less likely than boys to be charged with criminal offenses, they were more than twice as likely to be committed to institutions (p. 109). Some years later, a study of a juvenile court in Delaware found that first-time female status offenders were more harshly sanctioned (as measured by institutionalization) than males charged with felonies (Datesman & Scarpitti, 1977, p. 70). For repeat status offenders, the pattern became even starker, with females six times more likely than male status offenders to be institutionalized.

Careful studies of the juvenile courts well into the second half of the 20th century suggest that judges and other court workers participate rather directly in the judicial enforcement of the sexual double standard. The baldest evidence for this is found in the courts' early years, but there is evidence that this pattern continues in many parts of the country. Ironically, these abuses continued, although the same decades ushered in a series of Supreme Court decisions sharply critical of the courts' handling of youthful offenders. Most of this is because the landmark decisions of that era extended to youth charged with crimes—so boys' and not girls' problems were the subject of judicial scrutiny (Chesney-Lind & Shelden, 2004). However, the juvenile justice system's abuse of the status offense category was severely tested, and in some locales eroded, during the 1970s when court critics around the world mounted a major push to "deinstitutionalize and divert" status offenders from formal court jurisdiction.

DEINSTITUTIONALIZATION AND JUDICIAL PATERNALISM: CHALLENGES TO THE DOUBLE STANDARD OF JUVENILE JUSTICE

By the mid-1970s, correctional reformers in many parts of the world became concerned about abuse of the status offense category by juvenile courts. In Victoria, Australia, for example, the 1978 Community Welfare Services Act attempted to remove the more explicitly sexual grounds of some status offenses (notably "exposed to moral danger") and emphasized youths' lack of adequate care and their neglect and abandonment. Limitations were also placed on the courts' authority to find a child "beyond control" of his or her parents (Hancock & Chesney-Lind, 1982, p. 182). South Australia went even further and, in 1979, passed the Children's Protection and Young Offender's Act, which essentially abolished status offenses (Naffine, 1989, p. 10). In Canada, the Province of British Columbia repealed the act permitting incarceration of youth in training schools in 1969 and actively encouraged the "disuse" of that portion of the Federal Juvenile Delinquents Act that dealt with youth found to be "beyond the control of their parents" (Province of British Columbia, 1978, pp. 16–19). Ultimately, Canada replaced the Juvenile Delinquents Act with the Young Offenders Act (1982), which removed status offenders entirely from federal legislation.

In the United States, the Juvenile Justice and Delinquency Prevention (JJDP) Act of 1974 required that states receiving federal delinquency-prevention money begin to divert and deinstitutionalize their status offenders. Despite erratic enforcement of this provision and considerable resistance from juvenile court judges, girls were the clear beneficiaries of the reform. Incarceration of young women in training schools and detention centers across the country fell dramatically in the decades following its passage, in distinct contrast to the patterns found early in the century.

National statistics on girls' incarceration reflect both the official enthusiasm for the incarceration of girls during the early part of the 20th century and the effect of the JJDP Act of 1974. Girls' share of the population of juvenile correctional facilities increased from 1880 (when girls were 19% of the population) to 1923 (when girls were 28%). By 1950, girls had climbed to 34% of the total, and in 1960, they were still 27% of those in correctional facilities. By 1980, this pattern appeared to have reversed, and girls were again 19% of those in correctional facilities (Calahan, 1986, p. 130). In 1991, girls made up 11% of those held in public detention centers and training schools (Moone, 1993a, p. 2).

A separate and more recent analysis shows a leveling off of this pattern. Poe and Butts (1995) report that girls made up 19% of admissions to detention facilities in the years 1988 through 1992 and 11% of the admissions to long-term facilities (p. 15). By 2006, these figures grew: Girls comprised 22% of detention admissions and 15% of long-term commitments (Sickmund et al., 2008).

These mixed patterns are perhaps a product of the fact that court officials have always been critical of deinstitutionalization (Schwartz, 1989; see also Sprott & Doob, 2009). Not surprisingly, then, although there were great hopes when the Juvenile Justice and Delinquency Prevention Act was passed, a 1978 General Accounting Office (GAO) report concluded that the Law Enforcement Assistance Administration (LEAA), the agency given the task of implementing the legislation, was less than enthusiastic about the deinstitutionalization provisions of the act. Reviewing LEAA's efforts to remove status offenders from secure facilities, the GAO concluded that during certain administrations, LEAA had actually "downplayed its importance and to some extent discouraged states from carrying out the Federal requirement" (General Accounting Office, 1978, p. 10).

Just how deep the antideinstitutionalization sentiment was among juvenile justice officials became clear during the House hearings on the extension of the act held in March of 1980. Judge John R. Milligan, representing the National Council of Juvenile and Family Court Judges, argued the following:

> The effect of the Juvenile Justice Act as it now exists is to allow a child ultimately to decide for himself whether he will go to school, whether he will live at home, whether he will continue to run, run, run, away from home, or whether he will even obey orders of your court. (United States House of Representatives, 1980, p. 136)

Ultimately, the judges were successful in narrowing the definition of a status offender in the amended act so that any child who had violated a "valid court order" would no longer be covered under the deinstitutionalization provisions (United States Statutes at Large, 1981). This change, which was never publicly debated in either the House or the Senate, effectively gutted the 1974 JJDP Act by permitting judges to reclassify a status offender who violated a court order as a delinquent. This meant that a young woman who ran away from a court-ordered placement (a halfway house, foster home, etc.) could be relabeled a delinquent and locked up.

Before this change, judges apparently engaged in other, less public efforts to "circumvent" the deinstitutionalization component of the act. These included "bootstrapping" status offenders into delinquents by issuing criminal contempt citations to elevate status offenders into law violators, referring or committing status offenders to secure mental health facilities, and developing "semisecure" facilities (Costello & Worthington, 1981, p. 42).

One study that reviewed the effect of these contempt proceedings in Florida (Bishop & Frazier, 1992) found them to work to the disadvantage of female status offenders. This study, which reviewed 162,012 cases referred to juvenile justice intake units during 1985 to 1987, found only a weak pattern of discrimination against female status offenders compared to the treatment of male status offenders. However, when they examined the effect of contempt citations, the pattern changed abruptly. Bishop and Frazier found that female offenders referred for contempt were more likely than girls referred for other criminal offenses to be petitioned to court and substantially more likely than boys referred for contempt to be petitioned to court. Moreover, the girls were far more likely than boys to be sentenced to detention. Specifically, the typical female offender in their study had a 4.3% probability of incarceration, which increased to 29.9% if she was held in contempt. This pattern was not observed for the boys in the study. The authors conclude that

> the traditional double standard is still operative. Clearly neither the cultural changes associated with the feminist movement nor the legal changes illustrated in the JJDP Act's mandate to deinstitutionalize status offenders have brought about equality under the law for young men and women. (Bishop & Frazier, 1992, p. 1186)

Hearings held in conjunction with a later and historic reauthorization of the Juvenile Justice and Delinquency Prevention Act, in March 1992, addressed for the first time the "provision of services to girls within the juvenile justice system" (U.S. House of Representatives, 1992, p. 1). At this hearing, the double standard of juvenile justice and the paucity of services for girls were discussed. Representative Matthew Martinez opened the hearing with the following statement:

> In today's hearing we are going to address female delinquency and the provisions of services to girls under this Act. There are many of us that believe that we have not committed enough resources to that particular issue. There are many of us who realize that the problems for young ladies are increasing, ever increasing, in our society and they are becoming more prone to end up in gangs, in crime, and with other problems they have always suffered. (U.S. House of Representatives, 1992, p. 2)

Martinez went on to comment on the high number of girls arrested for status offenses, the high percentage of girls in detention as a result of violation of court orders, and the failure of the system to address girls' needs. He ended with the question, "I wonder why, why are there no other alternatives than youth jail for her?" (U.S. House of Representatives, 1992, p. 2). Testifying at this hearing were also representatives from organizations serving girls, such as Children of the Night, Pace Center for Girls, and Girls Incorporated, in addition to girls active in these programs.

Perhaps as a result of this landmark hearing, the 1992 reauthorization of the JJDP Act of 1974 included specific provisions requiring plans from each state receiving federal funds to include

> an analysis of gender-specific services for the prevention and treatment of juvenile delinquency, including the types of such services available and the need for such services for females and a plan for providing needed gender-specific services for the prevention and treatment of juvenile delinquency. (Public Law 102-586, November 1992)

Additional money was set aside as part of the JJDP Act's challenge grant program for states wanting to develop policies to prohibit gender bias in placement and treatment and to develop programs that ensure girls equal access to services. As a result, 25 states embarked on such programs—by far the most popular of the 10 possible challenge grant activity areas (Girls Incorporated, 1996, p. 26). The act also called for the GAO to conduct a study of gender bias within state juvenile justice systems, with specific attention to

> the frequency with which females have been detained for status offenses . . . as compared to the frequency with which males have been detained for such offenses during the 5 year period ending December, 1992; and the appropriateness of the placement and conditions of confinement. (U.S. House of Representatives, 1992, p. 4998)

This mandate will not produce a clear measure of the presence or absence of sexism in the juvenile justice system because it controls for elements of the system that are gendered. Specifically, because girls are overrepresented among those charged with status offenses, "controlling" for status offenses (or, more specifically, for the type of status offense) permits discrimination to remain undetected. The mandate does, however, recognize the central role played by status offenses in girls' delinquency (see Chesney-Lind & Shelden, 2004, for a discussion of this problem).

Finally, although not specifically related to gender, the reauthorization of the act moved to make the "bootstrapping" of status offenders into delinquents more difficult. The act specified that youth who were being detained due to a violation of a "valid court order" had to have appeared before a judge and made subject to the order and had to have received, before issuance of the order, "the full due process rights guaranteed to such juvenile by the Constitution of the United States." The act also required that before issuance of the order, "both the behavior of the juvenile being referred and the reasons why the juvenile might have committed the behavior must be assessed." In addition, it must be determined that all dispositions (including treatment), other than placement in a secure detention facility or secure correctional facility, have been exhausted or are clearly inappropriate. Finally, the court has to receive a "written report" stating the results of the review (U.S. House of Representatives, 1992, p. 4983).[2]

Perhaps the most significant changes in the juvenile justice system's handling of girls came indirectly, through the monies Congress made available to states. The 1992 reauthorization, through the "Challenge E" section of this act, set aside funds for states to assess their services to girls. More than 25 states across the United States applied for and received funding to address these goals, the most popular of the 10 possible challenge grant activity areas (Girls Incorporated, 1996, p. 26). This state-level funding produced a groundswell of studies, conferences, and programs for girls in states all over the nation (see Chesney-Lind & Belknap, 2002).

Another outcome of the 1992 reauthorization was funding for a research group to identify "promising practices" and programs regarding delinquent girls. Greene, Peters, and Associates (1998, p. 8) identified five needs that girls require for healthy development: (1) physical safety and healthy development; (2) trust, love, respect, and validation from caring adults; (3) positive female role models; (4) safety to explore their sexual development at their own pace; and (5) feelings of competency, worthiness, and that they "belong." This report also identifies the many hurdles girls face in meeting these needs, including poverty, family violence, inadequate health care, negative messages about females (particularly their sexuality), and negative community, school,

---

[2]Recently, the juvenile justice reforms signaled in these hearings have been challenged by congressional initiatives that make it easier to detain girls for status offenses and to eliminate the small amount of money set aside for girls' programs (Howard, 1996).

and peer experiences. Stated alternatively, a summary of U.S. and Canadian research identifies "a consistent multi-problem profile of the female young offender," consisting of high rates of both physical and sexual abuse, severe drug addiction, low academic and employment achievement, and chronically dysfunctional and abusive families (Corrado, Odgers, & Cohen, 2000, p. 193). Not surprisingly, as recently as 1998, judges in Ohio reported extremely limited sentencing options for delinquent girls, with almost two-thirds disagreeing with the statement "There are an adequate number of treatment programs for girls." (Less than one-third disagreed with this statement about boys; Holsinger, Belknap, & Sutherland, 1999.)

While there was optimism, however, that the passage of these 1992 requirements would give birth to a new national focus on girls, the results were actually somewhat uneven. As an example, the JJDPA required states receiving federal money "to analyze current needs and services for girls and to present a plan for meeting girls' needs" in their state plans. Yet a review of plans completed in 2002 by the Children's Defense Fund (CDF) and Girls, Inc. concluded that "many states had not taken significant steps toward implementing this framework. An overview of current state approaches finds that (1) a significant percentage of states acknowledge the need for gender-specific services; and (2) the majority of current state plans are lacking and inappropriate pertaining to gender issues" (Children's Defense Fund & Girls Inc., 2002, p. 3). Beyond this, federal efforts to fund grants on girls' issues (both research and practitioner oriented) were initially issued by the Clinton Administration and subsequently cancelled by the Bush Administration on the heels of the September 11 attacks (Ray, 2002).

Ultimately, a scaled-back version of the initiative was issued by the Bush Administration's OJJDP in 2003. In 2004, the for-profit Research Triangle Institute was funded to convene the Girls Study Group with a budget of $2.6 million (Larence, 2010). However, the activities of the group and the benefits to furthering girl-responsive programming it was supposed to generate have come under criticism. The group's activities were the subject of a GAO examination in part because of concern about the group's composition (12 academics and one practitioner), its overly restrictive definition of what constitutes evidence of effective programming, and its failure to produce work that was relevant to the field and helpful for direct service providers (Larence, 2010). Fortunately, there has been a more recent set of monies awarded to the National Council on Crime and Delinquency to establish a National Girls Institute, both to remedy these deficiencies and to produce work that is relevant to the emerging field of gender-responsive programming nationally (Ravoira, 2011).

Certainly, these developments mark a distinct departure from previous policies that ignored the situation of girls who found their way into the juvenile justice system. This visibility is clearly needed, because a review of the characteristics of girls in detention centers and training schools still reflects problems with the juvenile justice system's treatment of girls. Specifically, recent research suggests that the new fascination with girls' violence has greatly increased the likelihood that girls will be detained (now for "criminal" offenses like assault). In addition, there is continued evidence that at the level of long-term incarceration, deinstitutionalization has produced a racialized, two-track system of juvenile justice in which white girls are placed in mental hospitals and private facilities, whereas girls of color are institutionalized in public training schools and youth correctional institutions.

RISING DETENTIONS AND RACIALIZED JUSTICE

Although Deinstitutionalization of Status Offenders (DSO) stressed the need to deinstitutionalize status offenders, we have seen that the numbers of girls and boys arrested for these noncriminal offenses continue to remain high, and arrests of girls are still increasing. Most worrisome are reports of increasing use of detention. National data indicate that between 1988 and 2007, detentions involving girls increased by 82% compared to a 36% increase in boys' detentions (Puzzanchera & Kang, 2010). These same national data reveal that a large increase in the detention of girls is due to the growing number of delinquency cases involving females charged with person offenses. In the last 20 years, girls' formal referrals to juvenile court for person offenses increased by 300%, while their detentions for person offenses increased by 250% (Puzzanchera & Kang, 2010).

Increases in the detention of girls have also been affected by state initiatives to recriminalize status offenses. As an example, in 1995, the state of Washington passed "Becca's Bill" in the wake of the death of 13-year-old Rebecca Headman, a chronic runaway who was murdered while on the run. Under this legislation, parents can call the police and allege that their daughter has run away. Each time this happens, the girl can be detained in a secure "crisis residential center" for up to 5 days or up to 7 days for contempt if she violated court-ordered conditions. As a result of the passage of this bill, the number of youth placed in detention rose 835% between 1994 and 1997, and estimates are that 60% of the youth taken into custody under Becca's Bill are girls "for whom few long-term programs exist" (Sherman, 2002, pp. 78–79).

An analysis of official Canadian delinquency data and interviews with Canadian youth probation officers indicate that the rationale used to incarcerate youthful girls is primarily protective, but it is useful to examine this "protection" (Corrado et al., 2000; Sprott & Doob, 2009). Corrado and colleagues (2000) hypothesized that although controlling young female offenders' sexuality is part of the patriarchal discrimination, "the sentencing recommendations made by youth justice personnel are primarily based on the desire to protect female youth from high-risk environments and street-entrenched lifestyles" (p. 193). Excusing the practice of detaining in order to protect delinquent girls, then,

> is based partly on the inability of community-based programs to protect certain female youth, the difficulties that these programs have in getting young female offenders to participate in rehabilitation programs, such as drug and alcohol rehabilitation, when they are not incarcerated, and the presence of some, albeit usually inadequate, treatment resources in custodial institutions. As well, cost-effective issues concerning the provision of intervention programs for females engaged in minor offences must also be considered. (Corrado et al., 2000, p. 193)

This study found that when they examined new charges of girls once incarcerated, three-quarters were for "administrative offenses," which are typically probation violations (e.g., failing to attend treatment, obey curfew, and abstain from alcohol).

Thus, although we previously discussed the "bootstrapping" or relabeling (and recasting) of status-offending girls into the system, it is also important to address another current bootstrapping procedure that is often related to status offending and appears to be affecting girls more than boys: serious punishment/sentences for violating court orders. A review of processing girls in the United States is strikingly similar to that of Canadian reports:

> The distinction between delinquency and status offenses has been further muddied by "bootstrapping." A 1980 amendment to the JJDPA allows secure detention for violation of a valid court order, on the basis that such an action

(or inaction) constitutes the delinquent offense of contempt. The valid court order holds even when the original offense that brought the young person into the juvenile justice system was a status offense. (Girls Incorporated, 1996, p. 19)

This report recommends that bootstrapping be abolished, given "evidence [that] strongly suggests that bootstrapping results in harsh and inequitable treatment of girls charged with status offenses" (Girls Incorporated, 1996, p. vi). A study by the American Bar Association and the National Bar Association (2001) concluded that girls are not only more likely than boys to be detained

> but to be sent back to detention after release. Although girls' rates of recidivism are lower than those of boys, the use of contempt proceedings and probation and parole violations make it more likely that, without committing a new crime, girls will return to detention. (p. 20; see Chesney-Lind & Belknap, 2002, for a full discussion of these issues)

San Francisco researchers (Shorter, Schaffner, Schick, & Frappier, 1996) examined the situation of girls in their juvenile justice system and concluded that the girls in their system were "out of sight, out of mind" (p. 1). Specifically, girls would languish in detention centers waiting for placement, while the boys were released or put in placement. As a result, 60% of the girls were detained for more than 7 days, compared to only 6% of the boys (Shorter et al., 1996).

In their study of 267 juvenile probationers in Hawaii, Pasko and Chesney-Lind (2010) found that 88% of female probationers had spent some time in detention. Specifically, those who were deemed by probation officers and/or judges to be repeatedly out of control (e.g., recurring probation violations) and in need of protection were placed in a correctional environment that had few alternative programs and placements. Juvenile justice decision makers felt that the "end of the line" option—commitment—was the appropriate and singular "child-saving" response to girls' troubled behaviors.

Indeed, Acoca and Dedel interviewed 200 girls in county juvenile halls in California. They report "specific forms of abuse" experienced by girls including "consistent use by staff of foul and demeaning language, inappropriate touching, pushing and hitting, isolation, and deprivation of clean clothing" (Acoca, 1999, p. 6). Most disturbing, they report that "some strip searches of girls were conducted in the presence of male officers, underscoring the inherent problem of adult male staff supervising adolescent female detainees" (p. 4).

What of youth in court? According to national estimates provided by the National Center for Juvenile Justice, in 2007, boys constituted 73% of all delinquency referrals to juvenile courts (Puzzanchera et al., 2010). Tables 4.1 and 4.2 reveal that although delinquency referrals vary surprisingly little by gender, the status offense categories are gendered. Nearly 60% of the youth referred for runaway offenses are girls, the only status offense category in which girls represented a larger proportion than did boys (Puzzanchera et al., 2010, p. 77).

National statistics also show that juvenile courts handled nearly two million cases (1,876,856) compared to about 150,700 "petitioned" status

Table 4.1 National Delinquency Referrals by Sex, 2007

Offense Type	Male (%)	Female (%)
Person	24	27
Property	36	35
Drug	13	8
Public order	27	30
Delinquency	100	100
Total	1,217,100	448,900

SOURCE: Puzzanchera and Kang (2010).

Table 4.2 Offense Profile of Petitioned Status Offense Cases by Gender, 2007

Most serious offense	Male	Female
Runaway	9%	16%
Truancy	36	40
Curfew	11	7
Ungovernability	13	13
Liquor	24	19
Miscellaneous	8	5
Total	100%	100%

SOURCE: Puzzanchera, Adams, and Stahl (2010).

offenders (although this figure is described as an estimate). When comparing Table 4.2 to arrests statistics (see Table 2.1 in Chapter 2), these figures indicate that many youth arrested for status offenses are no longer appearing formally before juvenile court judges. In addition, a number of studies now show more evenhanded treatment of boys and girls appearing before court charged with status offenses (see Carter, 1979; Clarke & Koch, 1980; Cohen & Kluegel, 1979; Dungworth, 1977; Johnson & Scheuble, 1991; Mallicoat, 2007; Teilmann & Landry, 1981).

The picture, however, is not entirely rosy. The number of girls arrested for these and other offenses, for example, continues to climb (see Table 2.1 in Chapter 2). Population growth cannot explain these differences because boys' and girls' growth rates do not differ; the juvenile male and female populations have each grown by 10% since 1990. In addition, the gendered nature of juvenile arrests also continues. As we saw earlier, although about four boys are arrested for every girl, the ratio for serious crimes of violence is about nine to one. Looking at these figures differently, two status offenses (runaway and curfew violations) composed about 1 out of 5 arrests of girls but less than 1 in 10 arrests of boys. These arrest figures mean a considerable "front end" pressure on a juvenile justice system that has been told to "divert" and "deinstitutionalize" these youth.

What is also important to recognize is the racial and ethnic character of this "diversion" movement for the juvenile justice system. Tables 4.3 and 4.4 illustrate the racial/ethnic composition of the juvenile correctional population. Girls of color comprise 55% of the female detainee population and close to 60% of committed girls.

A growing number of studies have examined the development of a two-track juvenile justice system—one track for girls of color and another for white girls. In a study of investigation reports from one area office in Los Angeles, Jody Miller (1994) analyzed the effect of race and ethnicity on the processing of girls' cases during 1992 to 1993. Comparing the characteristics of the youth in Miller's group with Schlossman's earlier profile of girls in Los Angeles in the 1950s shows how radically (and racially) different the current girls in the Los Angeles juvenile justice system are from their earlier counterparts. Latinas made up the largest proportion of the population (43%), followed by white girls (34%) and African American girls (23%; Miller, 1994, p. 11).

Predictably, girls of color were more likely to be from low-income homes, but this was especially true of African American girls (53.2% were from AFDC families, compared to 23% of white girls and 21% of Hispanic girls).

Table 4.3 Census of Detained Juveniles, Race by Sex, 2006

Count	White	Black	Hispanic	American Indian	Asian	Pacific Islander	Other	Total
Male	19,799	22,339	11,438	968	580	112	620	55,856
Female	3,902	2,884	1,346	322	57	23	168	8,702
Total	23,701	25,223	12,784	1,290	637	135	788	64,558

SOURCE: Sickmund, Sladky, Kang, and Puzzanchera (2008).

Table 4.4 Census of Committed Juveniles, Race by Sex, 2006

Count	White	Black	Hispanic	American Indian	Asian	Pacific Islander	Other	Total
Male	6,308	9,395	5,095	367	237	82	169	21,653
Female	1,859	1,694	898	146	35	13	46	4,691
Total	8,167	11,089	5,993	513	272	95	215	26,344

SOURCE: Sickmund, Sladky, Kang, and Puzzanchera (2008).

Most important, Miller (1994) found that white girls were significantly more likely to be recommended for a treatment rather than a "detention-oriented" placement than either African American or Latina girls. In fact, 75% of the white girls were recommended for a treatment-oriented facility, compared to 34.6% of the Latinas and only 20% of the African American girls (p. 18).

Examining a portion of the probation officers' reports in detail, Miller (1994) found key differences in the ways that girls' behaviors were described—reflecting what she called "racialized gender expectations." In particular, African American girls' behavior was often framed as the product of "inappropriate 'lifestyle' choices," whereas white girls' behavior was described as the result of low self-esteem, being easily influenced, and "abandonment" (p. 20). Latina girls, Miller found, received "dichotomized" treatment, with some receiving the more paternalistic care white girls received and others receiving more punitive treatment (particularly if they committed "masculine" offenses, such as car theft).

Robinson (1990), in her in-depth study of girls in the social welfare (Child in Need of Supervision, or CHINS) and juvenile justice system (Department of Youth Services—DYS) in Massachusetts, documents the racialized pattern of juvenile justice quite clearly. Her social welfare sample ($N = 15$) was 74% white/non-Hispanic, and her juvenile justice system sample ($N = 15$) was 53% black or Hispanic.

Her interviews document the remarkable similarities of the girls' backgrounds and problems. As an example, 80% of the girls committed to the Massachusetts Department of Youth Services (DYS) reported being sexually abused, compared to 73% of the girls "receiving services as a child in need of supervision" (Robinson, 1990, p. 311). The difference between these girls was in the offenses for which they were charged; all the girls receiving services were charged with traditional status offenses (chiefly running away and truancy), whereas the girls committed to DYS were charged with criminal offenses. Here, however, her interviews reveal clear evidence of bootstrapping. Take, for example, the 16-year-old girl who was committed to DYS for "unauthorized use of a motor vehicle." In this instance, "Beverly," who is black, had "stolen" her mother's car for 3 hours to go shopping with a friend. Prior to this conviction, according to Robinson's interview, she had been at CHINS for "running away from home repeatedly." "Beverly" told Robinson that her mother had been "advised by the DYS social worker to press charges for unauthorized use of a motor vehicle so that 'Beverly' could be sent to secure detention whenever she was caught on the run" (p. 202).

Other evidence of this pattern is reported by Bartollas (1993) in his study of youth confined in juvenile "institutional" placements in a Midwestern state. His research sampled female adolescents in both public and private facilities. The "state" sample (representing the girls in public facilities) was 61% black, whereas the private sample was 100% white. Little difference, however, was found in the offense patterns of the two groups of girls. Seventy percent of the girls in the state sample were "placed in a training school as a result of a status offense" (p. 473). This state, like most, does not permit youth to be institutionalized for these offenses. However, Bartollas noted that "they can be placed on probation, which makes it possible for the juvenile judge to adjudicate them to a training school" (p. 473). In the private sample, only 50% were confined for status offenses; the remainder were there for "minor stealing and shoplifting-related offenses" (p. 473). Bartollas also noted that both of these samples of girls had far less extensive juvenile histories than did their male counterparts.

Other evidence, though less direct, points to much the same pattern. As deinstitutionalization has advanced over the past three decades, there has been a distinct rise in the number of youth confined in private and public facilities or institutions. In comparing public and private facilities, some clear gender and race differences emerge. Although the majority of the youths in all institutional populations are male, there is a noticeable gender difference between youth held in public and private facilities. In 2006, girls constituted 12% of those juveniles in public institutions, compared to 16% in private institutions (Sickmund et al., 2008; see also Moone, 1993a, 1993b, and Office of Juvenile Justice and Delinquency Prevention, 2001, for earlier analysis). See Tables 4.5 and 4.6.

There are also gender differences in the offenses or activities that bring youth to private facilities. In 2006, 40% of girls and 8% percent of boys were committed to private facilities for status offenses. Likewise, in public facilities, 19% of girls were committed for technical violations, compared to only 12% of boys. Tables 4.5 and 4.6 reveal that girls are still far more likely than boys to be held for status offenses in either type of facility and that girls are far less likely to be held for violent offenses. Girls, in contrast, were often held for status offenses and "voluntary commitments," which take on a more sinister tone when one realizes that parents can "voluntarily" commit their children (Chesney-Lind & Shelden, 2004, p. 165).

Table 4.5   Commitment Offense by Sex, Private Facilities, 2006

Count	*Male*	*Female*	*Total*
Person offenses	6,704	1,106	7,810
Property offenses	5,077	710	5,787
Drug offenses	2,283	350	2,633
Public order offenses	2,573	300	2,873
Technical violations	2,813	445	3,258
Status offenses	1,747	1,199	2,946
Total	21,197	4,110	25,307

SOURCE: Sickmund, Sladky, Kang, and Puzzanchera (2008).

Table 4.6   Commitment Offense by Sex, Public Facilities, 2006

Count	*Male*	*Female*	*Total*
Person offenses	13,634	1,509	15,143
Property offenses	10,065	1,145	11,210
Drug offenses	2,692	343	3,035
Public order offenses	3,591	412	4,003
Technical violations	4,264	884	5,148
Status offenses	389	297	686
Total	34,635	4,590	39,225

SOURCE: Sickmund, Sladky, Kang, and Puzzanchera (2008).

With this push for confinement come ethnic and racial differences in the populations of these correctional institutions. Overall, minority youth constitute 33% of the population age 10 to 17 in the United States, but they represent 65% of youth in residential placements (Sickmund et al., 2008). Whites constituted about 32% of those held in public institutions in 2006 but 43% of those held in private facilities (Sickmund et al., 2008).

Other, more detailed work on this issue (Krisberg, Schwartz, Fishman, Eisikovits, & Guttman, 1986) suggests that there is a significant interaction between gender and ethnicity in incarceration rates. In addition, where increases have occurred in incarceration of youth, they have apparently been in the incarceration of minority youth, both male and female (Krisberg et al., 1986). Minority youth spend more time in facilities than their white counterparts; minority youth spend an average of 17 weeks in custody while white youth spend an average of 15 weeks.

In general, the numbers indicate that after a dramatic decline in the early 1970s, the number of girls held in public training schools and detention centers has not declined at all since 1979. Recent global data show this quite clearly. On one day in 1979, there were 6,067 girls in public facilities (mainly detention centers and training schools); in 2006, the figure had more than doubled to 13,943. Meanwhile, the number of girls held in private facilities had decreased by 41%—from 8,176 in 1979 to 4,797 in 2006 (Krisberg et al., 1991, p. 43; Moone, 1993a, 1993b; Sickmund et al., 2008).

OFFENSE PATTERNS OF GIRLS
IN CUSTODY—BOOTSTRAPPING

Looking again at Tables 4.5 and 4.6, a slightly richer picture of the girls in correctional institutions emerges from this national snapshot of the offenses for which girls and boys are held in public and private facilities. The large number of girls incarcerated for probation or parole violations and for person offenses is a measure of new efforts to bootstrap status offenders into delinquents by incarcerating them for these offenses (see Feld, 2009; Girls Incorporated, 1996).

Such new efforts to bootstrap status offenses into delinquent charges (for example, assault or technical violations) becomes apparent when changes over time in the female juvenile custody population are analyzed. In 2006, 8,560 girls were committed to public correctional facilities and 4,797 were committed to private ones. Compared to the female population in custody in 1991, this represents a 45% increase in the public facilities and a 55% decrease in private ones (Girls Incorporated, 1996; Sickmund et al., 2008). The percentage of nonoffenders and voluntary commitments in private facilities dropped from 65% of girls in private facilities in 1991 to 24% in 1999. Whereas status offenders were 19% of females in custody in 1991, they were only 12% in 2006. Furthermore, person offenders comprised only 8% of females in custody in 1991; in 2006, they comprised 31% of girls in custody.

The explanation behind these person offenses is complicated, however. Focus group data with incarcerated girls has shown that girls were being incarcerated for minor infractions, and in some cases, for defending themselves (Belknap et al., 1997). Similarly, Acoca and Dedel in their case file reviews of girls in the juvenile justice system found "a shocking distortion of the number of 'violent' girl offenders. Frustration, anger and a lack of impulse control are often shared by the adult caretakers and the girls and, in some cases, the adults were the aggressors" (Acoca & Dedel, 1998, p. 97). Listing the types of events that caused arrest reveals a clear pattern: "She returned from a runaway, mom started questioning her, so she threw a batch of cookies at her," "Father was hitting her, so she hit him back and kicked him in the groin," "My mom kept saying 'Hit me so I can call the police,'" and finally "She was trying to sneak out of the house at night, but mom caught her and pushed her against the wall. She slapped mom" (Acoca & Dedel, 1998, p. 97). The authors concluded that a "majority" of the violence charges against girls were "non-serious mutual combat situations with parents" (Acoca & Dedel, 1998, p. 15). One can also see that in many instances, these are either clearly child abuse cases or "status offense" cases that have been relabeled as violent offenses.

One explanation for this decline in voluntary commitments and nonoffenders in girls' private facilities lies in changes within the health care system. With the advent of health management organizations (HMOs), the approval for funding adolescents with behavioral problems became more difficult to achieve (see Pasko, 1997, for this discussion). Refusing payment for inpatient or residential treatment, HMOs shifted to intensive outpatient and family therapy for juveniles with "conduct problems." Parents could no longer voluntarily commit their "incorrigible" daughters with ease of approval from their health care insurances. Given the cost of inpatient treatment and the limited assistance from the health care insurance, parents turned to the juvenile justice system to institutionalize their daughters. In order to be committed via the justice system, girls' behaviors (such as fighting with a parent, running away, staying out after curfew) needed to be "upcrimed" and relabeled as delinquent offenses. This bootstrapping phenomenon explains both girls' increases in person offenses and in the custody populations in public facilities as well as their decrease in status offenses and in private institutions' populations.

Having access to private health care also works in different ways. In their Hawaii study, Pasko and Chesney-Lind (2010) found judges, probation officers, and other juvenile justice practitioners felt the institution of youth corrections has had to transform itself into a mental health and drug treatment facility because parents and adolescents have limited access to private care outside the system. Not only did having health care coverage potentially lead to the prevention or intervention of medical and mental health conditions that contribute to chronic delinquency and consequent court involvement, it also allowed decision makers to use their discretion more widely and find alternatives to juvenile justice programming, which otherwise would not be possible. Indeed, girls who had no health insurance had a 23% chance of being committed to a public facility, controlling for other factors. Girls who had private insurance had only 10% odds of being committed.

A study of girls committed to or in state care in Virginia further underscores this concern to focus on bootstrapping. The study found that minority girls, who comprise about 26% of Virginia's population, make up fully half of those committed to a secure facility. The most frequent offenses committed by these girls were misdemeanor offenses, followed by status offenses. Most revealing, though, were the responses of the probation counselors to the request that they rank the reason for the girls' commitments (see Table 4.7). The most common answer was "probation violation," followed by "repeated

Table 4.7 Virginia Secure Custody: Probation Office Reasons for
Recommending Commitment

Reasons for Commitment	Frequency
Probation violation	46
Repeated runaway	44
Self-victimization	43
Failure to participate in ordered treatment/service	29
Chronic delinquency	27
Punishment	8
Treatment not available locally	7
Heinous violent crime	7
Frustration/exasperation within system	5
Noncompliance with court-ordered fine, restitution, public service	5
Example to community/other juveniles	5

SOURCE: Task Force on Juvenile Females Offenders (1991).

runaway," "self-victimization," and "failure to participate in ordered treatment/ service." Far down the list was "heinous violent crime" and "punishment" (Task Force on Juvenile Female Offenders, 1991, pp. 2–3).

These patterns have also turned up in other countries. Reitsma-Street (1993) found that in Canada in 1991, "one in four charges laid against young females are against the administration of justice; the rate is one in six for males" (p. 445). In Canada, violation of a court order or failure to comply with decisions of the youth administration of justice are described as "offenses against the administration of justice," or, stated more simply, bootstrapping, Canadian style.

Taken together, the data on girls currently being held in public institutions show tremendous and high-level resistance to the notion that youth who have not committed any criminal act should not be held in institutions. Although the juvenile female population in private facilities has decreased over the years, girls are still 3.5 times more likely than boys to be nonoffenders or voluntary commitments in these institutions. Having said this, it would be remiss not to note that the deinstitutionalization movement has reduced the number of girls in detention centers and training schools. The movement may, however, have simply moved those girls into a private system of institutionalization—the mental health system.

DEINSTITUTIONALIZATION OR TRANSINSTITUTIONALIZATION? GIRLS AND THE MENTAL HEALTH SYSTEM

Despite considerable resistance, the incarceration of young women in public training schools and detention centers across the country fell dramatically after the passage of the Juvenile Justice and Delinquency Prevention Act of 1974. Prior to the passage of the act, nearly three-quarters (71%) of the girls and 23% of the boys in the nation's training schools were incarcerated for status offenses (Schwartz, Steketee, & Schneider, 1990). Between 1974 and 1979, the number of girls admitted to public detention facilities and training schools dropped by 40%. Since then, however, the deinstitutionalization trend has slowed in some areas of the country, particularly at the detention level, as the number of girls held in public facilities has increased since 1979 (Moone, 1993b; Office of Juvenile Justice and Delinquency Prevention, 2001; U.S. Department of Justice, 1989, p. 43).

In addition, there has been considerable gender disparity in the commitment of girls to private facilities—8% of the entire girls' custody populations are voluntary commitments or nonoffenders, compared to 2% for boys (Moone, 1993a; Office of Juvenile Justice and Delinquency Prevention, 2001; U.S. Department of Justice, 1989, p. 43). Although some of this is doubtless good news (at least for white girls), others have taken a more critical look at this trend. Schwartz, Jackson-Beeck, and Anderson (1984) have called this a system of "hidden," private juvenile correction in which incarceration can occur without any legal procedure and without the consent of the youths (because they are underage). Costs are covered by third-party health care insurance plans; indeed, as previously discussed, the reliance on this funding structure is one reason that the trend has slowed.

The clearest problems with private institutions arise in the case of private psychiatric hospitals. Although the number of juveniles institutionalized for inpatient psychiatric conditions went down in the latter half of the 1990s, this has not always been the case. Between 1980 and 1984, adolescent admissions to psychiatric units of private hospitals increased fourfold (Weithorn, 1988, p. 773). There had also been a marked shift in the pattern of juvenile mental health incarceration. In 1971, juvenile admissions to private hospitals accounted for 37% of all juvenile admissions, but by 1980, this figure had risen to 61% (p. 783). Finally, it is estimated that fewer than one-third of juveniles admitted for inpatient mental health treatment were diagnosed as having severe or acute mental disorders, in contrast to between half and two-thirds of adults admitted to these sorts of facilities (pp. 788–789). A closer look by Weithorn at the youth in such institutions in Virginia suggests that 36% to 70% of the state's hospital population "suffer from no more than 'acting out' problems and a range of less serious difficulties" (p. 789). Despite this, juvenile psychiatric patients remain in the hospital approximately twice as long as adults (p. 789).

Given the problems that public systems of control have had with sexist interpretations of status offense labels, it should come as no surprise that a number of the examples of egregious abuse of institutionalization provided by Weithorn (1988) involved girls. Some of these cases made the link directly between status offenses and these incarcerations. The case of "Sheila," for example, involved a 12-year-old girl who was hospitalized in a state psychiatric facility after spending a week in a juvenile detention center on the basis that she was a "child in need of supervision." In another case ("Lisa"), a 16-year-old girl was admitted into a private psychiatric hospital because she "'seduced' older men, drank vodka, skipped school, ran way from home, and disobeyed her divorced mother" (p. 790). Ironically, as noted earlier, it was not a concern with the rights of girls that has slowed this practice of institutionalizing girls in private facilities for these sorts of behaviors, but instead a desire to contain costs in medical care during a period of managed care.

Other privately funded programs should also be scrutinized carefully for evidence of gender bias and abuse. An extreme example of abuse turned up in a "tough love" type of boot camp in Colorado. Youth complained that counselors "spit in their faces, made them eat their own vomit, challenged them to fight, screamed racial and sexist slurs at them and made them carry human feces in their pockets" (Weller, 1996, p. 1). Investigators discovered the abuse when two youth were found to have a flesh-eating virus and a girl lost a finger. Youth spent "between two and 12 weeks" at the camp because "their parents had problems with them and wanted them in a regimented environment" (p. 2).

In another case, Mystie Kreimer, a 15-year-old resident of a 161-bed youth "shelter and treatment center," died en route to a hospital. Mystie had been placed as a "resident" in one of a "fast-growing chain of for-profit congregate care children's facilities" (Szerlag, 1996, p. 48). Started by a politically connected multimillionaire who launched Jiffy Lube, Youth Services International now operates such homes in 10 states. The facility that held Mystie, Forest Ridge, had been investigated by the Iowa Department of Human Services after former staff reported that "teens were frequently physically and emotionally abused by inexperienced youth workers." In addition, a former staff member pled guilty to "sexually exploiting a minor" (p. 48).

Mystie landed at Forest Ridge because she had a "history of substance abuse and sexual adventuring" (Szerlag, 1996, p. 42). She entered the facility in March 1995 weighing 145 pounds. When she was visited by her mother in September of that same year, she complained of leg and chest pains. Her mother recalls asking to have her daughter hospitalized but was told by the facility that she was not "sick enough to warrant that kind of medical attention" (p. 42). The mother of another girl reports seeing Mystie lying on a couch and commenting to her daughter that Mystie looked sick. Her daughter replied, "Oh, Mom, she is so sick and they still expect her to do her chores" (p. 42). Mystie died while being transported by helicopter to a Sioux Falls hospital. At the autopsy, it was determined that she died of a "massive blood clot in her lung." At the time of her death, she weighed 100 pounds (p. 42).

Although the data are far from complete, the evidence seems to indicate that girls, particularly middle-class white girls, were being incarcerated in private hospitals and treatment programs for much the same behavior that, in previous decades, placed them in public institutions. Given the lack of procedural safeguards in these settings, some might even argue that there is greater potential for sexist practices and even abuse to flourish in these closed and private settings. Although girls are still "voluntarily" committed to private institutions more often than boys, the frequency of this appears to be changing since the late 1990s. Perhaps an unintended consequence from managed care is the beginning cessation of voluntary commitments for girls with "conduct" problems. This unintended consequence, however, may very well mean a reversal to the practices of previous decades—more girls in public institutions.

GIRLS' SEXUALITY IN INSTITUTIONAL ENVIRONMENTS

Sexuality continues to be a complicated issue in girls' correctional environments. Concentrating on sexual minority girls in custody, current research also shows how girls regularly experience heteronormative policies and overall homophobia from both staff and other inmates. Majd and colleagues' (2009) and Curtin's studies (2002) demonstrate how lesbian and bisexual identities are often ignored in juvenile court and corrections, with staff assuming youth are always "straight." In addition, girls in lockup are often encouraged to develop a heterosexual understanding of themselves and their sexuality and engage in heterofeminine forms of gender conformity. Such forms of conformity include pressuring them to wear makeup and "feminine" clothing, prohibiting them from shaving their heads, using "reparative therapy" to address sexual identity confusion, and offering them only heterosexual life skills and safe-sex education. When girls in Curtin's study did engage in consensual same-sex relationships and express their LBQ (lesbian, bisexual, or questioning) orientation, staff treated them with distrust, fear, negative remarks, and occasional punishments, such as being denied roommates, being held in isolation, and being forbidden to shower with other girls (2002, p. 4). Consequently, such policies enforced inmates' homophobic responses: "Every participant reported witnessing openly homophobic peer behavior such as anti-gay name calling and threats of violence. Some reported that girls 'out' lesbian or bisexual girls to staff to get them in trouble or to have them removed from their rooms" (Curtin 2002, p. 9).

Pasko's research (2010a, 2010b) also sheds light on the difficulties sexual minority girls navigate in correctional facilities. Using 55 in-depth interviews with juvenile correctional staff (e.g., directors, therapists, line staff, etc.), she found that while staff were sensitive to issues surrounding sexual minority girls in custody, over all, what took priority was a need to create a treatment-oriented, asexual environment in which alternative sexuality is seen as part of a pathology (stemming from sexual abuse), part of the institutionalization experience ("gay while you stay"), and always criminal, due to the zero-tolerance policies of the Prison Rape Elimination Act.

In addition, Pasko (2010a, 2010b) found sexuality was frequently reduced to action and choice, privilege and freedom, which girls in custody were not allowed to "enjoy." Indeed, many staff insisted that girls were heterosexual and that their same-sex attraction was temporary and a method of manipulation and power over other girls and staff. Rarely did staff conceptualize or acknowledge girls' LBQ behavior as identity. In addition to being emotionally abusive, such staff responses and practices also served to alienate LBQ girls and push them further to the margin within the institution and upon release.

HUMAN RIGHTS ABUSES IN GIRLS' INSTITUTIONS?

Several recent scandals suggest that like their adult counterparts (women's prisons), juvenile prisons are often unsafe for girls in ways that are uniquely gendered. Take a recent investigation of conditions in the Hawaii Youth Correctional Facility in the summer of 2003 by the American Civil Liberties Union (ACLU). The ACLU inquiry found that abusive discipline, overcrowding, inadequate staff, poor facility conditions, lack of proper mental health and medical care, lack of privacy, as well as sexual harassment, exploitation, and assault by some of the youth correctional officers on female wards were occurring at the facility (see Department of Justice, 2005). Additionally, there were no female guards on duty at night in the girls' ward. Consequently, one case of rape of a girl by a male guard and several reports of girls exchanging sex with guards for cigarettes were reported. The report also noted that male guards made sexual comments to female wards, talked about their breasts, and discussed raping them. While wards noted that rape comments decreased after the rape incident, White (2003, p. 16) wrote, "Wards expressed concern that the night shift is comprised entirely of male guards and they feel vulnerable after the rape because male guards could enter their cells at any time."

The ACLU report also discovered that female wards reported being watched by male guards while they changed clothes and used the toilet. Male guards were also present when girls took showers. And, like their counterparts in detention, girls had not received outdoor recreation for a week due to lack of supervising staff and girls were told that the situation may last for up to a month (White, 2003). While critics of the ACLU report commented that the wards made up stories and severely exaggerated tales of abuse, in April of 2004, the ACLU sued the State of Hawaii in order to improve the safety and overall living conditions at the facility. Additionally, the guard implicated in the rape charge pleaded guilty to three counts of sexual assault and one count of "terroristic threatening of a female ward" (Dingeman, 2004). Although comprising a plea bargain, the legal rape case uncovered details indicating that the sexual abuse was more severe and alarming than wards originally reported to the ACLU.

More recently, the ACLU's Women's Rights Project and Human Rights Watch (HRW) conducted an investigation of the conditions of girls sent to two juvenile facilities in New York (Lansing and Tryon; HRW & ACLU, 2006). They found many of the same problems identified in the Hawaii investigation, despite more limited access to wards and staff. Most notable among their findings was "use of inappropriate and excessive force by facilities staff against girls" (HRW & ACLU, 2006, p. 4).

Girls who were former wards of the facility complained specifically about excessive use of a "forcible face down 'restraint' procedure" that often resulted in the girls having "rug burns" and other abrasions as well broken limbs as a result of this restraint process. Said one young girl: "You see kids walking around with rug burns on their faces from their temple all the way to the bottom of their chin, with crutches, one girl was in crutches and a cast because they broke her arm and leg" (HRW & ACLU, 2006, p. 48). While such procedures are supposed to be reserved for extreme situations, the girls alleged that staff used the procedure in response to all sorts of minor infractions (such as not eating something they were allergic to, "improperly making their bed or not raising their hands before speaking"; HRW & ACLU, 2006, p. 5).

Girls also complained about sexual abuse at the hands of male staff as well as verbal abuse and degrading "strip searches," a severe lack of educational and vocational programming, and excessive idleness and security. As an example, "ill girls are bound in some combination of handcuffs, leg-shackles, and leather restraint belts any time they leave the facility" (HRW & ACLU, 2006, p. 5).

Again, as we have seen in other profiles, African American girls (who are only 18% of New York's youth population) comprised 54% of the girls sent to these facilities (HRW & ACLU, 2006, p. 43). Many of these girls had histories of victimization and resultant mental health issues. Roughly a third of all the girls were incarcerated for "property" crimes (mainly larceny); of the girls imprisoned for "crimes against person," more than a third of these girls were there for "assaults," many of which involved family members (HRW & ACLU, 2006, p. 36).

While one might think that the excesses noted in these three states are unusual (or linked to one geographic region), that is sadly not the case. HRW earlier issued very critical reports that the organization did on youth facilities in Georgia (HRW, 1996), Louisiana (HRW, 1995), and Colorado (HRW, 1997), and more recently, there have been scandals in Ohio and Texas as well. In Texas, where the Texas Youth Commission has had to fire more than 90 employees since 2000, a 16-year-old girl was granted early release after she attempted suicide as a result of being "molested repeatedly" by a male guard, who had earlier been accused of having raped four other girls (Fantz, 2008, p. 3).

HRW also notes that internal monitoring and oversight of the juvenile facilities in the United States are "dysfunctional" and independent, outside monitoring is "all but non-existent" (HRW & ACLU, 2006, pp. 3–4). As a result, virtually all youth facilities in the United States are "shrouded in secrecy and the girls who suffer abuse have little meaningful redress" (HRW & ACLU, 2006, p. 4). Sadly, scandals have long surfaced at girls' institutions (see Chesney-Lind & Shelden, 2004), and all of these incidents suggest that while authorities often use institutionalization as a means of "protecting" girls from the dangers of the streets and in their homes, many

of the institutions that house girls not only perpetuate the gendered victimization that pervades girls' lives outside of these institutions, in some of the
worst instances, the abuse that they suffer rivals that found in the most
horrific of adult prisons.

Indeed, more and more girls are actually doing time in adult prisons.
Beginning in the early 1990s, "get-tough-on-crime" attitudes promoted by
politicians and reinforced by the media's portrayal of youthful offenders as
increasingly dangerous, out-of-control super-predators ushered in an era of
prosecutorial direct files and waivers to adult court (Gaarder & Belknap,
2004). During this time, 49 states (Nebraska excluded) changed their statutes to make it easier to try juveniles as adults (Hartney, 2006). The result
was a dramatic increase in the number of youth waived to adult court and
sent to adult prison; from 1990 to 2004, the number of youth under the age
of 18 doing time in adult facilities increased by 208% (Gaarder & Belknap,
2004; Hartney, 2006). Although many states did not factor in the effect of
such policy and statute changes on girls, other states purposely planned for
their inclusion. For example, after passing their "get tough" policy, Arizona
immediately began prison expansion (30 beds) for female juveniles sentenced
to adult time (Austin et al., 2000).

Since 2000, adult prisons have housed roughly 7,200 juveniles every
year, with girls comprising 4% of that population (Hartney, 2006). The
consequences are dire. Compared to those held in juvenile detention centers,
youth held in adult facilities are more likely to be beaten by staff, to commit
suicide, and to be attacked with a weapon (Young & Gainsborough, 2000).
In particular, girls incarcerated in adult prisons are more likely to be sexually
assaulted and to be physically restrained by staff (Austin et al., 2000;
Gaarder & Belknap, 2004). In addition to pointing out abuses, research has
also critically questioned the quality of prison programming for girls, especially in the areas of education, psychiatric services, health care, life skills,
and work training (Gaarder & Belknap, 2004).

The new millennium has signaled a dramatic reversal of previous
decades of emphasis on the deinstitutionalization of girls. Today, girls are
more likely to be arrested for violence and, once arrested, they are more likely
to be detained or committed to residential facilities, often secure facilities
with prisonlike atmospheres and serious problems of abuse. Moreover,
girls' detentions and commitments are longer now, and once serving their
time, girls are more likely than before to return to detention and residential

placement thanks to recent legislative changes. One feature of girls and justice has not changed: Girls continue to experience rampant abuse and neglect at the hands of their justice system protectors—abuse that is in violation of international standards of human rights (HRW & ACLU, 2006). The persistence of neglect and abuse, as well as the increase in girls' arrests, court appearances, detentions, and commitments, seems truly ironic given that since the 1970s, advocates, researchers, and legislators have pressed for increased services for and the decreased institutionalization, abuse, and neglect of girls.

INSTEAD OF INCARCERATION: WHAT COULD BE DONE TO MEET THE NEEDS OF GIRLS?

Girls on the economic and political margins, particularly those who find their way into the juvenile justice system, share many problems with their male counterparts. They are likely to be poor, from disrupted and violent families, and having trouble in school. In addition, however, girls also confront problems unique to their sex: notably sexual abuse, sexual assault, dating violence, depression, unplanned pregnancy, and adolescent motherhood. Their experience of the problems they share with boys and the additional problems they face as girls are both conditioned by their gender, class, and race. Because families are the source of many of the serious problems that girls face, solutions must take into account the possibility that some girls may not be able to stay safely at home.

Programming for girls clearly needs to be shaped by girls' unique situations and to address the special problems girls have in a gendered society. Unfortunately, traditional delinquency treatment strategies, employed in both prevention and intervention programs, have been shaped largely by commonsense assumptions about what youth—generally boys—need, and even then, these problems fail to recognize boys' gender-management strategies and problematic dimensions. Sometimes girls will benefit from these notions, and sometimes their problems will not be addressed at all.

There is a tremendous shortage of information on programs that have been proven effective with girls (see Chesney-Lind & Shelden, 2004). Indeed, many studies that have evaluated particular approaches do not deal with special gender issues, and frequently, programs do not even serve girls. In addition, programs that have been carefully evaluated are often set in training schools (clearly not the ideal place to try any particular strategy). Finally, careful evaluation of most programs shows that even the most determined efforts to intervene and help often have very poor results. Of course, the last two points may be related; programs set in closed, institutional settings are clearly at a disadvantage and, as a consequence, tend to be less effective (Lipsey, 1992). Unfortunately, community-based programs for girls have been few and far between.

One such gender-responsive community program that has been evaluated as effective is Honolulu Girls Court (Davidson et al., 2011). Girls Court in Honolulu is a court-based program established to give visibility to girls and to meet their specific needs while minimizing the use of detainment or commitment. Girls Court began in the fall of 2004 with an initial cohort of 10 girls. Generally, the program works as follows: The girls attend hearings every 5 weeks at which they appear, with their parent(s), before the same judge, who consistently shows concern and involvement in the girls' lives. With their probation officers and the rest of their cohort looking on, the girls explain their behavior, achieved goals, setbacks, and stressors during the past 5 weeks. They receive praise for their successes and advice and possible consequences for their infractions. After the hearings, the girls attend activities that include, but are not limited to, HIV/STDs education, community service projects, family fun events, life skills projects, vocational training, academic counseling, physical exercise, and group and individual counseling with a therapist who specializes in girl-sensitive issues. They also receive psychiatric consultations and drug treatment when necessary (Pasko, 2008, p. 12).

With heightened discipline, access to girl-sensitive rehabilitation, and more connection to and investment in the girls' lives, Girls Court programming addresses those issues that perpetuate girls' pathways to delinquency and status offending (namely, running away), probation revocations, and commitment. Additionally, the structure of Girls Court seeks to minimize the fragmentation that girls typically experience in the juvenile justice system, since their low-level offending often affords them marginal services. Overall, the evaluation outcomes showed that participants felt programming improved their lives. In addition, Girls Court did reduce girls' recidivism, especially in the runaway offense category (which previously often segued to girls' probation revocations). The fact that Girls Court reduced runaway behaviors (coupled with positive commentary by the girls them-selves) intimates that such family stressors, previous trauma, and other risk factors were mediated by the program participation (Davidson et al., 2011).

Indeed, the evaluation's interview and focus group research revealed that girls' engagement in other risk factors was also minimized. Girls dem-onstrated less drug use, improved academic functioning, and awareness of healthy relationships. They also reported a connection to the other girls—sometimes the first connection girls have had. Girls reported that Girls Court was able to successfully foster an environment in which similarly situated girls openly encouraged each other to avoid making harmful choices. Moreover, parents also reported healthier relationships with their daughters, less fighting, and greater overall family functioning. That the qualitative data did reveal high marks from both the girls and their parents is consistent with other recent work that suggests that gender-responsive programming, when delivered properly, avoids the overall pitfalls of more punitive intensive supervision efforts (Morash, 2010).

Programs such as Girls Court are in the minority, however. Furthermore, programs for young women in general (and delinquents in particular) have been of low priority in our society, as far as funding is concerned. For instance, a report written in 1975 by the Law Enforcement Assistance Administration revealed that only 5% of federally funded juvenile delin-quency projects were specifically directed at girls and that only 6% of all local monies for juvenile justice were spent on girls (Female Offender Resource Center, 1977, p. 34). A 1990 review of 75 private foundations revealed that funding "targeted specifically for girls and women hovered around 3.4 percent" (Valentine Foundation and Women's Way, 1990, p. 5). More recently, the OJJDP Girls Study Group's examination of 62 girls' delinquency programs found that only 17 had published evaluations, with only four meeting the criteria of "promising" programming. None of the 17 had been evaluated as effective because most programs had insufficient evidence (Zahn et al., 2008). While the GAO criticized the study group's methodology as "unrealistically high" (Larence, 2010, p. 5), there is a more profound problem. As of 2009, many of the programs they examined were no longer in existence due to the absence of funding and lack of political support. Unfortunately, even Girls Court risks the same fate as lack of fund-ing and support become increasingly problematic (Judge Radius, personal communication, 2011).

What are the specific needs of young women—in particular, those who come into contact with the juvenile justice system as victims or offenders? Researchers and girls paint a picture of complex needs that include the daunting problems of lacking a family that can support adolescent development or provide basic safety, dangerous neighborhoods, individual trauma from sexual and other abuse, involvement in prostitution, relationships with older men with high potential for exploitation, academic failure, substance abuse, and lack of preparation to earn a living and live on one's own. Services must be comprehensive and adapted to a particular girl's family and neighborhood context, and they must be available to girls before they penetrate deeply into the juvenile justice system, during those vulnerable years from 9 to 14, and after they are in serious trouble.

The Minnesota Women's Fund noted that the most frequent risk factors for girls and boys differ, and that for girls the list includes emotional stress, physical and sexual abuse, negative body image, disordered eating, suicide, and pregnancy. For boys, the list included alcohol, polydrug use, accidental injury, and delinquency (Adolescent Female Subcommittee, 1994). Although not all girls at risk will end up in the juvenile justice system, this gendered examination of youth problems sets a standard for the examination of delinquency prevention and intervention programs.

Among other needs that girls' programs should address are dealing with the physical and sexual violence in their lives (from parents, boyfriends, pimps, and others); confronting the risk of AIDS; dealing with pregnancy and motherhood; countering drug and alcohol dependency; facing family problems; obtaining vocational and career counseling; managing stress; and developing a sense of efficacy and empowerment. Many of these needs are universal and should be part of programs for all youth (Schwartz & Orlando, 1991). However, most of these are particularly important for young women.

Alder (1986, 1995) points out that serving girls effectively will require different and innovative strategies because "young men tend to be more noticeable and noticed than young women" (Alder, 1995, p. 3). When girls go out, they tend to move in smaller groups, there are greater proscriptions against girls "hanging out," and they may be justly fearful of being on the streets at night. Finally, girls are subject to many more domestic expectations than their male counterparts, and these may keep them confined to their homes. Alder notes that this may be a particular issue for immigrant girls.

Despite the lack of evaluation research and the obvious necessity to recognize the special and unique needs of girls, there is also some encouraging news as girl-serving organizations (such as the YWCA, Girls Incorporated, etc., and Dress for Success) realize they have a responsibility for girls who are in the juvenile justice system. Recent reviews of promising programs for girls (Girls Incorporated, 1996; OJJDP Girls Study Group, 2009; Schwartz & Orlando, 1991; Zahn et al., 2010) indicate that programs that specifically target the housing and employment needs of youth while also providing them with the specific skills they need to survive on their own are emerging. These often include built-in caseworker/service broker and counseling components. Clearly, many girls will require specialized counseling to recover from the ravages of sexual and physical victimization, but the research cautions that approaches that rely simply on the provision of counseling services are not likely to succeed (see Chesney-Lind & Shelden, 2004). Programs must also be scrutinized to ensure that they are culturally specific. As increasing numbers of girls of color are drawn into the juvenile justice system (and bootstrapped into correctional settings) while their white counterparts are deinstitutionalized, there is a need for programs rooted in specific cultures. Because girls of color have different experiences of their gender and different experiences with the dominant institutions in the society (Amaro, 1995; Amaro & Agular, 1994; LaFromboise & Howard-Pitney, 1995; Orenstein, 1994; Schaffner, 2006), programs to divert and deinstitutionalize must be shaped by the unique developmental issues confronting minority girls and must build in the specific cultural resources available in ethnic communities. Programs such as Diineegwasii in Fairbanks, Alaska (Alaskan Native girls), and Nuevo Dia in Salt Lake City, Utah (Hispanic girls), are examples of gender-specific programming designed for minority girls. Each program works to develop both a positive gender as well as ethnic identity (Office of Juvenile Justice and Delinquency Prevention, 1998).

Innovative programs must also receive the same sort of stable funding generally accorded their more traditional "best practices" and institutional counterparts (which are generally far less innovative and flexible). Many novel programs relied on federal funds or private foundation grants; pitifully few survived for any length of time. To survive and thrive, innovative programs must be able to count on stable funding. The recent pressure exerted by Congress on states to conduct an inventory of programs that are specifically

FIVE

TRENDS IN WOMEN'S CRIME

—————◆•◆•◆—————

Women's crime, like girls' crime, is deeply affected by women's place. As a result, women's contribution to serious and violent crime—like that of girls—is minor. Of those adults arrested for serious crimes of violence in 2009 (murder, forcible rape, robbery, and aggravated assault), only 19% were female. Indeed, women constituted only 24.4% of all arrests during that year (FBI, 2010a, p. 239). This also means that adult women are an even smaller percentage of those arrested than their girl counterparts (who now comprise nearly one out of three juvenile arrests).

Moreover, the majority of adult women offenders, like girls, are arrested and tried for relatively minor offenses. In 2009, women were most likely to be arrested for larceny theft (which alone accounted for 15.2% of all adult women's arrests), followed by driving under the influence (10.9%) and drug abuse violations (9.9%). This means that more than a third of all the women arrested in the United States that year were arrested for one of these three offenses. Women's offenses, then, are concentrated in just a few criminal categories, just as women's employment in the mainstream economy is concentrated in a few job categories. Furthermore, these offenses, as we shall see, are closely tied to women's economic marginality and the ways women attempt to cope with poverty.

UNRULY WOMEN: A BRIEF HISTORY
OF WOMEN'S OFFENSES

Women's concentration in petty offenses is not restricted to the present. A study of women's crime in 14th-century England (Hanawalt, 1982) and descriptions of the backgrounds of the women who were forcibly transported to Australia several centuries later (Beddoe, 1979) document the astonishing stability in patterns of women's lawbreaking.

The women who were transported to Australia, for example, were servants, maids, or laundresses convicted of petty theft (stealing, shoplifting, and picking pockets) or prostitution. The number of women transported for these trivial offenses is sobering. Between 1787 and 1852, no fewer than 24,960 women, fully a third of whom were first offenders, were sent to relieve the "shortage" of women in the colonies. Shipped in rat-infested holds, the women were systematically raped and sexually abused by the ships' officers and sailors, and the death rate in the early years was as high as one in three. Their arrival in Australia was also a nightmare; no provision was made for the women and many were forced to turn to prostitution to survive (Beddoe, 1979, pp. 11–21).

Other studies add different but important dimensions to the picture. For example, Bynum's (1992) research on "unruly" women in antebellum North Carolina adds the vital dimension of race to the picture. She notes that the marginalized members of society, particularly "free black and unmarried poor white women," were most often likely both to break social and sexual taboos and to face punishment by the courts. Indeed, she observes that "if North Carolina lawmakers could have done so legally, they would have rid society altogether" of these women (p. 10). As it was, they harshly enforced laws against fornication, bastardy, and prostitution in an attempt to affect these women and their progeny.

The role of urbanization and class is further explored in Feeley and Little's (1991) research on criminal cases appearing in London courts between 1687 and 1912, and Boritch and Hagan's (1990) research on arrests in Toronto between 1859 and 1955. Both of these studies examine the effect of industrialization and women's economic roles (or economic marginalization) on women's offenses. Both works present evidence that women were drawn to urban areas, where they were employed in extremely low-paid work. As a result, this forced many into forms of offending, including disorderly conduct, drunkenness, and petty thievery. Boritch and Hagan make special note of the large numbers of women arrested for property offenses, "drunkenness," and "vagrancy," which can be seen as historical counterparts to modern drug offenses. But what of women who committed "serious" offenses such as murder? Jones's (1980) study of early women murderers in the United States reveals that many of America's early women murderers were indentured servants. Raped by calculating masters who understood that giving birth to a "bastard" would add 1 to 2 years to a woman's term of service, these desperate women hid their pregnancies and then committed infanticide. Jones also provides numerous historical and contemporary examples of desperate women murdering their brutal lovers or husbands. The less dramatic links between forced marriage, women's circumscribed options, and women's decisions to kill, often by poison, characterized the Victorian murderesses. These women, though rare, haunted the turn of the century, in part because women's participation in the methodical violence involved in arsenic poisoning was considered unthinkable (Hartman, 1977).

In short, research on the history of women's offenses, and particularly women's violence, is a valuable resource for its information on the level and character of women's crime and as a way to understand the relationship between women's crime and women's lives. Whenever a woman commits murder, particularly if she is accused of murdering a family member, people immediately ask, "How could she do that?" Given the enormous costs of being born female, that may well be the wrong question. The real question, as a review of the history of women's crime illustrates, is not why women murder but rather why so few murder.

Take a look at some facts. Every 15 seconds, a woman is beaten in her own home (Bureau of Justice Statistics, 1989). One in every three women reports having been physically attacked by an intimate partner at some time in her life (Wilt & Olson, 1996). Women were three times more likely to be killed by their intimate partners than were men and accounted for 86% of all victims of domestic violence (Rennison, 2001, p. 1; Smith & Farole, 2009). A National Institute of Mental Health study (based on urban-area hospitals) estimated that 21% of all women using emergency surgical services had been injured in a domestic violence incident; that half of all injuries presented by women to emergency surgical services occurred in the context of partner abuse; and that more than 40% of rapes had been perpetrated by an intimate partner (Stark et al., 1981; Truman & Rand, 2010).

In addition, other studies have shown that marital rape is often more violent and repetitive than other forms of sexual assault and is often not reported (Richie, 2000, p. 4). In the United States, for example, former Surgeon General C. Everett Koop (1989) estimated that 3 to 4 million women are battered each year; roughly half of them are single, separated, or divorced (Rennison, 2001). According to the 2008 National Crime Victimization Survey (Rand, 2009), women separated from their husbands are victimized at higher rates than married, divorced, or single women, with females aged 16 to 24 experiencing the highest rate of intimate partner violence—151 per 1,000 women (Rennison, 2001, p. 5). Battering also tends to escalate and become more severe over time. Almost half of all batterers beat their partners at least three times a year (Straus, Gelles, & Steinmetz, 1980). This description of victimization doesn't address other forms of women's abuse, such as incest and sexual assault, which have rates as alarmingly high (see Center for Policy Studies, 1991; Truman, 2011).

The real question is why so few women resort to violence in the face of such horrendous victimization in their homes—even to save their lives. In 2009, in the United States, only 10.7% of those arrested for murder were women—meaning that murder, like other forms of violent crime, is almost exclusively a male activity. In fact, women murderers, as both Jones (1980) and Hartman (1977) document, are interesting precisely because of their rarity. The large number of women arrested for trivial property and moral offenses, coupled with the virtual absence of women from those arrested for serious property crimes and violent crimes, provides clear evidence that women's crime parallels their assigned role in the rest of society (Klein & Kress, 1976). In essence, women's place in the legitimate economy largely relegates them to jobs that pay poorly and are highly sex segregated (such as secretarial and sales jobs). Likewise, in the illicit or criminal world, they occupy fewer roles and roles that do not "pay" as well as men's crime. There is, however, little understanding of why this is the case and, until recently, little scholarship devoted to explaining this pattern. This chapter attempts to address both the reality of women's crime and the fascination with the atypical woman offender who is violent and defies her conventional role in both the mainstream and the criminal world.

TRENDS IN WOMEN'S ARRESTS

Over the years, women have typically been arrested for larceny theft, drunk driving, fraud (the bulk of which is welfare fraud and naive check forgery), drug abuse violations, and buffer charges for prostitution (such as disorderly conduct and a variety of petty offenses that fall under the broad category of "other offenses"; Steffensmeier, 1980; Steffensmeier & Allan, 1995; see Table 5.1 for summary of women's arrests for Index Offenses).

Table 5.1   Adult 10-Year Index Offense Arrest Trends by Sex, 2000–2009

Index Offense Charged	Men			Women		
	2000	*2009*	*% Change*	*2000*	*2009*	*% Change*
Total	5,443,682	5,366,469	−1.4%	1,446,691	1,733,291	+19.8%
Murder*	6,179	5,838	−5.5	764	703	−8.0
Forcible rape	13,487	10,667	−20.9	147	120	−18.4
Robbery	43,582	50,564	+16.0	5,131	7,390	+44.0
Aggravated assault	208,978	186,393	−10.8	51,204	50,989	−0.01
Burglary	99,294	118,120	+18.9	16,484	24,024	+45.7
Larceny-theft	308,787	344,898	+11.7	172,780	264,843	+53.3
Motor vehicle theft	44,237	29,575	−33.1	7,756	6,544	−15.6
Arson	3,898	3,294	−15.5	894	823	−7.9
Total violent crime	272,226	253,462	−6.8	57,246	59,202	+3.4
Total property crime	456,216	495,887	+8.7	197,914	296,234	+49.7

SOURCE: Federal Bureau of Investigation (2010b, p. 239).

*Includes nonnegligent manslaughter

Arrest data certainly suggest that the war on drugs has translated into a war on women. Between 2000 and 2009, arrests of adult women for drug abuse violations increased by 15.4%, which was more than double the increase (7.7%) men experienced (FBI, 2010a, p. 239). The past decade (2000–2009) has also seen increases in arrests of women for "other assaults" (up 21.3%)—not unlike the pattern seen in girls' arrests. Arrest rates show much the same pattern. In the past decade, arrests of women for drug offenses and other assaults have replaced fraud and disorderly conduct as the most common offenses for which adult women are arrested.

These figures, however, should not be used to support notions of dramatic increases in women's crime. As an example, although the number of adult women arrested between 2000 and 2009 did increase by 19.8%, that increase followed a decline in women's arrests that started in 1997 but crept back up again, beginning in 2005 (FBI, 1998, 2006, 2010a).

Moreover, looking at these offenses differently reveals a picture of stability rather than change over the past two decades. Women's share of these arrests (as a proportion of all those arrested for these offenses) rose from 23% to 26% between 1992 and 2001 and then sank back to 24.4% in 2009. From 2000 to 2009, women's share of arrests for index violent offenses only rose from 17% to 19% (FBI, 2010a, p. 239). The lion's share of these serious violent crimes is not due to murder or rape arrests, but, rather, it is due to aggravated assault. At the other extreme is the pattern found in arrests for prostitution—the only crime among the 29 offense categories tracked by the FBI for which arrests of women account for the majority (68.8%) of all arrests.

Overall, the increase in women's official arrest statistics is largely accounted for by a similar pattern noticed in their juvenile counterparts— increases in other assaults, drug abuse violations, and property offenses, such as check forgery and embezzlement. Despite an increase in robbery, aggravated assaults, and other assaults, women's crime is mostly nonviolent in nature—30% of all women offenders are arrested for some type of property crime (compared to 13% of men). Here, both property and drug violation arrests are real, because the base numbers are large and, as a result, these offenses make up a large portion of women's official deviance. Whether the increase in robbery, other assaults, and drug violation arrests (coupled with a consistently large number of arrests for property offenses) are the product of actual changes in women's behavior over the past decade or changes in law enforcement practices is an important question, and one to which we now turn.

HOW COULD SHE? THE NATURE
AND CAUSES OF WOMEN'S CRIME

In summary, adult women have been and continue to be arrested for minor crimes (generally shoplifting, bad checks, and welfare fraud) and what might be called "deportment" offenses (prostitution, disorderly conduct, and, arguably, "driving under the influence"). Their younger counterparts are arrested for essentially the same crimes, in addition to status offenses (running away from home, incorrigibility, truancy, and other noncriminal offenses for which only minors can be taken into custody). Arrests of adult women, like arrests of girls, have increased for both aggravated and other assaults. Finally, and most important, adult women's arrests for drug offenses have soared. In 1986, 91,813 women in the United States were arrested for drug abuse violations (FBI, 1995). By 2009, that number had more than doubled to 189,039 women (FBI, 2010a).

Where there have been increases in women's arrests for offenses that sound nontraditional, such as embezzlement, careful examination reveals the connections between these offenses and women's place.

Embezzlement

In the case of embezzlement, for which women's arrests have also doubled during the past 25 years, careful research disputes the notion of women moving firmly into the ranks of big-time, white-collar offenders. Because women are concentrated in low-paying clerical, sales, and service occupations (Renzetti & Curran, 1995), they are "not in a position to steal hundreds of thousands of dollars but they [are] in a position to pocket smaller amounts" (Simon & Landis, 1991, p. 56). Moreover, their motives for such theft often involve family responsibilities rather than a desire for personal gain (Daly, 1989; Zietz, 1981).

Daly's (1989) analysis of gender differences in white-collar crime is particularly useful. In a review of federal "white-collar" crime cases in seven federal districts (which included people convicted of bank embezzlement, income tax fraud, postal fraud, etc.), she found that gender played a substantial role in the differences between men's and women's offenses. For example, of those arrested for bank embezzlement, 60% of the women were tellers and 90% were in some sort of clerical position. By contrast, about half of the men charged with embezzlement held professional and managerial positions (bank officers and financial managers). Therefore, it is no surprise that for each embezzlement offense, men's attempted economic gain was 10 times higher than women's (Daly, 1989). In commenting on this pattern, Daly notes, "the women's socioeconomic profile, coupled with the nature of their crimes, makes one wonder if 'white collar' aptly described them or their illegalities" (p. 790).

Embezzlement is a particularly interesting offense to "unpack" because it is one of the offenses for which, if present trends continue, women may comprise about half of those charged (Renzetti & Curran, 1995, p. 310). In fact, slightly more women ($n = 5,844$) than men ($n = 5,519$) were arrested for embezzlement in 2009 (FBI, 2010a, p. 239). Yet these increases cannot be laid at the door of women breaking into traditionally "male" offense patterns. Women's increased share of arrests for embezzlement is probably an artifact of their presence in low-level positions that make them more vulnerable to frequent checking and hence more vulnerable to detection (Steffensmeier & Allan, 1995). Combining this with these women's lack of access to resources to "cover" their thefts prompts Steffensmeier and Allan to draw a parallel between modern women's involvement in embezzlement and increases in thefts by women in domestic service a century ago.

Driving Under the Influence

Arrests of women driving under the influence (DUI) account for more than 1 arrest in 10 of women (FBI, 2010a, p. 239). One study (Wells-Parker, Pang, Anderson, McMillen, & Miller, 1991) found that women arrested for DUI tended to be older than men (with nearly half of the men but less than a third of the women under 30), more likely to be "alone, divorced or separated," and to have fewer serious drinking problems and fewer extensive prior arrests for DUI or "public drunkenness" (Wells-Parker et al., 1991, p. 144). Historically, women were arrested for DUI only if "the DUI involved a traffic accident or physical/verbal abuse of a police officer" (Coles, 1991, p. 5). These patterns have probably eroded in recent years because of public outrage over drinking and driving and an increased use of roadblocks. Changes in police practices and more women driving in general, rather than changes in women's drinking, could easily explain the prominence of this offense in women's official crime patterns.

Women tend to drink alone and deny treatment (Coles, 1991). Also, in contrast to men, they tend to drink for "escapism and psychological comfort" (Wells-Parker et al., 1991, p. 146). For these reasons, intervention programs that attempt to force women to examine their lives and the quality of relationships, which tend to work for male DUI offenders, are not successful with women. Indeed, these interventions could "exacerbate a sense of distress, helplessness and hopelessness" that could, in turn, trigger more drinking (Wells-Parker et al., p. 146).

Larceny Theft/Shoplifting

Women's arrests for larceny theft are composed largely of arrests for shoplifting. Steffensmeier (1980) estimates that perhaps as many as four-fifths of all arrests on larceny charges are for shoplifting. Cameron's (1953) early study of shoplifting in Chicago explains that women's prominence among those arrested for shoplifting may not reflect greater female involvement in the offense but, rather, differences in the ways men and women shoplift. Her research revealed that women tend to steal more items than men, to steal items from several stores, and to steal items of lesser value. Store detectives explained this pattern by saying that people tended to "steal the same way they buy" (Cameron, p. 159). Men came to the store with one item in mind. They saw it, took it, and left the store. Women, on the other hand, shopped around. Because the chance of being arrested increases with each item stolen, Cameron felt that the stores probably underestimated the level of men's shoplifting.

Although women stole more items than men, the median value of adult male theft was significantly higher than that of women (Cameron, 1953, p. 62). In addition, more men than women were defined as "commercial shoplifters" (people who stole merchandise for possible resale).

Perhaps as a result of women's shopping and shoplifting patterns, studies done later (Lindquist, 1988) have found that women constitute 58% of those caught shoplifting. Steffensmeier and Allan (1995) go so far as to suggest that shoplifting may be regarded as a prototypically female offense. Shopping is, after all, part of women's "second shift" of household management, housework, and child care responsibilities (Hochschild, 1989). Shoplifting can be seen as a criminal extension of expected and familiar women's work.

Even the reasons for shoplifting are gendered. Men, particularly young men, tend to view stealing as part of a broader pattern of masculine display of "badness" and steal items that are of no particular use to them (Steffensmeier & Allan, 1995). At the other extreme, they may be professional thieves and thus more likely to escape detection (Cameron, 1953).

Girls and women, on the other hand, tend to steal items that they either need or feel they need but cannot afford. As a result, they tend to steal from stores and to take things such as clothing, cosmetics, and jewelry. Campbell (1981) notes that women—young and old—are the targets of enormously expensive advertising campaigns for a vast array of personal products. These messages, coupled with the temptations implicit in long hours spent "shopping," lead to many arrests of women for these offenses.

Despite some contentions that women actually shoplift more than men, self-report data in fact show few gender differences in the prevalence of the behavior (see Chesney-Lind & Shelden, 2004, for a review of these studies).

What appears to be happening is that girls and women shoplift in different ways than men. In addition, they are more often apprehended because store detectives expect women to shoplift more than men and thus watch women more closely (Morris, 1987).

BIG TIME/SMALL TIME

English (1993) approached the issue of women's crime by analyzing detailed self-report surveys she administered to a sample of 128 female and 872 male inmates in Colorado. She examined both "participation rates" and "crime frequency" figures for a wide array of different offenses. She found few differences in the participation rates of men and women, with the exception of three property crimes. Men were more likely than women to report participation in burglary, whereas women were more likely than men to have participated in theft and forgery. Exploring these differences further, she found that women "lack the specific knowledge needed to carry out a burglary" (p. 366).

Women were far more likely than men to be involved in "forgery" (it was the most common crime for women and fifth out of eight for men). Follow-up research on a subsample of "high crime"-rate female respondents revealed that many had worked in retail establishments and therefore "knew how much time they had" between stealing the checks or credit cards and having them reported (English, 1993, p. 370). The women said that they would target "strip malls" where credit cards and bank checks could be stolen easily and used in nearby retail establishments. The women reported that their high-frequency theft was motivated by a "big haul," which meant a purse with several hundred dollars in it, in addition to cards and checks. English concludes that "women's over representation in low-paying, low status jobs" increases their involvement in these property crimes (p. 171).

English's (1993) findings with regard to two other offenses, for which gender differences did not appear in participation rates, are worth exploring here. She found no difference in the "participation rates" of women and men in drug sales and assault. However, when examining the frequency data, English found that women in prison reported making significantly more drug sales than men but not because they were engaged in big-time drug selling. Instead, their high number of drug sales occurred because women's drug sales were "concentrated in the small trades (i.e., transactions of less than $10)" (p. 372).

Because they made so little money, English found that 20% of the active women dealers reported making 20 or more drug deals per day (p. 372).

A reverse of the same pattern was found when English (1993) examined women's participation in assault. Here, slightly more (27.8%) women than men (23.4%) reported assaulting someone in the past year. However, most of these women reported making only one assault during the study period (65.4%), compared to only about a third of the men (37.5%).

English (1993) found that "economic disadvantage" played a role in both women's and men's criminal careers. Beyond this, however, gender played an important role in shaping women's and men's response to poverty. Specifically, women's criminal careers reflect "gender differences in legitimate and illegitimate opportunity structures, in personal networks, and in family obligations" (p. 374).

PATHWAYS TO WOMEN'S CRIME

As with girls, the links between adult women's victimization and crimes are increasingly clear. As was noted in earlier chapters, the backgrounds of adult women offenders hint at links between childhood victimization and adult offending. Experiencing gender and racial oppression, those groups of women who are most socially marginalized are particularly vulnerable to both problems—abuse/victimization and involvement in illegal activity (DeHart, 2009; Richie, 2000; Salisbury & Van Voorhis, 2009). For example, a 1996 survey of women in prison reported that at least half of them experienced sexual abuse before their incarceration—a much higher rate than what is reported in the general population (Richie, 2000, p. 5). Other studies have documented the link between women's experiences with physical and/or sexual violence and their involvement with illegal drugs (DeHart, 2009; Harlow, 1999).

Widom (2000) demonstrates in her work the importance of understanding women's experiences of abuse and neglect during childhood and their entrance into criminal activity. Abused and neglected girls are nearly twice as likely to be arrested as juveniles, twice as likely to be arrested as adults, and 2.4 times more likely to be arrested for violent crimes (p. 29). They are "more likely to use alcohol and other drugs and turn to criminal and violent behaviors when coping with stressful life events" (p. 33). Widom explains (as previously mentioned in Chapter 2) that victimization prompts girls' entry into delinquency as they try and flee their abusive environments. With deficits in cognitive abilities and achievement and few positive relationships or social controls, these girls end up on the streets with hardly any legitimate survival skills (p. 30). Their experiences with victimization and violence may result in lowered self-esteem, a lack of sense of control over one's life, and behavioral inclinations for crime and violence. Consequently, they become women with few social or psychological resources for successful adult development.

Family problems and violence—such as death, disruption, abuse and neglect, poverty, and drug/alcohol addiction—produce gendered effects for boys and girls. Although both boys and girls who grow up in family environments riddled with crime and violence have higher propensities to model such behavior (Widom, 2000), girls must also negotiate gender oppression. Such oppression confines girls and women to a dichotomous characterization: weak and dependent as well as sexually uncontrollable (Gelsthorpe, 1989; Girshick, 1999). Girshick (1999, p. 30), in her stories of women in prison, points out an important consequence: Abused females are the least likely to have been affected in a positive way by the challenge of the women's movement to traditional gender roles and expectations. In a desperate need to have someone close to them, they often feel powerless, have limited options for change, and meet with continued abuse and violence. These women are trapped by patriarchy (and for women of color, racial and ethnic discrimination), their gender identity, their loyalty to their partners, and the violence itself (Girshick, 1999, p. 58; Richie, 1996).

DeHart's (2009) study also demonstrates the importance of understanding the connection between abuse and trauma in women's criminality. In her interviews of 60 female prisoners, women shared how victimization and mistreatment had direct links to their offending: that is, adults and caregivers in early childhood forcing them to use drugs, steal, or prostitute, which became ways of life in adulthood (p. 1365). Her interviews also showed how indirect links of prior abuse to adult offending were apparent in these women's lives: from experiencing profound effects on mental and physical health to viewing maltreatment in relationships as a normal part of life (p. 1370).

Other studies have also demonstrated this important link between childhood trauma and adult criminality. Gilfus (1992) interviewed 20 incarcerated women and documented how such childhood injuries were linked to adult crimes in women. Gilfus extends the work of Miller (1986) and Chesney-Lind and Rodriguez (1983) on the ways in which women's backgrounds color their childhoods and ultimately their adulthoods. She conducted in-depth interviews in 1985 and 1986 with the women in a Northeastern women's facility that, at the time, served as both a jail and a prison. From these lengthy interviews, she reconstructed "life event histories" for each of the women. The group had a mean age of 30 (ranging from 20 to 41 years of age), and included 8 African American and 12 white women. All of the women had life histories of what Gilfus characterized as "street crimes"—by which she meant prostitution, shoplifting, check or credit card fraud, and drug law violations. Their current offenses included assault and battery; accessory to rape; breaking and entering; and multiple charges of drug possession, larceny, and prostitution (Gilfus, p. 68). Sentence lengths ranged, for this group, from 3 months to 20 years.

Most of the women were single mothers, three-quarters were intravenous drug users, and almost all (17) had histories of prostitution (7 of the women had begun as teenage prostitutes). Most of these women had grown up with violence; 13 of the 20 reported childhood sexual abuse, and 15 had experienced "severe child abuse" (Gilfus, 1992, p. 70). There were no differences in the levels of abuse reported by black and white respondents, although African American women grew up in families that were more economically marginalized than those of their white counterparts. Although some women's childhood memories were totally colored by their sexual abuse, for most of the women in Gilfus's sample, coping with and surviving multiple victimization was the more normal pattern. In the words of one of these women, "I just got hit a lot. . . . 'Cause they would both drink and they wouldn't know the difference. Mmm, picked up, thrown against walls, everything, you name it" (p. 72).

Despite the abuse and violence, these women recall spending time trying to care for and protect others, especially younger siblings, and attempting to do housework and even care for their abusive and drug- or alcohol-dependent parents. They also recall teachers who ignored signs of abuse and who, in the case of African American girls, were hostile and racist. Ultimately, 16 out of the 20 dropped out of high school (Gilfus, 1992, p. 69). The failure of the schools to be responsive to these young women's problems meant that the girls could perceive no particular future for themselves. Given the violence in their lives, drugs provided these girls with a solace found nowhere else.

Many (13) ran away from home as girls. "Rape, assault, and even attempted murder" were reported by 16 of the 20, with an average of three "rape or violent rape attempts" per woman; many of these occurred in the context of prostitution, but when the women attempted to report the assault, the police simply "ridiculed" the women or threatened to arrest them. In some cases, the police would demand sexual services for not arresting the woman (Gilfus, 1992, p. 79).

Violence also characterized these women's relationships with adult men; 15 of the 20 had lived with violent men. The women were expected to bring in money, generally through prostitution and shoplifting. These men functioned as the women's pimps but also sold drugs, committed robberies, or fenced the goods shoplifted by the women. Thirteen of the women had become pregnant as girls, but only four kept their first baby. Most of the women had subsequent children whom they attempted to mother despite their worsening addictions, and they tended to rely on their mothers (not their boyfriends) to take care of their children while they were in prison. The women continued to see their criminal roles as forms of caretaking, taking care of their children and of their abusive boyfriends. As Gilfus (1992) puts it, "the women in this study consider their illegal activities to be a form of work which is undertaken primarily from economic necessity to support partners, children, and addictions" (p. 86). Gilfus further speculates that violence "may socialize women to adopt a tenacious commitment to caring for anyone who promises love, material success, and acceptance" (p. 86), which, in turn, places them at risk for further exploitation and abuse.

The interviews Arnold (1995) conducted, based on this same hypothesis, with 50 African American women serving sentences in a city jail and 10 additional interviews with African American women in prison, are an important addition to the work of Gilfus (1992). Arnold notes that African American girls are not only sexually victimized but are also the victims of "class oppression." Specifically, she notes that "to be young, Black, poor and female is to be in a high-risk category for victimization and stigmatization on many levels" (p. 139). Growing up in extreme poverty means that African American girls may turn earlier to deviant behavior, particularly stealing, to help themselves and their families. One young woman told Arnold that "my father beat my mother and neglected his children. . . . I began stealing when I was 12. I hustled to help feed and clothe the other [12] kids and help pay the rent" (p. 139).

Thus, the caretaking role noted in women's pathways to crime is accentuated in African American families because of extreme poverty. Arnold (1995) also noted that economic need interfered with young black girls' ability to concentrate on schoolwork and attend school. Finally, Arnold (p. 140) noted, as had Gilfus (1992), that African American girls were "victimized" by the school system; one of her respondents said that "some [of the teachers] were prejudiced, and one had the nerve to tell the whole class he didn't like black people" (p. 140). Most of her respondents said that even if they went to school every day, they did not learn anything. Finally, despite their desperate desire to "hold on . . . to conventional roles in society," the girls were ultimately pushed out of these, onto the streets, and into petty crime (p. 141).

The mechanics of surviving parental abuse and educational neglect were particularly hard on young African American girls, forcing them to drop out of school, onto the streets, and into permanent "structural dislocation" (Arnold, 1995, p. 143). Having no marketable skills and little education, many resorted to "prostitution and stealing" while further immersing themselves in drug addiction.

BEYOND THE STREET WOMAN: RESURRECTING THE LIBERATED FEMALE CROOK?

Issues of women's violence and the relationship between that violence and other changes in women's environment are recurring themes in discussions of women's crime. As we saw in Chapter 3, a persistent theme in women's criminality is the presumed link between efforts to improve women's economic and political position and levels of girls' and women's crime—particularly violent crime. We also saw that there is nothing particularly "new" about the concern. During the early 1970s, newspapers and periodicals were full of stories about the "new female criminal" (Foley, 1974; Klemesrud, 1978; Los Angeles Times Service, 1975; Nelson, 1977; Roberts, 1971). Presumably inspired by the women's movement, the female criminal supposedly sought equality in the underworld just as her more conventional counterparts pursued their rights in more acceptable arenas.

Such media accounts, like contemporary "girlz in the hood" and "girls gone wild" stories, generally relied on two types of evidence to support the alleged relationship between the women's rights movement and increasing female criminality: FBI statistics showing dramatic increases in the number of women arrested for nontraditional crimes and sensationalistic accounts of women's violence. In the 1970s, the activities of female political activists such as Leila Khaled, Bernardine Dohrn, and Susan Saxe were featured. Of course, women's involvement in political or terrorist activity is nothing new, as the activities of Joan of Arc and Charlotte Corday demonstrate.

Arrest data collected by the FBI seem to provide more objective evidence that dramatic changes in the number of women arrested were occurring during the years associated with the second wave of feminist activity. For example, between 1960 and 1975, arrests of adult women went up 60.2% and arrests of juvenile women increased a startling 253.9%. In specific, nontraditional crimes, the increases were even more astounding. For example, between 1960 and 1975, the number of women arrested for murder was up 105.7%, forcible rape arrests increased by 633.3%, and robbery arrests were up 380.5% (FBI, 1973, p. 124; 1976, p. 191).

Law enforcement officials were among the earliest to link these changes to the movement for female equality. "The women's liberation movement has triggered a crime wave like the world has never seen before," claimed Chief Ed Davis of the Los Angeles Police Department (Weis, 1976, p. 17). On another occasion, he expanded on his thesis by explaining that the "breakdown of motherhood" signaled by the women's movement could lead to "the use of dope, stealing, thieving and killing" (Los Angeles Times Service, 1975, p. B4). Other officials, such as Sheriff Peter Pitchess of California, made less inflammatory comments that echoed the same general theme: "As women emerge from their traditional roles as housewife and mother, entering the political and business fields previously dominated by males, there is no reason to believe that women will not also approach equality with men in the criminal activity field" (Roberts, 1971, p. 72).

Law enforcement officials were not alone in holding this position; academics like Adler (1975a, 1975b) also linked increases in the number of women arrested to women's struggle for social and economic equality. Adler noted, for example, that

> in the middle of the twentieth century, we are witnessing the simultaneous rise and fall of women. Rosie the Riveter of World War II has become Robin the Rioter or Rhoda the Robber of the Vietnam era. Women have lost more than their chains. For better or worse, they have lost many of the restraints which kept them within the law. (1975b, p. 24)

Such arguments, it turns out, are nothing new. The first wave of feminism also saw an attempt to link women's rights with women's crime. Smart (1976), for example, found the following comment by W. I. Thomas written in 1921, the year after the ratification of the 19th Amendment guaranteeing women the right to vote:

> The modern age of girls and young men is intensely immoral, and immoral seemingly without the pressure of circumstances. At whose door we may lay the fault, we cannot tell. Is it the result of what we call "the emancipation of woman," with its concomitant freedom from chaperonage, increased intimacy between the sexes in adolescence, and a more tolerant viewpoint towards all things unclean in life? (Smart, 1976, pp. 70–71)

Students of women's crime were also quick to note that the interest in the female criminal after so many years of invisibility was ironic and questioned why the new visibility was associated with "an image of a woman with a gun in hand" (Chapman, 1980, p. 68). Chapman concluded that this attention to the female criminal was "doubly ironic" because closer assessments of the trends in women's violence did not support what might be called the "liberation hypothesis" and, more to the point, data showed that the position of women in the mainstream economy during those years was "actually worsening" (pp. 68–69).

To be specific, although what might be called the "liberation hypothesis" or "emancipation hypothesis" met with wide public acceptance, careful analyses of changes in women's arrest rates provided little support for the notion. Using national arrest data supplied by the FBI and more localized police and court statistics, Steffensmeier (1980, p. 58) examined the pattern of female criminal behavior for the years 1965 through 1977 (the years most heavily affected by the second wave of feminist activity). By weighting the arrest data for changes in population and comparing increases in women's arrests to increases in men's arrests, Steffensmeier concluded that "females are not catching up with males in the commission of violent, masculine, male-dominated, serious crimes (except larceny) or in white collar crimes" (p. 72). He did note increases in women's arrests in the Uniform Crime Report categories of larceny, fraud, forgery, and vagrancy, but by examining these increases more carefully, he demonstrated that they were due almost totally to increases in traditionally female crimes, such as shoplifting, prostitution, and passing bad checks (fraud).

Moreover, Steffensmeier (1980) noted that forces other than changes in female behavior were probably responsible for shifts in the numbers of adult women arrested for these traditionally female crimes. The increased willingness of stores to prosecute shoplifters, the widespread abuse of vagrancy statutes to arrest prostitutes combined with a declining use of this same arrest category to control public drunkenness, and the growing concern with "welfare fraud" were all social factors that he felt might explain changes in women's arrests without necessarily changing the numbers of women involved in these activities.

Steffensmeier's (1980) findings confirm the reservations that had been voiced earlier by Simon (1975), Rans (1975), and others about making generalizations solely from dramatic percentage increases in the number of women's arrests. These reservations are further justified by current arrest data that suggest that the sensationalistic increases of the early 1970s were not indicative of a new trend. Between 1976 and 1979, for example, the arrests of all women rose only 7.1%, only slightly higher than the male increase of 5.8% for the same period (Chesney-Lind, 1986).

Finally, as previously mentioned, women offenders of the 1970s were unlikely targets for the messages of the largely middle-class women's movement. Women offenders tend to be poor, members of minority groups, with truncated educations and spotty employment histories. These were precisely the women whose lives were largely unaffected by the gains, such as they were, of the then white, middle-class women's rights movement (Chapman, 1980; Crites, 1976). Crites, for example, noted that "these women rather than being recipients of expanded rights and opportunities gained by the women's movement, are, instead, witnessing declining survival options" (1976, p. 37). Research on the orientations of women offenders to the arguments of the women's movement also indicated that, if anything, these women held very traditional attitudes about gender (see Chesney-Lind & Rodriguez, 1983, for a summary of these studies).

To summarize, careful work on the arrest trends of the 1970s provided no support for the popular liberation hypothesis of women's crime. Changes in women's arrest trends, it turned out, better fit arguments of woman's economic marginalization than of her liberation (Simon & Landis, 1991).

THE REVIVAL OF THE "VIOLENT FEMALE OFFENDER"

The failure of careful research to support notions of radical shifts in the character of women's crime went almost completely unnoticed in the popular press. As a result, there was apparently nothing to prevent a recycling of a revised "liberation" hypothesis a decade and a half later.

As noted earlier, one of the first articles to use this recycled hypothesis was a 1990 article in the *Wall Street Journal,* titled "You've Come a Long Way, Moll," that focused on increases in the number of women arrested for violent crimes. This article opened with a discussion of women in the military, noting that "the armed forces already are substantially integrated" and moved from this point to observe that "we needn't look to the dramatic example of battle for proof that violence is no longer a male domain. Women are now being arrested for violent crimes—such as robbery and aggravated assault—at a higher rate than ever before recorded in the U.S." (Crittenden, 1990, p. A14).

As noted in Chapter 3, many of the articles to follow dealt with young women (particularly girls in gangs), but there were some exceptions. For example, "Hand That Rocks the Cradle Is Taking Up Violent Crime" (Kahler, 1992) focused on increases in women's imprisonment and linked this pattern to "the growing number of women committing violent crimes" (p. 3A). In April 2000, in the *New York Times*'s series on "Rampage Killers," the author was quick to point out by the third sentence of the story that rampage killers are "mostly white men, but a surprising number are women" (Fessenden, 2000), when in fact, it is even rarer for women to commit multiple-victim homicides than single-victim ones (about 4% of all such crimes). And on July 28, 2009, New Jersey Attorney General Anne Milgram announced that law enforcement officials dismantled an all female-led, gang-involved narcotics ring. Dubbing the investigation "Operation Bloodette," Milgram went on to state that she wished "this was not one (glass) ceiling women were breaking" and that "women are taking over dominant roles in traditionally male-dominated gangs" (Read, 2009).

Comparing the arrest rates that prompted the first media surge of reporting on the "liberation" hypothesis with the arrest rates from the second wave of media interest, it is evident that little has changed. As noted earlier in this chapter, women's share of violent crime has remained more or less stable, though arrests of women for "other assaults" did climb by 21% and robbery increased by 44% in the past decade (FBI, 2010a). In the past 5 years, however, women's arrests for robbery (a relatively small number of arrests in the first place) only increased 15.8% and other assaults climbed only 5.5%, while all other categories of violent crime arrests, including aggravated assault and weapons carrying, decreased for women (p. 241).

The news media were not alone in their interest in women's violence—particularly violent street crime. In a series of articles (Baskin, Sommers,

& Fagan, 1993; Sommers & Baskin, 1992, 1993), the authors explore the extent and character of women's violent crime in New York. Prompted by an account in their neighborhood paper of two women who shot another woman in a robbery, the authors note that their research "has led us to the conclusion that women in New York City are becoming more and more likely to involve themselves in violent street crime" (Baskin et al., 1993, p. 401). Some of the findings that brought them to this conclusion follow.

In one study, Sommers and Baskin (1992) used arrest data from New York City (and arrest histories of 266 women) to argue that "black and Hispanic females exhibited high rates of offending relative to white females." They further argue that "violent offending rates of black females parallel that of white males" (p. 191). Included in their definition of "violent" crimes is murder, robbery, aggravated assault, and burglary (apparently classified as a violent crime in New York City, but classified as a property crime by the FBI).

The authors explain that this pattern is a product of "the effects of the social and institutional transformation of the inner city" (Sommers & Baskin, 1992, p. 198). Specifically, the authors contend that "violence and drug involvement" are adaptive strategies in underclass communities that are racked by poverty and unemployment. Both men and women, they argue, move to crime as a way of coping with "extreme social and economic deprivation" (p. 198).

A second study (Sommers & Baskin, 1993) further explores women's violent offenses by analyzing interview data from 23 women arrested for a violent felony offense (robbery or assault) and 65 women incarcerated for such an offense. Finding a high correlation between substance abuse and the rate of violent crime (particularly for those who committed robbery and robbery with assault), they also noted that "the women in our study who were involved in robbery were not crime specialists but also had a history of engagement in nonviolent theft, fraud, forgery, prostitution, and drug dealing" (p. 142). In fact, they comment that "these women are not roaming willy-nilly through the streets engaging in 'unprovoked' violence" (p. 154).

Just how involved these women were in more traditional forms of female crime was not apparent in the text of this article. In an appendix, however, the role played by a history of prostitution in the lives of these women offenders is particularly clear. As an example, the women who reported committing both robbery and assault also had the highest rate of involvement with prostitution (77%; Baskin & Sommers, 1993, p. 159).

In a third paper, Baskin and colleagues (1993) explore "the political economy of street crime." This work, which appears to be based on the New York arrest data and a discussion of the explosion of crack selling in the city, explores the question, "Why do black females exhibit such relatively high rates of violence?" (p. 405). Convinced that the concentration of poverty is associated positively with the level of criminal activity, regardless of race, the authors then conclude that "the growing drug markets and a marked disappearance of males" combine with other factors in underclass communities "to create social and economic opportunity structures open to women's increasing participation in violent crime" (p. 406).

The authors further suggest that traditional theories of women's offenses, particularly those that emphasize gender and victimization, do not adequately explain women's violent crime. Their work, they contend, "confirms our initial sense that women in inner city neighborhoods are being pulled toward violent street crime by the same forces that have been found to affect their male counterparts (e.g., peers, opportunity structures, neighborhood effects)" (Baskin et al., 1993, p. 412). They conclude that the socioeconomic situation in the inner city, specifically as it is affected by the drug trade, creates "new dynamics of crime where gender is a far less salient factor" (p. 417).

These authors argue that in economically devastated inner cities such as New York, women's violence—particularly the violence of the women of color—does not need to be considered in terms of the place of these women in patriarchal society (e.g., the effect of gender in their lives). Instead, they contend that these women (like their male counterparts) are being drawn to violence and other forms of traditionally male crimes for the same reasons as men.

This turns the "liberation" hypothesis on its head. Now, it is not presumed economic gain that promoted "equality" in crime, but rather it is economic marginalization that causes women to move out of their "traditional" roles into the role of criminal. Is that really what is going on?

This chapter has already cast doubt on the notion that there has been any dramatic shift in women's share of violent crime (at least as measured by arrest statistics). This chapter has also provided evidence that women's participation in offenses that sound "nontraditional" (such as embezzlement, DUI, and larceny theft) is deeply affected by the "place" of women in society. Both of these findings cast doubt on claims for the existence of a new, violent street criminal class of women—at least without first providing a more detailed exploration of trends in women's involvement in crimes such as robbery and drug selling. Because these offenses, particularly drug use and sale, feature so prominently in the debate about the nature of adult women's offenses, they are explored in detail in the next chapter.

Has there been an increase in women's participation in traditionally male types of crime, such as violent crime? Does women's search for "equality" with men have a darker side, as suggested by some of the arrest statistics reviewed in this chapter? To answer this question fully, the next chapter explores the offenses that bring women to prison. It shows the while a third of incarcerated women were convicted for "crimes against a person," the majority (58.2%) were imprisoned for property and/or drug offenses (Bureau of Justice Statistics, 2010a, 2010c). Indeed, it is not that women are becoming more violent and more "like men"—it is the masculinist system that punishes them that is becoming harsher.

SIX

SENTENCING WOMEN TO PRISON

Equality Without Justice

—————◆•◆•◆—————

More than one million women in the United States are under some form of criminal justice supervision in the United States (Glaze & Bonzcar, 2007). By 2009, the number of women imprisoned in the United States increased 800% over the past three decades, bringing the number of women behind bars to more than 105,000 (West, 2010). From 1995 to 2009 alone, the number of women behind prison bars increased 87%, and women now account for nearly 7% of the total prison population (see Table 6.1; Stephan, 2008; West & Sabol, 2010). More than a third of them served time in the nation's three largest jurisdictions: Texas, the federal system, and California (Glaze & Bonzcar, 2010; West, 2010; see also Chesney-Lind, 2002, pp. 80–81). Currently, women also account for 23% of the probation population, 12% of the jail population, and 12% of the parole population in the United States (Glaze & Bonzcar, 2010; Minton, 2010).

Increases in the number of women in prison surpassed those of men over this period as well. The number of women in prison has increased at nearly double the rate of men since 1985 (Sentencing Project, 2007). A similar pattern can be found in the number of women in jail, where a 32% increase was seen between 2000 and 2009; for men, the increase was 22% (Minton, 2010).

The soaring numbers of women under lock and key are not simply products of the increasing reliance in the United States on imprisonment, although that

Table 6.1   Number of Female Prisoners Under the Jurisdiction of State or
Federal Correctional Authorities, December 31, 2000–2009

Year	Total	Federal	State	Percentage of sentenced prisoners
2000	85,044	8,397	76,647	6.4%
2001	85,184	8,990	76,194	6.3
2002	89,066	9,308	79,758	6.5
2003	92,571	9,770	82,801	6.6
2004	95,998	10,207	85,791	6.7
2005	98,688	10,495	88,193	6.7
2006	103,343	11,116	92,227	6.9
2007	105,786	11,528	94,258	6.9
2008	106,358	11,578	94,780	6.9
2009	105,197	11,780	93,417	6.8

SOURCE: West and Sabol (2010).

has played a role in the pattern. Nationally, the rate of women's imprisonment is also at an all-time high. In 1925, women's rate of incarceration was 6 per 100,000. In 2001, the rate climbed to 58 per 100,000, and by 2009, the rate had reached a historical high of 67 per 100,000, with Hispanic and African American women experiencing even higher rates of incarceration (see Table 6.2). Taken together, these figures signal a major policy change in society's response to women's crime, one that has occurred with virtually no public discussion.

So, as the number of people imprisoned in the United States continues to climb, our nation has achieved the dubious honor of having the highest incarceration rate in the world, with Russia following as a distant second (Mauer, 1999, 2006). Along the way, America's love affair with prisons has claimed some hidden victims—economically marginalized women of color and their children.

TRENDS IN WOMEN'S CRIME: A REPRISE

Is the dramatic increase in women's imprisonment a response to a women's crime problem spiraling out of control? As seen in previous chapters, a look at the pattern of women's arrests provides little evidence of a dramatic change in

Table 6.2   Estimated Number of Sentenced Prisoners Under State or Federal
Jurisdiction per 100,000 U.S. Residents, by Sex, Race, Hispanic
Origin, and Age, December 31, 2009

| | *Female Prisoners* | | | |
Age	*Total*	*White*	*Black*	*Hispanic*
Total	67	50	142	74
18–19	23	17	42	24
20–24	109	86	186	124
25–29	149	115	287	164
30–34	188	155	361	178
35–39	206	164	426	187
40–44	172	131	360	171
45–49	94	67	205	107
50–54	45	32	101	60
55–59	22	18	42	29
60–64	11	9	22	22
65 or older	3	2	6	4

SOURCE: Bureau of Justice Statistics (2010a).

the composition of women's crime. One crude measure will serve to make this
point again. The number of arrests of adult women for serious violent crime
has only marginally increased (3.4%) between 2000 and 2009 (FBI, 2010a,
p. 239). However, the number of women incarcerated during the past decade
has increased by 24% (West & Sabol, 2010).

WOMEN, VIOLENT CRIMES, AND THE WAR ON DRUGS

Another indication that the increase in women's imprisonment is not explained
by a shift in the character of women's crime comes from information about the
offenses for which women are being imprisoned (see Table 6.3). For the past
decade and a half, roughly a third of women's incarceration is due to violent
crimes. Indeed, the proportion of women in state prisons for violent offenses has

Table 6.3 Estimated Number of Sentenced Prisoners Under State Jurisdiction, by Offense and Sex, Year-end 2006

	All Inmates	Male	Female
Total	1,331,100	1,238,900	92,200
Violent offenses	693,400	661,600	31,800
Murder	168,600	158,200	10,200
Manslaughter	16,100	14,200	1,600
Rape	65,800	65,300	500
Other sexual assault	93,600	92,500	1,300
Robbery	178,900	171,600	7,500
Assault	133,900	125,500	7,800
Other violent	37,100	34,400	2,800
Property offenses	258,200	230,700	27,500
Burglary	126,100	119,800	6,000
Larceny	49,500	41,900	7,800
Motor vehicle theft	22,700	21,000	1,600
Fraud	33,600	23,700	9,800
Other property	26,400	24,400	2,200
Drug offenses	264,300	238,600	26,200
Public order offenses	101,300	95,700	5,500
Other/unspecified	13,300	12,300	1,200

SOURCE: Bureau of Justice Statistics (2010a, p. 13).

declined since 1979: from 48.95% to 32% in 2001 to 34% in 2006 (Bureau of Justice Statistics, 1988, 2002a, 2010). In states that have seen large increases in women's imprisonment, such as California, the decline is even sharper. In 2009, only 16% of the women admitted to the California prison system were being incarcerated for violent crimes, compared to 37.2% in 1982 (Bloom, Chesney-Lind, & Owen, 1994; Department of Corrections and Rehabilitation, 2010, p. 44).

Other recent figures suggest that without any fanfare, the war on drugs has become a war on women and has contributed to the explosion in women's prison populations. More than one out of four women in U.S. prisons in 2006 was doing time for drug offenses (up from 1 in 10 in 1979), whereas fewer than one out of five men were imprisoned for drug convictions (Bureau of Justice Statistics, 2002a, p. 13; 2010a; Snell & Morton, 1994, p. 3). Although the intent of "get tough" policies was to rid society of drug dealers and so-called kingpins, more than a third (35.9%) of the women serving time for drug offenses in the nation's prisons are serving time solely for "possession" (Bureau of Justice Statistics, 1988, p. 3).[1] In California, more than half (52%) of the women admitted to prison for drug crimes were convicted for possession only (Department of Corrections and Rehabilitation, 2010, p. 45).

The war on drugs, coupled with the development of new technologies for determining drug use (e.g., urinalysis), plays another, less obvious role in increasing women's imprisonment. Many women parolees are being returned to prison for technical parole violations because they fail to pass random drug tests. Of the 7,117 women incarcerated in California in 2009, approximately one in five was imprisoned for parole violations (Department of Corrections and Rehabilitation, 2010, p. 30). In Oregon, during a 1-year period (October 1992–September 1993), only 16% of female admissions to Oregon institutions were incarcerated for new convictions; the rest were probation and parole violators. This pattern was not nearly so clear in male imprisonment; 48% of the admissions to male prisons were for new offenses (Anderson, 1994). Finally, in Hawaii, other data underscore this point further: Of individuals released during 1998 and tracked for 2 years on parole, nearly half (43%) were returned to prison. When examining the reasons for parole revocation, a gender difference emerges: 73% of the women were returned to prison for technical violations (as opposed to new crimes); this was true for a smaller yet significant percentage (64%) of male parolees (Chesney-Lind, 2002, p. 90).

Nowhere has the drug war taken a larger toll than on women sentenced in federal courts. In the federal system, the passage of harsh mandatory minimums for federal crimes, coupled with sentencing guidelines intended to "reduce

---

[1]In 1979, 26% of women doing time in state prisons for drug offenses were incarcerated solely for possession (Bureau of Justice Statistics, 1988, p. 3).

race, class and other unwarranted disparities in sentencing males" (Raeder, 1993), have operated to the distinct disadvantage of women.[2] They have also dramatically increased the number of women sentenced to federal institutions. From 2000 to 2009, approximately 2,700 women a year have been sentenced to imprisonment in federal court for drug trafficking (U.S. Sentencing Commission, 2010). Drugs that have come under amplified surveillance by the federal government within the last decade, such as methamphetamine and marijuana, have also greatly impacted women. From 1995 through 2009, the number of women convicted of federal methamphetamine offenses increased by nearly 200% (from 239 offenders in 1996 to 700 in 2009), and female federal marijuana offenders were up by 51% (from 495 in 1996 to 751 in 2000; see Table 6.4). Indeed, women now account for one out of every five arrests

Table 6.4   Number of Female Drug Offenders Sentenced in Federal Court by Drug Type, 2009

Powder cocaine	589
Crack cocaine	508
Heroin	240
Marijuana	751
Methamphetamine	700
Other	219

SOURCE: United States Sentencing Commission (2010).

---

[2]Raeder (1993) notes, for example, that judges are constrained by these federal guidelines from considering family responsibilities, particularly pregnancy and motherhood, which in the past may have kept women out of prison. Yet the effect of these "neutral" guidelines is to eliminate from consideration the unique situation of mothers, especially single mothers, unless their situation can be established to be "extraordinary." Nearly 90% of male inmates report that their wives are taking care of their children; by contrast, only 22% of mothers in prison could count on the fathers of their children to care for the children during the mother's imprisonment (p. 69). This means that many women in prison, the majority of whom are mothers, face the potential, if not actual, loss of their children. This is not a penalty that men in prison experience. Additionally, although the *United States v. Booker* (2005) decision allowed for more judicial discretion and for judges to depart from the guidelines more easily, application of federal sentencing guidelines continued at a steady pace. Pre-*Booker* courts sentenced roughly 70% of offenders within the guidelines. In post-*Booker* years, about 60% are still sentenced within the guidelines (see U.S. Sentencing Commission, 2010).

for methamphetamine in the federal system (Motivans, 2008). The number of women convicted of powder cocaine offenses and the number of female crack cocaine offenders also remained at a steady high of more than 500 offenders in each drug category. In state prisons, women are 47% more likely to be doing time for a drug offense than are men (Bureau of Justice Statistics, 2010a).

Additionally, drugs such as methamphetamine and crack cocaine come attached with mandatory minimum prison sentences for relatively small amounts of drug trafficking. The consequence is that more and more women no longer receive probation for low-level offenses but, rather, receive prison. Thirty years ago, nearly two thirds of the women convicted of federal felonies were granted probation, but by 1991, only 28% of women were given straight probation (Raeder, 1993, pp. 31–32). By 2009, fewer than 1 in 10 female felons convicted in federal court received straight probation (U.S. Sentencing Commission, 2010). The mean time to be served by women drug offenders increased from 27 months in July 1984 to a startling 67 months in June 1990 (p. 34). Taken together, these data explain why the number of women in federal institutions has skyrocketed since the 1980s. In 2008, women made up 6.7% of those in federal institutions, with 11,988 women behind bars (Motivans, 2010).

What about property offenses? Roughly 30% (29.8%) of the women in state prisons were doing time for these offenses in 2009 (West & Sabol, 2010). California, again, merits a closer look: More than a third (34.6%) of women in California state prisons in 2009 were incarcerated for property offenses (Department of Corrections and Rehabilitation, 2010, p. 15). These generally included low-level burglary, fraud, and petty theft with a prior record. Taken together, this means that nearly one woman in three (30.5%) is incarcerated in California for simple drug possession, petty theft with a prior, fraud, or low-level burglary (Department of Corrections and Rehabilitation, 2010, p. 15).

GETTING TOUGH ON WOMEN'S CRIME

Data on the offenses for which women are in prison and an examination of trends in women's arrests suggest that factors other than a shift in the nature of women's crime are involved in the dramatic increase in women's imprisonment. Simply put, the criminal justice system now seems more willing to incarcerate women.

What has happened in the last two decades? Although explanations are necessarily speculative, some reasonable suggestions can be advanced. First, it appears that mandatory sentencing for specific kinds of offenses—especially drug offenses—at both state and federal levels has affected women's incarceration. Legislators at the state and national levels, perhaps responding to a huge increase in media coverage of crime but not necessarily the nation's actual crime rate, are escalating penalties for all offenses, particularly those associated with drugs (Mauer, 2006; Mauer & Huling, 1995).

Beyond this, sentencing "reform," especially the development of sentencing guidelines and mandatory minimums resulting from "Three Strikes and You're Out" and "Truth in Sentencing" legislation, also has been a problem for women. In California, this has resulted in increasing the number of prison sentences for women who, due to such "Truth in Sentencing" policies, will be required to do at least 85% of their sentence behind bars (Blumstein, Cohen, Martin, & Tonry, 1983; Department of Corrections and Rehabilitation, 2010; Mauer, 2006). Sentencing reform has created some problems because the reforms address issues that have developed in the handling of male offenders and are now being applied to female offenders.[3] Daly's (1994) review of this problem notes, for example, that federal sentencing guidelines ordinarily do not permit a defendant's employment or family ties/familial responsibilities to be used as a factor in sentencing. She notes that these guidelines probably were intended to reduce class and race disparities in sentencing, but their effect on women's sentencing was not considered. Bush-Baskette's (1999) analysis of the war on drugs resonates a similar theme: "Sentencing guidelines that disallow the use of drug addiction and family responsibilities as mitigating circumstances subject Black females to prison and long sentences under criminal justice supervision, as they do White females" (p. 222).

Finally, the criminal justice system has simply become tougher at every level of decision making. Langan (1991) notes that the chance of receiving a prison sentence following arrest has risen for all types of offenses, not simply those typically targeted by mandatory sentencing programs (p. 1569). This is specifically relevant to women because mandatory sentencing laws (with the exception of those regarding prostitution and drug offenses) typically have targeted predominantly male offenses, such as sexual assault, murder, and weapons offenses. Thus, Langan's research confirms that the whole system is now "tougher" on all offenses, including those that women traditionally have committed.

---

[3]Blumstein and colleagues (1983) note that California's Uniform Determinate Sentencing Law "used the averaging approach, one consequence of which was to markedly increase the sentences of women—especially for violent offenses" (p. 114).

A careful review of the evidence on the current surge in women's incarceration suggests that this explosion may have little to do with a major change in women's behavior. This surge stands in stark contrast to the earlier growth in women's imprisonment, particularly to the other great growth of women's incarceration at the turn of the 20th century.

Perhaps the best way to place the current wave of women's imprisonment in perspective is to recall earlier approaches to women's incarceration. Historically, women prisoners have been few in number and were apparently an afterthought in a system devoted to the imprisonment of men. In fact, early women's facilities were often an outgrowth of men's prisons. In those early days, women inmates were seen as "more depraved" than their male counterparts because they were viewed as acting in contradiction to their whole "moral organization" (Rafter, 1990, p. 13).

The first large-scale, organized imprisonment of women occurred in the United States when many women's reformatories were established between 1870 and 1900. Women's imprisonment was justified not because the women posed a public safety risk, but because women were thought to need moral revision and protection. Important to note, however, is that the reformatory movement that resulted in the incarceration of large numbers of white working-class girls and women for largely noncriminal or deportment offenses did not extend to women of color. Instead, as Rafter (1990) has carefully documented, African American women, particularly in the southern states, continued to be incarcerated in prisons where they were treated much like the male inmates. They frequently ended up on chain gangs and were not shielded from beatings if they did not keep up with the work (pp. 150–151). This racist legacy, the exclusion of black women from the "chivalry" accorded white women, should be kept in mind when the current explosion of women's prison populations is considered.

The current trend in adult women's imprisonment seems to revisit the earliest approach to female offenders: Women are once again an afterthought in a correctional process that is punitive rather than corrective. Women are also, however, no longer being accorded the benefits, however dubious, of the chivalry that had characterized the reformatory movement. Rather, they are increasingly likely to be incarcerated, not because society has decided to crack down on women's crime specifically, but because women are being swept up in a societal move to "get tough on crime" that is driven by images of violent criminals (almost always male and often members of minority groups) "getting away with murder."

A look at capital punishment demonstrates this point further. Although historically, women have received the death penalty far less frequently than men, the advent of "get tough" approaches to crime ushered in a dramatic increase in the number of death sentences imposed on women (Morgan, 2000, p. 280; Streib, 2010; see Table 6.5). A total of 167 death sentences have been imposed upon female offenders from 1973 through late 2010 (Streib, 2011, p. 9). Five states (Texas, California, Florida, North Carolina, and Ohio) account for essentially half (83/167) of all such sentences, while the annual death sentencing rate for female offenders during the last decade has averaged four per year (Streib, 2010, pp. 3–6). As of 2010, 55 women remained on death row in the

Table 6.5   Women Executed in the United States, 1984–2010

Year	Inmate	Race	State	Victim
11/2/1984	Velma Barfield	White	NC	Boyfriend, by poison (also admitted to killing four others, including her mother and husband)
2/3/1998	Karla Faye Tucker	White	TX	Acquaintance, by pick-ax
3/30/1998	Judy Buenoano	White	FL	Husband, by poison
2/24/2000	Betty Lou Beets	White	TX	Husband, by gunshot
5/2/2000	Christina Riggs	White	AR	Two children, by poison (intended suicide, but was revived)
1/11/2001	Wanda Jean Allen	Black	OK	Girlfriend, by gunshot
5/1/01	Marilyn Plantz	White	OK	Husband, beaten and burned (hired boyfriend, who also received death)
12/4/01	Lois Nadean Smith	White	OK	Son's ex-girlfriend, by gunshot
5/10/02	Lynda Lyon Block	White	AL	Police officer, by gunshot (committed crime with husband, also executed)
10/9/02	Aileen Wuornos	White	FL	Stranger by gunshot (a "john"; 7 victims total)
9/15/05	Frances Newton	Black	TX	Husband, son, daughter by gunshot
9/23/10	Teresa Lewis	White	VA	Husband, stepson by gunshot (hired boyfriend and accomplice)

SOURCE: Based on Streib (2010).

United States, while the remaining 112 either were executed, died from natural causes, or received commuted life sentences. Despite the fact that domestic homicide is not a capital offense in most jurisdictions that utilize the death penalty, one-quarter (14/55) of these 55 women received the death penalty for killing their husbands or boyfriends. Another one-fifth killed their children or a child in their care (Streib, 2010, p. 10).

From 1990 to 2010, the total number of women executed exceeded the combined total of the previous four decades, despite declines in murder arrests for women. From 1984 to 2010, 12 women were executed in the United States (Streib, 2011). Table 6.5 summarizes the race, location, and victim(s) of these 12 women.

This public mood, coupled with a legal system that now espouses "equality" for women with a vengeance when it comes to the punishment of crime, has resulted in this punitive attitude surrounding the death penalty and women and, in general, much greater use of imprisonment in response to women's crime. There also seems to be a return to the imagery of women's depravity for those women whose crimes (and race) put them outside of the ranks of "true women." As evidence, consider the new hostility signaled by bringing child abuse charges against women who use drugs before the birth of their children (Chavkin, 1990; National Advocates for Pregnant Women (NAPW), 2011; Noble, 1988).

The fact that many of the women incarcerated in U.S. prisons are women of color who are doing time for drug offenses further distances them from images of womanhood that require protection from prison life. For this reason, when policymakers are confronted with the unanticipated consequences of the new "get tough" mood, their response is all too frequently to assail the character of the women they are jailing rather than to question the practice itself.

BUILDING MORE WOMEN'S PRISONS

As a result of the surge in women's imprisonment, our country has gone on a building binge with regard to women's prisons. Prison historian Nicole Hahn Rafter (1990) observes that between 1930 and 1950, roughly two or three prisons were built or created for women each decade. In the 1960s, the pace of prison construction picked up slightly, with seven units opening, largely in southern and western states. During the 1970s, 17 prisons opened, including units in states such as Rhode Island and Vermont, which once relied on transferring women prisoners out of state. In the 1980s, 34 women's units or prisons were established; this figure is 10 times larger than the figures for earlier decades (Rafter, 1990, pp. 181–182).

To put this dramatic shift in another important historical context, consider the fact that only 30 years ago, the majority of states did not operate separate women's prisons. In 1973, only 28 states (including Puerto Rico and the District of Columbia) had separate institutions for women. Other states handled the problem differently; women were either housed in a portion of a male facility or, like Hawaii, Rhode Island, or Vermont, were imprisoned in other states (Singer, 1973). Looking backward, this pattern was very significant. The official response to women's crime during the 1970s was heavily influenced by the relative absence of women's prisons, despite the fact that some women were, during these years, committing serious crimes.

What has happened in the past few decades, then, signals a major and dramatic change in the way the country is responding to women's offenses. Without much fanfare and with little public discussion, the model of men's incarceration has been increasingly applied to women. Some of this punitive response to women's crime can be described as "equality with a vengeance"—the dark side of the equity or parity model of justice that emphasizes the need to treat women offenders as though they were "equal" to male offenders. As one correctional officer said at a national meeting, "an inmate is an inmate is an inmate."

But who are these "inmates," and does it make sense to treat women in prison as though they were men? The next section examines what is known about the backgrounds of women currently doing time in state and federal prisons across the country.

PROFILE OF WOMEN IN U.S. PRISONS

Childhoods of Women in Prison

The most recent research on the characteristics of women doing time in state prisons across the country underscores the salience of themes identified early in this book—particularly the role of sexual and physical violence in the lives of women who come into the criminal justice system. This research also argues forcefully for a national discussion of the situation of women in our jails and prisons.

Snell and Morton (1994) surveyed a random sample of women and men ($N = 13,986$) in prisons around the country during 1991 for the Bureau of Justice Statistics. For the first time, a government study asked questions about women's and men's experiences of sexual and physical violence as children. They found, when they asked these questions, that women in prisons have experienced far higher rates of physical and sexual abuse than men. Forty-three percent of the women surveyed "reported they had been abused at least once" before their current admission to prison; the comparable figure for men was 12.2% (Snell & Morton, 1994, p. 5). A look at women in jail and prison in 1998 shows even higher estimates: 48% of women in jail and 57% in state prisons report prior histories of sexual or physical abuse (see Table 6.6).

Table 6.6   Characteristics of Adult Women on Probation, in Jail, and in Prison

	Probation	*Jails*	*State Prisons*
Race/Ethnicity			
White	62%	36%	33%
Black	27	44	48
Hispanic	10	15	15
Other	1	5	4
Age			
24 and younger	20	21	12
25–34	39	46	43
35–44	30	27	34
45–54	10	5	9
55 and older	1	1	2
Median Age	32 years	31 years	33 years
Marital Status			
Married	26	15	17
Widowed	2	4	6
Separated	10	13	10
Divorced	20	20	20
Never married	42	48	47

(Continued)

Table 6.6 (Continued)

	Probation	Jails	State Prisons
Education			
8th grade or less	5	12	7
Some high school	35	33	37
High school graduate/GED	39	39	39
Some college or more	21	16	17
Report ever physically or sexually abused	41	48	57

SOURCE: Bureau of Justice Statistics (1999, pp. 7–8).

For about a third of all women in prison (31.7%), the abuse started when they were girls and continued as they became adults. A key gender difference emerges here. A number of young men who are in prison (10.7%) also report abuse as boys, but it did not continue into adulthood. One in four women reported that their abuse started as adults, compared to only 3% of male offenders. Fully 33.5% of the women surveyed reported physical abuse, and a slightly higher number (33.9%) had been sexually abused either as girls or young women, compared to relatively small percentages of men (10% of boys and 5.3% of adult men in prison).

This survey also asked women about their relationships with those who abused them. Predictably, both women and men reported that parents and relatives contributed to the abuse they suffered as children, but female prisoners were far more likely than their male counterparts to say that domestic violence was a theme in their adult abuse; fully half of the women said they had been abused by a spouse or ex-spouse, compared to only 3% of male inmates.

The survey found ethnic differences in the role played by the juvenile and criminal justice system in the lives of women in prison. Overall, white women were slightly more likely to report having been in the foster care system or other institutions (21.1%) than African American or Hispanic women (14.1% and 14.4%, respectively). African American women and Hispanic women, by contrast, were far more likely than white women to report a family member (usually a brother) in prison (Snell & Morton, 1994).

Contrary to some stereotypes about drug use, more white and Hispanic women than African American women reported parental involvement with alcohol and drug abuse when they were girls. More than 4 out of 10 white women and about a third of the Hispanic women reported parental drug abuse, compared to only a quarter of the African American women. This underscores the need to focus on the specific interaction among culture, gender, and class in women's pathways to prison.

Current Offenses

A look at the offenses for which women are incarcerated quickly puts to rest the notion of hyperviolent, nontraditional women criminals. "Nearly half of all women in prison are currently serving a sentence for a nonviolent offense and have been convicted in the past of only nonviolent offenses" (Snell & Morton, 1994, p. 1). In fact, the number of women in prison for violent offenses, as a proportion of all female offenders, has fallen steadily over the past decades, whereas the number of women in prison has soared. In 1979, about half of the women in state prisons were incarcerated for violent crimes (Bureau of Justice Statistics, 1988). By 1986, the number had fallen to 40.7%, and in 2001, it was at 32.2% (Bureau of Justice Statistics, 2002a; Snell & Morton, p. 3). In 2009, one out of three women in U.S. prisons was there for a violent crime, compared to about 40% of male prisoners (Bureau of Justice Statistics, 2010a).

Snell and Morton (1994) also probed the gendered nature of the women's violence that resulted in their imprisonment. They noted that women prisoners were far more likely to kill an intimate or relative (50%, compared to 16.3%), whereas men were more likely to kill strangers (50.5%, compared to 35.1%). The last (1999) Bureau of Justice Statistics study that focused on women offenders showed similar findings. In 1998, more than 93% of female homicide offenders killed an intimate, family member, or acquaintance. For men, only 76% killed someone they knew (see Table 6.7). Given the information already discussed in this book regarding the nature of women's violence and its relationship to their own histories and experiences of abuse, women's violent acts take on quite a different significance than men's violence.

Drugs and their role in women's violence are also apparent in these data; generally speaking, women doing time for crimes of violence were less likely to report a link between drugs and violence than women serving time for property or drug offenses. For example, only 11% of the women convicted of violent crimes used drugs at the time of their crime, compared to 25% of those

Table 6.7 Relationship of Offender to Victim for Murder Offenses, 1998

Victim	Female	Male
Spouse	28.3%	6.8%
Ex-spouse	1.5	0.5
Child/stepchild	10.4	2.2
Other family member	6.7	6.9
Boyfriend/girlfriend	14.0	3.9
Acquaintance	31.9	54.6
Stranger	7.2	25.1
Number, 1976–1997	59,996	395,446

SOURCE: Bureau of Justice Statistics (1999, p. 4).

serving time for property offenses and 32% of those serving time for drug offenses (Bureau of Justice Statistics, 1999, p. 9). In Snell and Morton's (1994) study, the one exception to this generalization was found for women incarcerated for robbery. Not only did these women report that they were under the influence of the drug at the time of the robbery, but they were virtually the only women serving time for a violent offense who reported that they committed the offense "to get money for drugs" (p. 8). Women serving time for homicide were also slightly more likely to report greater use of drugs the month before the offense for which they were imprisoned and to report being under the influence of drugs at the time of the offense, but they rarely said that getting money to buy drugs was a motive for the crime.

Property Crimes

Many women in state prisons are serving time for larceny theft. Indeed, of the women serving time for property offenses (25.1% of all women in prison), about a third (30.2%) are doing time for larceny theft. This compares to only 18.2% of men who are doing time for property crimes. Fraud is another important commitment offense for women, accounting for 35% of women's but only 10.3% of men's most serious property offenses. Men serving time for property offenses are more likely to be serving time for burglary (49.2%; Bureau of Justice Statistics, 2010a).

Drug Use Among Women in Prison

Given the history of the women in prison, it should come as no surprise that drug use, possession, and, increasingly, drug trafficking are themes in women's imprisonment. In 1979, only 10.5% of women in state prisons were serving time for drug offenses; by 1986, the proportion had increased to 12%; in 2006, 28.4% of all women in state prisons were doing time for drug offenses (Bureau of Justice Statistics, 1988, p. 3; 2010c, p. 29; Snell & Morton, 1994, p. 3). Currently, more than half of the women serving time for drug offenses are now serving time for drug trafficking. Although this offense sounds very serious, it must be placed in context. As we shall see later in this chapter, in a world in which big drug deals are controlled almost exclusively by men (Green, 1996), women, many of whom are from desperately poor countries or from our own impoverished communities, are being cast or coerced into the role of serving as drug mules or couriers, only to be swept up in the escalating penalties that have characterized the past decade's war on drugs (Mauer & Huling, 1995).

National data on women in prison confirm that women prisoners have more problems with drugs than their male counterparts. Snell and Morton (1994) found that, contrary to the stereotype of the male drug addict committing crimes, "women in prison in 1991 used more drugs and used those drugs more frequently than men" (p. 7). For example, more female prisoners used drugs daily before imprisonment than male prisoners (41.5%, compared to 35.7%), and women were more likely than men to be under the influence of drugs when they committed the offense for which they were imprisoned (36.3%, compared to 30.6%). Finally, about a quarter of women in prison but only a fifth of men committed the offense for which they were imprisoned to buy drugs. Ominously, about a quarter of all women in prison had some form of drug treatment prior to imprisonment, and of those using drugs, 41.8% had treatment the month before their offense. These figures suggest that most interventions are not sufficient to help these women with their drug problems.

Cobbina's research (2009, 2010) also illustrates the strong role of drugs in women offenders' lives, criminal pathways, and their chances for successful re-entry. In her interviews with 50 incarcerated or paroled women, 88% of incarcerated and 79% of paroled women reported using drugs in their lifetimes (p. 38).

> Of the women who used drugs, 74 percent of incarcerated women and 79 percent of paroled women had at least one member of their family who was drug addicted, indicating that women are more likely to use narcotic substances when members of their own family abuse drugs. (p. 38)

A number of incarcerated (23%) and paroled (25%) women in the study stated that their initiation into the drug world began as a result of their exposure to illicit substances by their family during childhood or adolescence. Most stated that their desire for approval and acceptance by their peers and male intimate partner also influenced their decision. Finally, some stated they used drugs as a way to cope with negative life events (pp. 37–38).

Women prisoners are also taking health risks by using drugs. Snell and Morton (1994) found that women prisoners were more likely than men to use needles to inject drugs (34%, compared to 24.3%) and to have shared needles with friends (18%, compared to 11.5%). Again, contrary to many stereotypes, these rates were highest among white and Hispanic women, compared to African American women. For example, 41.6% of white women and 45.9% of Hispanic women had ever used a needle, compared to only 24% of African American women.

Perhaps as a result of these patterns, at the turn of the 21st century, more women than men in prison were infected with HIV; in that year, 3.6% of all women in state prisons had the virus that causes AIDS, compared to 2.2% of male inmates. In New York, the state with the most HIV-positive female prisoners (600), the percentage of women inmates testing positive (18.2% of the female prison population) far outreached the percentage of male inmates testing positive for the virus (8%; Maruschak, 2002). Although the number of inmates with HIV is decreasing overall, the rate is faster for men. Between 1999 and 2000, 7% fewer men in prison were known to be HIV positive; for women, the decrease was 2% (Maruschak, 2001, 2002).

Mothers Behind Bars

Nearly two-thirds of women in prison have a child under the age of 18 (Glaze & Muraschak, 2008). Over the past two decades, the number of children who have a mother behind bars has increased 131% (Glaze & Muraschak, 2008). Many of these women will never see their children if this and other national studies (see Bloom & Steinhart, 1993) are accurate. Women in prison are five times more likely than men to have their children removed from immediate family members and placed into foster care or some other agency (Mumola, 2000). Even those women who retain custody of their children are unlikely to see them. Snell and Morton (1994) found that 52.2% of the women with children under 18 had never been visited by their children. Most of the women who were able to be visited by their children saw them "less than once a month" or "once a month." More women were able to send mail to or phone their children, but even here, one in five never sent or received mail from their children, and one in four never talked on the phone with their children. This is despite the fact that many of these women, prior to their incarceration, were taking care of their children (unlike their male counterparts). More than 64% of mothers behind bars lived with their children prior to incarceration (Glaze & Muraschak, 2008).

Moreover, because women's work is never done, it is more often the imprisoned woman's mother (the child's grandmother) who takes care of her children, whereas male inmates are more likely (89.7%) to be able to count on the children's mother to care of the child (Snell & Morton, 1994, p. 6).

These patterns are particularly pronounced among African American and Hispanic women. Black children are almost nine times more likely than white children to have a parent in prison, and Hispanic children are three times more likely (Mumola, 2000; Sentencing Project, 2007). By age 14, among children born in 1990, the cumulative risk of parental imprisonment is 25.1 to 28.4% for African American children, while only 3.6 to 4.2% for white children (Foster & Hagan, 2009). Additionally, white female inmates more often report access to husbands as primary caretakers of their children, whereas African American women do not identify this as an option (Enos, 2001, p. 55). Although black women and Hispanic women are more likely to share caretaking responsibilities with other family members and are less likely to rely upon foster care services, the ability of the family to effectively respond, both financially and emotionally, to the incarceration of a female family member with children is dependent upon social and economic status (Enos, 2001). This becomes highly problematic for women of color, because poverty and race are intertwined and families often have few resources to extend (Christian & Thomas, 2009).

Additionally, women of color are more likely to experience adverse parenting situations even before incarceration, as African American and Hispanic women more often live in communities that have intense exposure to dual modes of state intervention—the criminal justice system and child welfare services (Roberts, 2002). In Brown and Bloom's (2009) research on mothers on parole, nearly 24% ($n = 48$) of the women in this study had been involved with the state's Department of Human Services (DHS), Child Welfare Services

Division for child maltreatment (p. 317). In addition, the state (or some other jurisdiction) had terminated the parental rights of 17% ($n = 34$) of the mothers in this study for one or more children.

Race and Women's Imprisonment

Race as well as gender figures prominently in women's imprisonment. The numbers indicate that nearly half the women in the nation's prisons are women of color; notably, 30% are African American and 16% are Hispanic (Sentencing Project, 2007). Moreover, the incarceration rate for African American women is nearly twice that of Hispanic women and 2.5 times that of white women: In 2009, 1 in 703 black females was imprisoned, compared to about 1 in 1,987 white females and 1 in 1,356 Hispanic females (Bureau of Justice Statistics, 2010a, 2010c).

Hidden in these data is the fact that the surge in women's imprisonment has disproportionately hit women of color in the United States. Further analysis of these survey data and other national data (Bureau of Justice Statistics, 2010c; Mauer, 2006; Mauer & Huling, 1995) has thoroughly documented the way in which the surge in women's imprisonment has been driven almost completely by a dramatic increase in the imprisonment of women of color. Although white women comprise 62% of women on probation, it is African American women who are most represented in jails and prisons.

Between 1986 and 1991, all women saw an increase in what Mauer and Huling (1995) call the "control rate" (the proportion of women under some form of correctional supervision—probation, jail, prison, or parole), but this rate jumped most dramatically for African American women. Although much of the nation's attention has been correctly focused on the horrific overcontrol of African American males (whose control rate now approaches one out of every three young males between the ages of 20 and 29; Mauer & Huling, 1995), their sisters are also seeing increases in contact with the criminal justice system.

The "control rate" for African American women was 2.7% of all young women in 1989; by 1994, the rate had jumped 78% to 4.8% (or 1 out of 20 young African American women; Mauer & Huling, 1995, p. 5). The distance between the white and African American rates also widened, so that well over three times as many young black women have contact with the criminal justice system as do their white counterparts. Hispanic women have also seen their control rate increase by 18%, and their control rate is about double the rate for white women (2.2%).

Mauer and Huling (1995) present compelling evidence to support their contention that much of this increase can be laid at the door of the war on drugs, which many now believe has become a war on women, particularly on women of color. They also present a striking analysis of how the crackdown on drug use and trafficking has affected black and Hispanic women. Specifically, although the number of women in state prisons for drug sales has increased by 433% between 1986 and 1991, this increase is far steeper for Hispanic women (328%) and for African American women (828%) than for white women (241%; Mauer & Huling, 1995, p. 20).

Huling (1995), in a subsequent paper, directly links these increases in women's incarceration to the fact that the war on drugs has been particularly harsh on those using and selling crack cocaine. This has a significant effect on African American women because "there are indications that women are more likely to use crack and are more likely to be involved in crack distribution sales relative to other drugs" (p. 8). Thus, she contends that, without much public fanfare, the war on drugs, and particularly the harsh penalties for the sale of crack cocaine (relative to powder cocaine and other drugs), has had a dramatic effect on the incarceration patterns of African American women. With the major focus of the drug war on low-level street users of crack cocaine, black women, constructed by the media as "crack whores" and drug-addicted mothers, became "responsible" for crack's devastation in inner-city neighborhoods (see also Bush-Baskette, 1999, for similar argument). Consequently, black women entered the criminal justice system at exacerbated rates.

Recall the research by English (1993) on women's and men's self-reported drug selling, wherein she found that female prisoners were much more likely than their male counterparts to report numerous small drug sales. This could mean that the patterns of women's drug selling rather than the seriousness of their sales expose them to more risk of arrest and incarceration.

The other hidden victims of the war on drugs are the women, many from foreign countries, who are serving time in U.S. prisons for being drug couriers. Huling (1996) notes that the lack of repatriation treaties between most "drug-demand countries" and "drug-supply countries" has meant that many drug couriers end up serving long prison terms in the country of their arrest. Initially, women from foreign countries entering the United States at airports, such as John F. Kennedy in New York, were tried in federal court. As the federal prisons began to experience sharp increases in women's imprisonment, federal officials shifted the cases to state courts (Huling, 1996; see also English, 1993).

Reviewing the cases of women who were arrested at JFK airport during 1990 and 1991 for drug smuggling ($n = 59$), Huling (1996) found the following: First, almost all (96%) had no history of involvement with the criminal justice system. Most (95%) had not been convicted at trial but had instead pled guilty to a reduced charge. To avoid the New York laws that would have sentenced them to life terms, they pled guilty to a reduced charge that requires a "mandatory minimum" of 3 years to life in prison. Almost all of the women arrested were Hispanic (Huling, p. 53). Prosecutors, when asked about these patterns, argued that they had "no choice" but to pursue indictments for anyone found in possession of 4 ounces or more of an illegal drug.

Interviewing some of these women, Huling (1996) was able to document that many carried the drugs because of threats to their families, because they were trapped in abusive relationships with men involved in the drug trade, or because they had been duped or fooled. Despite this reality, Huling shows that New York politicians (including elected prosecutors) used the number of convictions of drug smugglers to document their "get tough on crime" stances, and despite a public outcry generated in part by Huling's work and the work of Sister Marion of Riker's Island, efforts to reform New York's harsh mandatory sentences failed.

Different Versus Equal?

Given situations like those experienced by women charged with being drug smugglers, it should come as no surprise that the continuing debate over whether equality under the law is a good thing for women has special immediacy for those looking at the situation of women in the criminal justice system. To recap this debate (see Chesney-Lind & Pollock-Byrne, 1995, for a full discussion), some feminist legal scholars argue that the only way to eliminate the discriminatory treatment and oppression that women have experienced in the past is to push for continued equalization under the law, that is, to champion equal rights amendments and to oppose any legislation that treats men and women differently. They argue that although this may hurt in the short run, in the long run it is the only way that women will ever be treated as equal playing partners in economic and social spheres. For example, MacKinnon (1987) writes, "For women to affirm difference, when difference means dominance, as it does with gender, means to affirm the qualities and characteristics of powerlessness" (pp. 38–39). Even those who do not view the experience of women as one of oppression conclude that women will be victimized by laws created from "concern and affection" that are designed to protect them (Kirp, Yudof, & Franks, 1986).

The opposing argument is that women are not the same as men, and because it is a male standard that equality is measured against, they will always lose. Therefore, one must consider differential needs (a sort of "separate but equal" argument). This would mean that women and men might receive differential treatment as long as it did not put women in a more negative position than the absence of such legislation. Conversely, the equalization proponents feel that, given legal and social realities, differential treatment for women will always be unequal treatment, and by accepting different definitions and treatments, women run the risk of perpetuating the stereotype of women as "different from" and "less than" men.

One might reasonably ask how this legal debate, which has to date largely focused on the rights of women as workers, bears on women as prisoners. In fact, as the next section will demonstrate, the experience of women prisoners starkly illuminates some of the shortcomings of the conventional extremes of the different-versus-equal debate, because at different points in our nation's history, those who have imprisoned women have used each perspective to deal with the women they confined. This review of the history and current issues surrounding women's imprisonment will also highlight severe problems with the gender-blind approach to jailing women.

Prisons and Parity

Initially, the differential needs approach was the dominant correctional policy. Almost from the outset, the correctional response to women offenders was to embrace the Victorian notion of "separate spheres" and to construct and manage women's facilities based around what were seen as immutable differences between men and women (Rafter, 1990). Women were housed in separate facilities, and programs for women prisoners represented their perceived role in society. Thus, they were taught to be good mothers and housekeepers; vocational education was slighted in favor of domestic training. Women were hired to supervise female offenders in the belief that only they could provide for the special needs of female offenders and serve as role models for them. To some degree, this legacy still permeates women's prisons today. Typically, these prisons have sex-typed vocational programming and architectural differences (such as smaller living units and decentralized kitchens) in recognition of gender roles.

In sentencing, too, one could observe that the system treated women and men differently. Women were much less likely than men to be imprisoned unless the female offender did not fit the stereotypical female role, for example, if she was a "bad mother" who abused or abandoned her children, or if she did not have a family to care for (Chesney-Lind, 1987; Eaton, 1986). This resulted in one of the most dramatic disproportional ratios in criminal justice—women composed roughly only 4% of the total prison population for years. Of course, part of this was because most women committed far fewer serious crimes than men, but at least some part of the difference was due to sentencing practices (see Blumstein et al., 1983).

Certainly, the differential treatment of women in sentencing and prison programming is a thing of the past. Partially as a result of prisoner rights litigation based on the parity model (see Pollock-Byrne, 1990), women offenders are being swept into a system that seems bent on treating women "equally." Currently, the emphasis on women's prison construction and the architecture of women's prisons suggest that women get the worst of both worlds, correctionally. A couple of well-publicized scandals can serve to highlight the severe problems with a "gender-blind" approach to women's imprisonment.

In Alabama, the state reinstated male "chain gangs" with much fanfare in 1995, after they had been dropped in 1932 because of accounts of brutality and abuse. The current practice involves men shackled in groups of five working along public highways, although some groups are assigned the job of breaking "large rocks into little ones" ("Chain Gang Death," 1996, p. 8A). The country's current "get tough on crime" mood provided Alabama officials with the opening to reinstate these workgroups and even to involve some groups in grueling "busy work."

Alabama corrections officials were threatened with a lawsuit brought by male inmates suggesting that the practice of excluding women from the chain gangs was unconstitutional. The response from the Alabama Corrections Commissioner was to include women in the chain gangs (Franklin, 1996, p. 3A). Ultimately, the governor forced the corrections chief to resign; the governor's spokesperson said simply, "It was just a philosophical difference. In his [the governor's] opinion, there is a difference in men and women (specifically) physically" (Hulen, 1996, p. A1).

Although the issue of chain gangs for women is moot in Alabama, it has surfaced in other states. Proclaiming himself "an equal opportunity incarcerator," an Arizona sheriff has started one for women "now locked up with three or four others in dank, cramped disciplinary cells" (Kim, 1996, p. 1A). To escape these conditions, the women can "volunteer" for the 15-woman chain gang. Defending his controversial move, the sheriff commented, "If women can fight for their country, and bless them for that, if they can walk a beat, if they can protect the people and arrest violators of the law, then they should have no problem with picking up trash in 120-degrees" (p. 1A).

Other routine institutional practices, such as strip searches (sometimes involving body-cavity searches), have also produced problems. In New York prisons, in response to complaints by male inmates that strip searches were often accompanied by beatings, video monitors (usually mounted on the wall) were installed in areas where searches occurred. When the women's prison (Albion Correctional Center) began to tape women's strip searches, though, fixed cameras were replaced by hand-held cameras (Craig, 1995, p. 1A).

Fifteen women prisoners incarcerated at Albion filed complaints based on their experiences with strip searches. Specifically, they said that doors to the search area were occasionally kept open, that male guards were sometimes seen outside the doors watching the searches, and that, unlike the men's videos, which surveyed the whole room where the searches occurred, according to the women's lawyer, "these videotapes were solely focused on the woman. That amplified the pornographic effect of it" (Craig, 1996, p. 1A). Said one woman who was searched while men were "right outside a door and could see the whole incident, 'I knew they was watching . . . I was so humiliated . . . I felt like I was on display. I felt like a piece of meat'" (p. A6). Advocates for the women stressed the traumatic effect of such searches, given the histories of sexual abuse and assault that many women bring with them to prison.

Moreover, the women inmates suspected that prison officials were viewing the tapes and eventually filed complaints to stop routine videotaping of women prisoners. In addition to receiving more than $60,000 in damages, the women were able to change the policy of routine videotaping of women's searches. As a result of their complaints, "a female inmate would be filmed only if officers believed she would resist the search" (Craig, 1996, p. A6). Presently, very few searches of women inmates are being videotaped in New York, but the possibility of abuse is present in almost all prisons.

Even without videotaping and other possible abuses, strip searches have quite different meanings for women and men. For example, a key point made by the Albion women was that, given the high levels of previous sexual abuse among women inmates, such searches had the possibility of being extremely traumatic. In fact, similar concerns have also surfaced in a Task Force Report to the Massachusetts Department of Health about the use of "restraint and seclusion" among psychiatric patients who have histories of sexual abuse (Carmen et al., 1996).

Finally, the most pervasive complaint that has accompanied women's imprisonment is the sexual abuse and harassment of women inmates by male guards. Owen's (1998) study of "women in the mix" includes the degrading experiences women encounter with male guards. Although the women in her study offered limited discussion about forced or consensual sexual relationships with staff, one woman illustrated the potential for harassment in day-to-day activities:

> If you are short, the officers, you can be seen from the (officer's) bubble. It is degrading. Sometimes you get a shower peeker. I told the other girls to block the shower. Then the officer got an attitude. You could tell. (p. 166)

As old as women's imprisonment (Beddoe, 1979), the sexual victimization of women in U.S. prisons is the subject of increasing news coverage and, more recently, international scrutiny. Scandals have erupted in California, Georgia, Hawaii, Ohio, Louisiana, Michigan, Tennessee, New York, and New Mexico (respectively, Stein, 1996; Meyer, 1992; Watson, 1992; Curriden, 1993; Sewenely, 1993; Craig, 1996; and Lopez, 1993), and the assumption has grown that prisons, here in the United States and elsewhere, are rife with this problem. So extensive is the concern that the issue has attracted the attention of Human Rights Watch (1993).

Details of these scandals yield the predictable charges and counter-charges, but the storyline remains essentially unchanged; women in prisons, guarded by large numbers of men, are vulnerable. As one advocate for women in prison has noted, "We put [women] into an environment where they're controlled by men and men are willing to put their hands on them whenever they want to" (Craig, 1996, p. A1). The story that prompted this observation dealt with one of a series of sexual assaults reported by a young woman in a New York prison:

> Correctional officer Selbourne Reid, 27, came into the cell of a 21-year-old inmate at the maximum security prison in Westchester County. The inmate, at first asleep, was startled to find him in her cell. . . . On this night, Reid forced the woman to perform oral sex on him, according to the Westchester

County district attorney's office. After he left, she spit the semen into a small bottle in her room. She told prison authorities about the attack, and gave them the semen for DNA analysis. (Craig, 1996, pp. 1A, 6A)

Similar accounts appear with distressing regularity, and even more disturbing is the fact that so few of the cases, unlike the one reported here, actually go to trial or result in the perpetrators being found guilty. Institutional subcultures in women's prisons that encourage correctional workers to "cover" for each other, coupled with inadequate protection accorded women who file complaints, make it unlikely that many women inmates will show the courage of the young woman in New York. Indeed, according to a memo filed by an attorney in the Civil Rights Division of the U.S. Department of Justice, the Division found "a pattern of sexual abuse by both male and female guards" in Michigan women's prisons (Patrick, 1995).

A judge reviewing the situation of women in Washington, D.C., jails noted that "the evidence revealed a level of sexual harassment which is so malicious that it violates contemporary standards of decency" (Stein, 1996, p. 24). If this is true, why do so few of these cases make it to court? Sadly, some of this involves the histories of women in prison, many of whom have engaged in prostitution, which allow the defendants to use the misogynist defense that it is impossible to rape a prostitute. Beyond this, the public stereotype of women in prison as "bad girls" means that any victim must first battle this perception before her case can be fairly heard. Finally, what little progress has been made is severely threatened by recent legislation that has drastically curtailed the ability of prisoners and advocates to sue over prison conditions (p. 24)—changes again likely to have been motivated by public perceptions of prisoners as violent men.

That women in prison are the recipients of "equity with a vengeance" does not necessarily mean that the abuses that used to exist in prisons that assumed gender difference have retreated completely. In fact, it appears that today's women in prison still receive some of the worst of the old separate spheres abuses, particularly in the area of social control. For example, McClellan (1994) examined disciplinary practices at men's and women's prisons in Texas. Using Texas Department of Corrections records, McClellan constructed two samples of inmates (271 men and 245 women) and followed them for a 1-year period (1989). She documented that although most men in her sample (63.5%) had no citation or only one citation for a rule violation, only 17.1% of the women in her sample had such clear records. Women prisoners were much more likely to receive numerous citations and received them for different sorts of offenses than men. Most commonly, women were cited for "violating posted rules," whereas men were cited most frequently for "refusing to work" (McClellan, 1994, p. 77). Finally, women were more likely than men to receive the most severe sanctions, including solitary confinement (p. 82).

McClellan's (1994) review of the details of women's infractions subsumed under the category "violation of posted rules" included such offenses as "excessive artwork ('too many family photographs on display'), failing to eat all the food on their plates, and for talking while waiting in the pill line" (p. 85). Possession of contraband could include such things as an extra bra or pillowcase, peppermint sticks, or a properly borrowed comb or hat. Finally, "trafficking" and "trading" included instances of sharing shampoo in a shower and lighting another inmate's cigarette (p. 85).

The author concluded by observing that there exists "two distinct institutional forms of surveillance and control operating at the male and female facilities . . . this policy not only imposes extreme constraints on adult women but also costs the people of the State of Texas a great deal of money" (McClellan, 1994, p. 87). Research like this provides clear evidence that women in prison are overpoliced and overcontrolled in institutional settings—a finding earlier researchers have noted, as well (see Burkhart, 1973; Mann, 1984). Whether this is an extension of historic interests in women's sexual behavior or whether, more prosaically, it is a function of the fact that, if men were controlled to the extent women were, they would probably riot, is unclear.

What is clear from all these accounts is that women in modern prisons may be subjected to the "worst of both worlds." If McClellan's (1994) findings can be extended to other states, women in modern prisons continue to be overpoliced and overcontrolled (a feature of the separate-spheres legacy of women's imprisonment). At the same time, they are also the recipients of a form of "equality" that results in abuses that are probably unparalleled in male institutions (e.g., sexual exploitation by guards and degrading strip searches). Beyond this, correctional leaders are, in some cases, implementing grossly inappropriate and clearly male-modeled interventions, such as chain gangs and even boot camps, to deal with women's offenses (Elis, MacKenzie, & Simpson, 1992).

The enormous and rapid increase in women's imprisonment has clearly overwhelmed correctional officials who must scramble to come up with space, let alone programs, for the thousands of women coming through the doors (see Morash & Bynum, 1996). Yet prior to these huge population increases, things were not necessarily good for women inmates. Women inmates have never had the same range of programs as male offenders (this was often justified by their low numbers; see Pollock-Byrne, 1990). Because the current imprisonment boom has affected men's and women's facilities, even with larger numbers in women's prisons, women's special needs are unlikely to receive serious attention any time soon.

Some efforts have been made nationally, especially in improving the connection of children with their incarcerated mothers. For example, in California, some nonviolent female drug offenders are sentenced to Family Foundations, a community-based, residential drug-treatment program, where they live with their children who are 6 and younger. The Women's Prison Association in New York assists women offenders in addressing the critical issues involved in women's pathways toward crime and in their successful return to the community after prison; these issues include substance abuse problems, victimization experiences, family disruption, housing needs, and vocational and employment issues (Conly, 1998). Lastly, the Children's Center in Belford Hills, New York, allows women offenders to reside with their children until the children are 1 year of age. The women learn "to be good mothers," and the focus is on the women's mental health needs (National Institute of Justice, 1998, p. 8).

Despite programs such as these, there still exists a paucity of alternative and innovative approaches available to address women offenders' issues. A National Institute of Justice (1998) study demonstrates this point: In the study, state and prison-level administrators were asked to identify innovative programs for women in prison in their jurisdictions. Only three states reported high levels of innovative programming for women; 34 states identified none or limited availability (National Institute of Justice, 1998, p. 6). On a more global level, given the differences between male and female prisoners, it seems extremely unlikely that women's experience of imprisonment will ever mirror men's experience—no matter how often the legal system insists on a gender-neutral stance. Nor, if the lessons are learned from these scandals, should women be treated as though they are men.

The abuses mentioned earlier force us to ask whether a gender-blind approach to imprisonment is fair or just. Is it the case that female prisoners are "disappearing" politically, in a country haunted by images of male drug kingpins and violent predators, because their convictions bolster those who are cynically manipulating the system and the public's fears to win an election? Finally, as the nation becomes increasingly aware of the surge in women's imprisonment from news accounts (LeBlanc, 1996), we need to question whether tax dollars spent on women's imprisonment could be better spent on programs for women in the community.

REDUCING WOMEN'S IMPRISONMENT THROUGH EFFECTIVE COMMUNITY-BASED STRATEGIES AND PROGRAMS

The expansion of the female prison population has been fueled primarily by increased rates of incarceration for drug offenses, not by commitments for crimes of violence. The majority of women in America's prisons are sentenced for nonviolent crimes that are all too often a direct product of the economic marginalization of the women who find their way through the prison doors.

As we have seen, changes in criminal justice policies and procedures over the past decade have contributed to the dramatic growth in the female prison population. Mandatory prison terms and sentencing guidelines are gender blind and, in the crusade to get tough on crime, criminal justice policymakers have gotten tough on women, pushing them into jails and prisons in unprecedented numbers.

Most of these female offenders are poor, undereducated, unskilled, victims of past physical or sexual abuse, and single mothers of at least two children. They enter the criminal justice system with a host of unique medical, psychological, and financial problems.

The data summarized in this chapter suggest that women may be better served in the community because of the treatable antecedents and less serious nature of their crimes. A growing number of states are beginning to explore nonincarcerative strategies for women offenders, such as the ones aforementioned. Commissions and task forces charged with examining the effect of criminal justice policies on women are recommending sentencing alternatives and the expansion of community-based programs that address the diverse needs of women who come into conflict with the law.

In California, the Senate Concurrent Resolution (SCR) 33 Commission on Female Inmate and Parolee Issues examined the needs of women offenders.

The Commission's upcoming report is based on three central concepts: (1) Female inmates differ significantly from males in terms of their needs, and these gender-specific needs should be considered in planning for successful reintegration into the community; (2) women are less violent in the community and in prison, and this fact provides opportunities to develop nonprison-based programs and intermediate sanctions without compromising public safety; and (3) communities need to share the responsibility of assisting in this reintegration by providing supervision, care, and treatment of women offenders (Bloom et al., 1994). Although coming under some criticism in its effectiveness, California began a more gendered approach to corrections by developing nonprison institutions that housed incarcerated mothers with their children (see Haney, 2010).

Despite the growth of the female prison population, there has not been a commensurate increase in research devoted to the needs of these women, nor in designing prison treatment, discharge, and reentry programs specifically for female prisoners (Balis, 2007). One study (Morash, 2010) compared two sorts of philosophical approaches to supervision on probation and parole: One focused on compliance with rules and "equality" between male and females and the other focused on "gender-responsive" issues in two Michigan counties. Reviewing probation and parole recidivism, Morash found that attention paid to women's unique problems and needs in a gender-responsive fashion (like focusing on domestic violence and the role of trauma in women's drug use) and building on women's strengths (e.g., the importance of relationships) produces better services and lower overall recidivism. More importantly, she did not find that the gender-responsive approach backfired, sending more women back to jail or prison because of the more intensive supervision offered low-level female offenders, as some feared, because earlier studies of intensive supervision had produced just that outcome (Morash, 2010, pp. 147–148).

Overcrowding and overuse of women's prisons can be avoided by planning creatively for reduced reliance on imprisonment for women while reimagining and reinventing probation and parole to focus on gendered needs as well as cutting-edge research on issues such as drug addiction, trauma, and other challenges that plague women in the criminal justice system. Many advocate a moratorium on the construction of women's prisons and a serious commitment to the decarceration of women. They believe that every dollar spent locking up women could be better spent on services that would prevent women from resorting to crime. As one prisoner at the Central California Women's Facility commented,

> You can talk to them about community programs. I had asked my P.O. for help—but his supervisor turned him down. I told him that I was getting into a drinking problem, asked if he could place me in a place for alcoholics but he couldn't get permission. I was violated with a DUI—gave me eight months. I think people with psychological problems and with drug problems need to be in community programs. (Bloom et al., 1994, p. 8)

There is a range of effective residential and nonresidential community-based programs serving women offenders throughout the nation. Austin, Bloom, and Donahue (1992) reviewed limited program-evaluation data and found the following common characteristics that appeared to influence successful program outcomes: continuum of care design, clearly stated program expectations, rules and sanctions, consistent supervision, diverse and representative staffing, coordination of community resources, and access to ongoing social and emotional support. They also suggested that promising approaches are multidimensional and deal specifically with women's issues.

DETENTION VERSUS PREVENTION

The United States now imprisons more people than at any time in its history and has the world's highest incarceration rate (Mauer, 1999). On any given day, more than a million people are locked up, and an unprecedented number of prison cells are being planned. As a result, the fastest-growing sector of state and local economies, nationally, is correctional employment, which increased 108% during the 1990s, whereas total employment increased by just 13.5% (Center for the Study of the States, 1993, p. 2). Women in conflict with the law have become the hidden victims of the nation's imprisonment binge. Women's share of the nation's prison population, measured in either absolute or relative terms, has never been higher. Women were 4% of the nation's imprisoned population shortly after the turn of the 20th century. By 1970, the figure had dropped to 3%. By 2001, however, more than 6.7% of those incarcerated in state prisons in the country were women.

Is this increase in women's imprisonment being fueled by a similarly dramatic increase in serious crimes committed by women? The simple answer is no. As has been shown, the proportion of women in prison for violent crimes has dropped steadily, and the numbers of women incarcerated for petty drug and property offenses have soared. Large increases in women's imprisonment are due to changes in law-enforcement practices, judicial decision making, and legislative mandatory sentencing guidelines rather than a shift in the nature of the crimes women commit.

As a nation, we face a choice. We can continue to spend our shrinking tax dollars on the pointless and costly incarceration of women guilty of petty drug and property crimes, or we can seek other solutions to the problems of drug-dependent women. Because so many of the women in prison in California are driven to drug use because of poverty and abuse, the real question before us is: detention or prevention?

As this and previous chapters have indicated, we know what to do about crime, particularly crime committed by women. Any review of the back-grounds of women in prison immediately suggests better ways to address their needs. Whether it be more funding for drug-treatment programs, more shelters for the victims of domestic violence, or more job-training programs, the solutions to their problems are obvious. The question remains: Do we as a society have the courage to admit that the war on drugs (and indirectly on women) has been lost and at a great price (see Baum, 1996)? The hidden victims of that war have seen their petty offenses criminalized and their personal lives severely disrupted. Is this our only choice?

This book has suggested another choice. By focusing on strategies that directly address the problems of women on the economic and political margins rather than expensive and counterproductive penal policies, the pointless waste of the nation's scarce tax dollars could be stopped. To do this, there must be changes in public policy, so that the response to women's offenses addresses human needs rather than the short-sighted objectives of lawmakers who often cannot see beyond the next sound bite or election. The greed of what might be called the "correctional industrial complex" must also be addressed. This term refers to those who benefit from prison construction (such as architectural and construction companies, unions representing prison guards, etc.), who might well seek to replace the mindless spending of the cold war with the equally mindless but profitable incarceration of the nation's poor and dispossessed.

Now that we have entered the new millennium, there are actually a few indications that some states are beginning to re-examine their incarceration practices. So, although the rate of women's imprisonment does stand at a historic high, the first decade of the new century saw several years in which the female rate of increase in imprisonment fell behind that of the male rate of increase. In 2009, fewer females (down 1%) were incarcerated than in 2008 (West & Sabol, 2010).

Several states long associated with the women's imprisonment boom—notably California and New York—actually saw decreases in the number of women in their prisons. In California, the decrease that accelerated in 2001 was clearly tied to the passage of Proposition 36. This initiative, passed in 2000, diverted most people convicted of nonviolent drug possession to programs instead of prison. In the short time since its inception, it has caused the number of women sent to California prisons to drop by 10% (Martin, 2002, p. 1). The drop actually encouraged two Democratic lawmakers to propose closing one or two of California women's prisons in an attempt to address the state's budget deficit (p. 1).

California's experience provides a valuable lesson to the rest of the nation. Given the characteristics of the women in prison, it is clear that the decarceration of almost all of the women in United States prisons would not jeopardize public safety. Furthermore, the money saved could be reinvested in programs designed to meet women's needs, which would enrich not only their lives but also the lives of many other women who are at risk for criminal involvement. Finally, by moving dollars from women's prisons to women's services, we will not only help women—we also help their children. In the process, we are also breaking the cycle of poverty, desperation, crime, and imprisonment rather than perpetuating it.

We also must dispense with a belief that gender does not matter in prison programming and that we can do effective corrections (especially gender-informed probation, parole, or other community re-entry programs) through an evidence-based gender-blind approach to supervisory practices. The next chapter explores this issue in depth, providing a careful and important review of a national best practice—contemporary risk- and needs-assessment tools—to explore how these sorts of approaches work and where they fall short in working effectively with female offenders in the community.

SEVEN

FEMALE OFFENDERS, COMMUNITY SUPERVISION, AND EVIDENCE-BASED PRACTICES

by Janet T. Davidson

———•◦•———

The women's problems isn't the f***ing addiction, it's what's behind the addiction.

—Zoe (Parolee)

The last two decades have witnessed a criminal justice system in which female offenders have comprised an ever-increasing portion of the correctional population, from jails and prisons to probation and parole. While there has been a corresponding increase in attention paid to women held in jail and prison settings, less attention has been given to women serving time in the community, on either probation or parole, and when attention has been paid to those under community supervision, the focus has usually surrounded male offenders (Bloom et al., 2003; Sabol & Couture, 2008; Schram et al., 2006). Considerably less concern has been directed toward the issue of female offenders, to the unique circumstances that bring them into the system, and to their gendered needs as they navigate life on probation or parole.

The pathways that bring women to offending also affect how they do time in the community. Women's histories of poverty, physical and sexual abuse, substance abuse, and familial obligations all impact whether women will reoffend (recidivism; Huebner, DeJong, & Cobbina, 2010; Neal, 2007). Yet such factors are infrequently taken into account in community correctional supervision and interventions; gender is rarely considered. This chapter examines the challenges and issues underscoring the female offender as she does her time in community corrections and survives life on probation/parole. Using research from a Hawaii study of male and female parolees, this chapter also explores contemporary risk-assessment tools and evidence-based practices and programs and whether such tools and programs take gender into account and meet the needs of female probationers and parolees.

TRENDS IN PROBATION, INCARCERATION, AND PAROLE

As can be seen in Table 7.1, supervision in the community is the most used yet seemingly least visible method of punishment in this country. And, while women make up 13% of the total U.S. jail population (Sabol & Minton, 2008) and 7% of the U.S. prison population, they comprise a full 24% of the U.S. probation and 12% of the U.S. parole population (Glaze & Bonczar, 2007).

Table 7.1 Trends in Correctional Populations by Sex

Population 1988–2009	Total	Percent Change Total	Male	Percent Change Male	Female	Percent Change Female
Probation	2,356,483– 4,203,967	78.4	1,714,114– 2,342,640	36.7	350,852– 740,253	111.0
Parole	407,977– 819,308	100.8	355,341– 718,982	102.3	26,816– 98,432	267.1
Jail	341,893– 767,620	124.5	313,158– 673,891	115.2	30,411– 93,729	208.2
Prison	606,810– 1,617,478	166.6	575,670– 1,502,499	161.0	31,140– 114,979	269.2

SOURCES: Bureau of Justice Statistics, Data Analysis Tools: http://bjs.ojp.usdoj.gov/content/dtdata.cfm#corrections; Glaze and Bonczar (2010); Minton (2010); West (2010).

NOTE: 1988 was used as a starting point since this represented the first year in which probation and parole data were readily available by sex.

It is also instructive to look at how the growth in correctional populations has specifically impacted male and female offenders. In every category—jail, prison, probation, and parole—female offender populations demonstrate the greatest percentage change. Indeed, the percentage change over the two-decade period outlined is more than double the male percentage change in two categories.

While women do recidivate at lower levels than men, their rates of success nonetheless should be taken with caution. More than one-half (58%) of women on parole are rearrested within 3 years of release from prison, more than one-third are convicted of a new crime (38%), and roughly 30% are returned to prison for either a new crime or a violation of community supervision (e.g., failure to find employment, to secure housing, to keep meetings with parole officer, and/or to stay drug-free; Deschenes et al., 2006). Yet, as we shall see, patterns of recidivism, much like pathways to offending, are not static across different groups. Gender matters in recidivism, just as it does in initial offending. The next section will outline the current framework for evidence-based best practices in effective management of offenders in the community as well as the manner in which gender factors into this framework.

EVIDENCE-BASED PRACTICES AND GENDER-NEUTRAL SUPERVISION

The increase in community correctional populations presented a pressing need to manage more people with fewer resources and to do so with a consideration of public safety and risk aversion. Over the past two decades, a coalition of researchers, policy makers, and practitioners have thus moved to research-based practices (i.e., program components that have been tested and evaluated as effecting change in offenders' behaviors) in order to get the most "bang for the buck" in terms of both cost savings and public safety assurances.

The model used by many states is one put forth by the National Institute of Corrections (NIC). According to NIC's model, there are eight principles for effective offender interventions, and jurisdictions that implement and follow the model are most likely to realize substantial gains in public safety and recidivism reduction (Crime and Justice Institute, 2004). Table 7.2 presents the eight principles.

These evidence-based policies and practices presume that the risk of reoffending is nongendered and that these risks can be accurately predicted with

Table 7.2 NIC's Eight Principles for Effective Offender Interventions

Principle	
Access Actuarial Risk/Needs	Use of an actuarial-based assessment tool to screen offenders for risk and to determine criminogenic (crime-causing) factors that can be changed through case management.
Enhance Intrinsic Motivation	Encourages the use of motivational interviewing to move offenders to want to change. Interpersonal interactions by all correctional staff, treatment providers, and others are meant to develop an internal motivation to change.
Target Interventions	There are five main pieces to this part of the model: (1) risk principle—supervision is prioritized for the highest-risk offenders; (2) need principle—interventions are targeted to the assessed criminogenic needs; (3) responsivity principle—officer should be responsive to temperament, learning style, motivation, gender, and culture when assigning offenders to programs; (4) dosage—high-risk offenders should have 40 to 70% of their time structured for at least 3 and up to 9 months; and (5) treatment principle—integrate treatment into the correctional sentence requirements.
Skill Train With Directed Practice	Calls for the use of cognitive-behavioral strategies in the provision of evidence-based programming. Correctional staff are to be trained in antisocial thinking, social learning, and appropriate communication techniques.
Increase Positive Reinforcement	Calls for the use of four positive to every one negative reinforcement in order to promote behavior change.
Engage Ongoing Support in Natural Communities	Engage community-based prosocial supports for the offenders.
Measure Relevant Processes/Practices	Collect data to measure case information, offender change, outcomes, and staff performance.
Provide Measurement Feedback	Use information collected in the previous step to monitor the process and progress and any change. Offenders should also be included in the feedback loop.

SOURCE: Crime and Justice Institute (2004).

the use of validated actuarial-based assessment tools for all offenders. Since female offenders constitute the minority of probationers and parolees, the issue of gender has been largely ignored in the development of these tools. Research, policy, and practice have centered on male offenders (Belknap, 2007; Blanchette

& Taylor, 2009; Bloom et al., 2003); thus, the model for effective offender intervention is also based on male offenders.

Indeed, gender and race are only mentioned, almost in passing, in one part of the NIC model. Namely, the responsivity principle states, "Be responsive to temperament, learning style, motivation, *gender*, and culture when assigning to programs" (Crime and Justice Institute, 2004, emphasis added). This is the only mention of gender in the entire model, and even then, there is no clarification as to what this might actually mean in practice. So while practitioners must use the instrument and be "responsive" to an individual's gender (and race, for that matter), what this guideline becomes in practice is left undefined.

Nonetheless, it should be understood that risk in this context means recidivism. But recidivism can be measured in myriad ways, although rearrests for new crimes or violations of community supervision are typically included. Female offenders are less likely to be convicted of violent offenses and, thus, less likely to incur violent recidivism offenses. Even when at risk, female offenders pose a much lower threat to public safety than do their male counterparts. Risk, albeit measured in the same fashion, simply does not represent the same level of public safety threat for men versus women. Specifically, miscalculating "risk" for male offenders could constitute a considerable public safety risk, but the same is not true for women.

Regardless, actuarial risk/need instruments have become the theoretical foundation of offender management for those serving time in the community. No offender is released to parole or placed on probation without the completion of a risk assessment that (1) instructs the probation/parole officer as to the kind and amount of supervision the offender needs and (2) supposedly gauges the risk the offender poses to the community as well as the risk the offender has of reoffending. Harcourt (2007, p. 1) best describes actuarial risk/need instruments as follows:

> The use of statistical rather than clinical methods on large datasets to determine different levels of criminal offending associated with one or more group traits, in order (1) to predict past, present, or future criminal behavior and (2) to administer criminal justice outcome. (p. 1)

The instruments that are currently in use are designed to both aid in risk management and case planning such that offenders' programmatic needs are aligned with their assessed needs. These instruments have evolved over time to move from mere risk management and the assessment of static (e.g., unchange-able) factors (such as criminal record) toward plans for case management and rehabilitation via the inclusion of dynamic, or changeable, factors (such as drug addiction or educational level), marking an improvement over past gen-erations of assessment tools (Hannah-Moffat & Shaw, 2003; Van Voorhis, 2005). The static factors on these instruments represent risks while the crimi-nogenic needs—the dynamic factors—are those factors both amenable to change and predictive of recidivism (Bonta, 1996). The latter allows for tar-geted case planning to take place.

However, as aforementioned, these instruments have been crafted based upon knowledge of male offending; thus, gendered factors have been largely neglected, ignored, or discounted (Belknap & Holsinger, 2006) in their cre-ation and application. Factors that are not assessed will not be targeted for programmatic services. The problem is seemingly transparent—if factors rel-evant to female offending are not assessed, then this population will be at a disadvantage via inappropriate or inadequate treatment, supervision, and sur-veillance. For example, Holtfreter and Cupp (2007) note that the majority of research used to support the validity of the most widely used instrument for risk and need assessment, the LSI-R (Level of Service Inventory-Revised), has been based solely on male offenders.

It is instructive to discuss the LSI-R in some greater detail. While more of the details of past and present research follow, it is important to fully understand how risk is measured via this particular instrument in order to understand the weaknesses in the current research and application. Addition-ally, the LSI-R represents just one actuarial risk instrument (among the most commonly used), yet other instruments measure risk in a similar fashion. Table 7.3 displays each of the 10 domains and what each one measures.

The LSI-R contains a total of 54 individual items that are collapsed into the 10 domains listed in Table 7.3. Each item is ultimately scored in a dichotomous fashion whereby the presence of a factor is scored as a 1 and the absence of the risk factor as 0. The sum of all scores provides the total, overall risk score. A person could score anywhere from 0 to 54 (theoreti-cally): the higher the score, the higher the assessed risk. This score is then used to manage offenders based on their likelihood of recidivism and, thus, drives the overall level of surveillance as well as provision of services. Those domains that are deemed most criminogenic—ones that place the offender at the greatest odds for recidivism—are targeted for treatment. The

Table 7.3   Descriptions of the LSI-R Domains

Domain	
Criminal History	This domain uses 10 separate questions to measure the nature and extent of past criminal histories.
Education & Employment	This domain uses 10 separate questions to measure current and past education and employment situations.
Financial	This domain uses two questions to measure the extent of financial distress or disruption.
Family & Marital	This domain uses 4 questions to measures the nature of current marital or equivalent and familial relationships.
Accommodation	This domain uses three questions to measure the nature of living arrangements as well as the stability thereof.
Leisure & Recreation	This domain uses two questions to measure the extent to which individuals are prosocially involved in the community and/or making good use of their time.
Companions	This domain uses five questions to measure the extent to which individuals have criminal and prosocial individuals in their lives as both friends and acquaintances.
Alcohol & Drug	This domain uses nine questions to measure whether the individual has now or has ever had an alcohol or a drug problem and the extent to which either has interfered with or affected their law violations, marital/family relationships, school/work, medical health, or other negative indicators.
Emotional & Personal	This domain uses five questions to measure histories of mental health treatment and other mental health disorders that interfere with daily life.
Attitudes & Orientation	This domain uses four questions to measure an individual's attitudes toward conventional lifestyle and toward their criminal punishment and supervision.

SOURCE: Davidson (2007, 2009).

treatment aspect is important because these instruments are thought to contain dynamic risk factors, those needs that should be targeted for intervention to reduce overall risk (Van Voorhis et al., 2008).

As with many studies of crime and justice, research on the LSI-R and similar risk-assessment tools has ignored female offenders and a serious consideration of how gender matters. Notably, only 11 of the 41 studies published between 1986 through 2006 report any statistics for female offenders. Holtfreter and Cupp (2007) go on to note that more than half of these studies (26) were based on male-only models and only five included female-only samples. Yet, many of the studies note gender neutrality in their findings.

In those studies that did include gender in their analyses, the findings have been mixed (Fagan et al., 2007; Manchak et al., 2009; Smith et al., 2009; Van Voorhis et al., 2008; Veysey & Hamilton, 2007). Funk (1999) found that the inclusion of gendered factors into a female-only model was able to explain more predictors of recidivism than was a male-only model. Specifically, child abuse, neglect, and running away emerged as significant predictors of recidivism. Others have discovered similar gender disparities in predictors of recidivism. Olson, Alderden, and Lurigio (2003) found gendered differences in predictors of recidivism, while Holtfreter and colleagues (2004) found that the LSI-R failed to predict women's reoffending once female poverty status was controlled. In a later study by Reisig, Holtfreter, and Morash (2006), researchers discovered that the LSI-R was only predictive for women whose offending context paralleled that of male offenders—in other words, if women and their offenses resembled those of men and those women did not have prior experiences with abuse and victimization. This risk assessment did not predict recidivism well for female offenders who followed a pathways approach to offending. Lastly, Van Voorhis and colleagues (2008) demonstrated that gender-relevant factors proved to be better predictors of various outcomes compared to gender-neutral (male) factors.

Even if some studies do support the gender neutrality of tools like the LSI-R (Harer & Langan, 2001; Smith et al., 2009, for example), gender does matter in some respect. Problems such as running away, poverty, prior victimization (especially sexual victimization), and economic marginalization do emerge. This is an important consideration because case-management and offender-treatment constraints will follow these risks and needs assessments—they will be guided by the results of these assessments.

Research conducted in the state of Hawaii demonstrates the importance of considering context. Data collected as part of an ongoing study related to NIC's model of effective corrections, including risk assessment, were used to evaluate any gender-related differences in overall LSI-R scores, domain scores, and recidivism prediction.[1] All offenders released to parole or sentenced to probation between January 1998 and February 2005 and who had an LSI-R assessment were tracked for at least one year. This sample included a sizeable number of females, 462, and 2,046 men. It should be noted that due to an LSI-R prescreening tool, the least risky offenders (based on current age, age at first arrest, and number of prior arrests) were not included as they did not have an LSI-R assessment.

Although the females demonstrated significantly lower rates of recidivism, the LSI-R as an overall predictor of recidivism did appear in line with the gender neutrality findings. Males and females scored similarly in overall LSI-R scores (21.91 and 21.63, respectively). And, while the correlation between the LSI-R total score and recidivism was slightly stronger for men ($r = .27, p < .001$) than for women ($r = .26, p < .001$), these differences were not significant.

Female offenders did score significantly higher on certain domains and initial items. Specifically, females scored *higher* than males on the following domains and items:

- Financial ($t = 5.704, p < .001$)
- Family and marital ($t = 3.598, p < .01$)
- Emotional and personal ($t = 4.716, p < .001$)
- Reliance on social assistance ($t = 8.313, p < .001$)
- Having a criminal spouse or family member ($t = 5.939, p < .001$)
- Having past ($t = 5.761, p < .001$) and current mental health treatment ($t = 4.524, p < .001$)
- Having a mental disorder that moderately interferes with daily living ($t = 2.087, p < .05$)
- Frequently unemployed ($t = 2.148, p < .05$)
- Never been employed for a full year ($t = 3.808, p < .001$)

Yet, in terms of correlations with outcome, the strongest domain correlation for women was the alcohol and drug domain ($r = .27, p < .001$), which was *stronger* than the correlation between the overall LSI-R score and recidivism (and a

---

[1]These data come from a study conducted as part of a doctoral dissertation. The dissertation, *Risky Business: What Standard Risk/Need Assessments Mean for Female Offenders*, was completed in 2007 by Janet T. Davidson.

domain in which the men actually scored higher). The females also demonstrated higher correlations with recidivism than the men on the following domains: financial, family and marital, leisure and recreation, and attitudes and orientation.

CHALLENGING GENDER-NEUTRAL RISK-DRIVEN SUPERVISION

The problem with relying on statistics alone, though, is that we may not fully conceptualize what these domains actually represent for female offenders. This is the side effect of operating within a gender-neutral (male) model. We may not be fully capturing specific risks and needs of female offenders, and this is partly evidenced via their stronger correlations with recidivism on domains in which males actually scored *higher* (e.g., alcohol and drug).

To assess whether this phenomenon may indeed have been a factor, interviews were conducted with 18 male and 13 female offenders who were under community correctional supervision (probation or parole; Davidson, 2007). Interviews were conducted between 2005 and 2006. These male and female offenders were interviewed to assess risks that are measured via the LSI-R from their perspectives and within the overall contexts of their lives. Even though this is a convenience sample, it is important that we listen to groups who have been traditionally neglected in research, especially female offenders, so that we can discover if and what quantitative analyses might have hidden (see Sprague, 2005).

While the offenders were interviewed on all aspects related to a typical LSI-R assessment, only some areas are highlighted here. First, this qualitative analysis was meant to get at the content validity of the LSI-R—an important consideration beyond the more common predictive validity studies. As such, interview data that did not challenge specific domains or in which no gender differences emerged are left out of this section. Specifically, the leisure and recreation, companions, and attitudes and orientations domains are excluded. The remaining domains are highlighted because the interview data revealed some cause for concern in the assessment process and challenge the notion that these assessment tools are gender neutral.

Criminal History

This LSI-R domain is largely concerned with the criminal history (both quality and quantity). Women did exhibit less serious criminal histories than the male counterparts. The majority of the men had committed either a person (56%) or property (35%) offense, while more than half (53.8%) of the women had committed a drug offense. The men largely explained that they committed their crimes in order to obtain money or goods (71%) or to settle personal problems (19%). Most of the men also committed their crimes alone (76%) and committed their first crimes as juveniles (88%). The majority of the men were on parole (65%) and had more arrests in their criminal histories than did women.

Women explained their criminality in terms that squarely place their offending within the context of intimate relationships or in substance use and abuse. Differently from the men, women's criminal acts often involved attempts to obtain drugs, use drugs, or get money to buy drugs. As will be discussed later, these data also help to substantiate that the pathway to drugs and crime is quite different for females than for males.

Education and Employment

Although this domain within the LSI-R is described as "straightforward" in terms of assessing risk for a community correctional population (Andrews & Bonta, 2000), the interviews suggest that this is not necessarily the case. Many were unemployed and in treatment (substance abuse and/or living in a clean and sober home, which often contains a treatment component). Thus, a good percentage of both males (44.4%) and females (61.5%) relied on social assistance. Unfortunately, unemployment and social assistance are considered risk factors per the LSI-R.

Many in the sample voiced that they were not working because they needed to finish their program and the program staff did not want them to work, at least in the initial stages of treatment. The interviews also revealed that the requirement or suggestion of mental health treatment, also considered a risk factor per the LSI-R, was part of treatment. Maka, a 21-year-old male on probation, explained his situation this way:

> Right now I stay in a substance abuse program, so I gotta be on welfare. I gotta be there. I don't really like it. . . . I don't like being with it [welfare] but, I got to, cause it's a condition I gotta follow through with. Once I complete treatment I can go work, which I like go work already, you know.

Unemployment, mental health treatment, and receipt of social assistance would appear to be protective actions in the context of both male and female offenders' lives. These factors are meant to help the individual become clean and sober, and, ultimately, independent and functioning enough to enter the workforce.

Many of the women in this sample revealed that they were abused as girls. This, in turn, led them to become truant and/or to run away from home. Like many other girls and women in the system, they either gave up on or were unable to continue their education. Rather, these girls found work in positions that placed them subservient to men (e.g., legal or semilegal sex industry work). Paulina, a 38-year-old female on parole, discusses her work in the sex industry:

> I was in the sex industry since I was 22, I started working in the hostess bars, and then I started stripping which, you know, uh, stripping and prostitution kind like, they offer you more money to go back with them. And even in the hostess bar situation if the rich Japanese offered me, you know, money to sleep with them I would do that. So I say sex industry cause it kinda covers the whole thing, and then when I started getting heavy into the heroin I just hit the streets at about, uh, God, 25, about 26, no about 25. And then the boyfriend of my first child, the one that turned me out cause, you know, he was on the run and we couldn't get like regular jobs so basically he was, like, boyfriend/pimp. Yeah, supporting his habit, so I was like the money maker, you know, so that's when I first got turned on to like, the street.

Rose, a 52-year-old female on parole, provides another example. She lost both of her parents when she was young—both passed away from liver disease due to alcoholism. She lived in an abusive home and began to run away at an early age, dropped out of school, and entered prostitution to earn money. Her first arrest for prostitution was at the age of 14. Although Rose did work, she had few legitimate jobs and a lack of education. She later earned her GED in prison. Her work trajectory was guided by the context of her life circumstances rather than by a lack of work ethic. As Paulina's and Rose's stories show, early abuse leads many female offenders to run away from their homes, to disengage from school, and to form otherwise unhealthy attachments, often with abusive or older men. The resulting lack of social capital makes it difficult for them to truncate pathways to criminality.

Financial

The LSI-R measures risk for recidivism via two questions: whether offenders have any financial problems (trouble meeting their basic needs, not just merely having debt) and whether they currently rely on social assistance. A greater percentage of the women (76.9%) voiced financial problems than did the men (61.1%). As mentioned previously, roughly three-fifths (61.5%) of the women and fewer than half of the men (44.4%) were dependent on social assistance.

The prior section highlights why this risk should be viewed with caution, especially when the context of social assistance and financial problems is considered. To reiterate, drawing social assistance often requires the recipient to obtain mental health treatment—a risk factor per the LSI-R. This domain simply does not match the *context* of social assistance for many in this sample. A substantial percentage of both males and females were typically on social assistance due to an addiction to drugs that *preceded* incarceration or probation. For many, living in a clean and sober home came with a requirement to attend treatment programs (some facility based) and remain unemployed through the completion of treatment. They are thus typically either on welfare or on Supplemental Security Income (SSI). In other words, it would be impossible for probationers/ parolees to complete treatment, live in sober-living home/center, *and* work.

Olivia, for example, was a 35-year-old French/Indian woman on probation for a drug offense. She had a GED along with a sporadic employment history. She was living in a clean and sober home that contained a substance-abuse treatment component. She received $418 per month from welfare, of which $360 went to rent in the home, along with all of her food stamp money. Olivia noted that while this was not enough to live on: "the rules of this house is that program first. Get your program done, next step is a job." At the time of these interviews, most of the interviewees who received social assistance did so because they were in a recovery program.

The LSI-R and similar tools simply do not capture the salient connections between social assistance (counted as a criminogenic risk factor) and treatment that occurs in the context of clean and sober homes, treatment, and/or mental health treatment. Holtfreter and colleagues (2004) found, for example, that economically disadvantaged female offenders who did not have their immediate needs satisfied with social assistance were more rather than less likely to reoffend. The content validity of this domain seems to be challenged by these and other data.

Family and Marital

The LSI-R scoring manual (Andrews & Bonta, 2000, p. 8) states that: "In general, this area is dynamic and is assessed on current marital/family interactions. There may well be historical issues from family/marital relationships that are present needs. Such needs may be noted in the Emotional/Personal area." Slightly more females (46.2%) than males (33.3%) were classified as being dissatisfied with their marital or equivalent situation. Almost all of the females (92.3%) compared to three-quarters of the males (72.2%) reported nonrewarding relationships with parents. Females (46.2%) also were more likely to have a nonrewarding relationship with other relatives than males (5.6%). Finally, 46.2% of the females interviewed but *none* of the males had a criminal spouse or significant other.

The interviews and prior literature suggest that women's histories of abuse—as both children and as adults—enable a sort of normalization of otherwise dysfunctional and bad relationships. In other words, verbally, emotionally, physically, and even sexually abusive relationships become the norm in female offenders' lives, and what is defined as a "healthy" relationship by parole officers, treatment providers, and the like seems unfamiliar, foreign, and uncomfortable. Since the LSI-R is conducted via motivational interviewing,[2] the assessor would need to be cognizant of women's more prevalent histories of abuse and what women may find acceptable in a relationship. In an interview, for example, women may appear satisfied because they tend to minimize or refute their own victimization (Belknap, 2007).

Indeed, the women interviewed as part of this study demonstrated that their current relationships were very much tangled with their histories of childhood abuse and problematic adult relationships (particularly parental relationships). While the LSI-R will document whether the female is currently dissatisfied with her relationship, the true dynamic nature of women's current relationships is shaped by their abusive pasts and how the women have (or have not) coped with that abuse. The myriad effects of past abuse, which are further connected to other areas measured in the LSI-R, are not likely to be captured—largely because the LSI-R does not ask such questions.

For example, Randi, a 40-year-old female on parole, explained that her inability to maintain employment was an unwanted consequence of victimization

---

[2]Motivational interviewing (MI) is part of the "best practices" model. MI is a method of interviewing and talking with offenders to give them internal motivation for positive change. The basic principles of MI involve the expression of empathy toward the offender, responding to offenders' resistance in nonargumentative ways, helping the offender find his or her own reasons for change, and supporting that the offender has self-efficacy (Walters et al., 2007).

at the hands of her intimate partner—relationships with abusive men led her to getting into trouble and losing jobs. She went on to say:

> Being in a bad relationship. I guess it started while I was pregnant, I was in a bad relationship, uhm, and then my husband was very abusive. So when I left him I ended up in a relationship with men, I guess I looked. . . . I, I'm attracted to punchy, raunchy, you know, like that uhm, and it always led to me getting in trouble, always.

Vicki, a 28-year-old female on parole, turned to drugs as a way of dealing with relationship-related trauma. Randi's unemployment and Vicki's substance abuse would simply count as criminogenic needs (and place them at assessed higher risk) without regard to what those factors really mean for them. The context of relationships for women is simply qualitatively more complex and, thus, more likely to interact with other measures.

Accommodation

This LSI-R domain measures the level of satisfaction with current accommodation, whether the offender has had three or more address changes in the prior year, and whether he or she lives in a high-crime area. Women were less likely (23.1%) than men (44.4%) to indicate that they had unsatisfactory accommodations. The women (46.2%) and men (44.4%) were equally likely to live in high-crime neighborhoods. Women were substantially more likely (53.8%), however, to have had three or more address changes during the past year or in the year prior to incarceration compared to men (11.1%).

Frequent address changes for female offenders often reflected relationship difficulties. Some women noted that they moved frequently in order to get away from abusive partners. Many women also noted that they were often homeless, living in high-crime neighborhoods.

Maile, a 50-year-old local woman convicted of theft and currently living in a clean and sober house, was homeless at the time of her arrest. Following is what Maile had to say about her situation:

> Before I came here [current clean and sober home] I was homeless for maybe . . . seven—eight years. Then because of the living situation, and the drugs, and, uhm, and I was doing prostitution just to get money and the drugs and stuff like that. And within those years by passing I was doing drugs I was getting into when I was doing, forging checks and stuff like that for get money and stuff.

Homelessness and frequent address changes do place offenders at greater risk for recidivism. For women, this pattern is compounded by the nature of their relationships with men and their substance abuse. Unsatisfactory accommodation, as currently assessed, may simply be a proxy for these problems.

Alcohol and Drug Problems

This LSI-R domain centers on whether the individual has now or has ever had an alcohol or a drug problem and the extent to which either alcohol or drugs have interfered with or affected her or his law violations, marital/family relationships, school/work, medical health, or other negative indicators. While most in this sample reported that they did not have an alcohol problem, more than half of the women (53.8%) versus 38.9% of the males reported having had a problem with alcohol at some point in their lives. However, a full 100% of the women and 83.3% of the men reported a drug problem at some period in their lives.

All of the women in this sample said that drugs or alcohol had affected their law violations; 84.6% noted that it had affected their family or marital situations; *all* noted impacts on their school or work; 53.8% noted problems with medical histories; and 69.2% had other indicators of interference (mainly homelessness). For men, the numbers are slightly different: 83.3% noted that their alcohol or drug problems had impacted their law violations; 72.2% demonstrated that their family or marital relationships were impacted; 61.1% had their school or work affected; 22.2% had a medical problem directly related to their substance use; and 11.1% had other indicators of serious interference.

In general, women mainly talked about self-medication and escape as their entrée into substance use, while the men discussed their use in terms of partying and hanging out with friends. Female offender substance use was often intertwined with issues of abuse (physical, sexual, and/or emotional) and isolation. Rose, for example, discussed the difficulties that drugs caused, including stealing from friends and family to support her habit. Rose began using drugs (heroin) at the age of 14. Rose had been placed into foster care at the age of 5 and ultimately ended up living with an aunt and uncle. The aunt physically abused her while the uncle repeatedly sexually abused her. The untreated trauma surrounding the sexual abuse ultimately led to her initial drug use, running away, and later entrée into the world of prostitution, pimps, and other crimes designed to support her drug habit. Although she had thoughts of suicide, she ultimately opted to use drugs to ease her pain. This is what Rose, whose first drugs at the age of 14 were barbiturates and heroin, had to say about what drugs did for her:

> The first time I stuck it in my arm, I fell in love . . . I was pretty miserable, I was being molested, and my aunt was very abusive, I wanted to be with my Dad. I loved my dad, regardless of how bad he was, you know. I just remember these young days driving around the country and with him while all his friends drinking, partying, and having fun, and that was the only images I had of him . . . happy guy . . . so I wanted that and, I was suffering where I was, you know, and uhm, when I shot up I didn't feel the pain that I was going through, you know, because there was times at a young age that I wanted to commit suicide.

While the LSI-R might do a good job in terms of identifying criminogenic risks for females in terms of their alcohol and drug abuse, the lack of *contextual* understanding renders this problematic for treatment purposes. This can have serious implications for the treatment of these problems. Here is what Rose has to say about one of her episodes in treatment:

> [after 16 months in residential treatment] I left there in a fit of rage, uhm, me and one of the male counselors . . . he's just very aggressive, very mean, and, uhm, I didn't know, I didn't have the, those skills to handle it, you know. So I left and I, uh, I went to [another treatment facility].

The aggressive style, mixed with Rose's abusive past history, rendered this type of treatment situation untenable. It seems feasible that any actuarial risk/need assessment instrument dealing with women would need to include histories of abuse and the impact of this with drug use.

Emotional and Personal

This section of the LSI-R measures moderate interference or emotional distress (signs of anxiety or depression), severe interference or active psychosis, past or present mental health treatment, and whether a psychological assessment is indicated in the past 12 months (or whether characteristics are present, such as excessive fears, hostility, impulse control problems, etc.). While only one of the males and none of the females in this sample exhibited either moderate or severe interference due to emotional and personal problems, there were other differences between males and females. All of the females reported past mental health treatment compared to roughly half of the men (55.6%). At the time of the interviews, 61.5% of the women were in receipt of mental health treatment compared to only 22.2% of the males.

Given the more prevalent histories of abuse in the lives of women, it is not surprising that they were more likely to have had mental health treatment. It appears that mental health treatment, past or present, would be a protective factor and should not count against the women as a risk factor. Yet the LSI-R does just that. It is the *lack* of treatment that seems to be a criminogenic risk factor for these women.

Zoe, a 38-year-old on parole for auto theft, exemplifies the need for mental health treatment. Zoe lived with her mom and dad until she was 8 years old, at which time her mother committed suicide in front of her. Her dad remarried and she lived with him and her new stepmother until the age of 12, at which time she permanently ran away from home. She dropped out of school in the seventh grade. She continued into a life of drugs, prostitution, abusive men, and crime. She was receiving mental health treatment at the time of the interview.

The men in this sample were less likely to have been in mental health treatment or to state that they felt they needed such help. Additionally, the context of their treatment was typically different than that of females. Women tended to voice their actual need for treatment, especially to deal with the trauma of their pasts. Men, however, did not see the utility of mental health treatment, outside of the technical requirement of a drug treatment program or for the provision of disability. Hector, for example, said that he never really sought mental health treatment but did see a psychiatrist once as a requirement of disability. He did not see this as helpful in any way.

In sum, the content validity of this section of the risk instrument for women is compromised on two fronts. First, most of the females in this sample *need* mental health treatment (because of trauma caused by prior and ongoing abuse in many cases). The lack of rather than the presence of mental health treatment is a real risk factor for these women. Second, for both men and women, the LSI-R does not take into account how some of the characteristics that are considered risk factors are connected. For many of these women (and men), the ability to seek treatment—both mental and substance—along with the financial ability to do so (albeit limited) appears quite protective and promising in the reduction of recidivism.

CHALLENGING GENDER-NEUTRAL SUPERVISION: WOMEN'S HISTORIES OF VICTIMIZATION, HEALTH PROBLEMS, AND CHILD CARE NEEDS

Histories of Abuse

The interviews with the women revealed quite striking histories of abuse. Almost three-quarters of the female offenders reported emotional abuse as children compared to about a third of the male offenders. A full 100% of the females reported having been emotionally abused as adults compared to none of the men.

Many of the women in this sample experienced sexual abuse as both children and adults. Almost two-thirds, 69.2%, of the females compared to 11.1% of the males experienced childhood sexual abuse. The abuse continued into adulthood for about a third of the females (38.5%) but for none of the males. Finally, 61.5% of the females experienced childhood physical abuse compared to 22.2% of the males. The physical abuse continued into adulthood for many of the women— 61.5% of the women were abused as adults compared to none of the men.

Jackie was a 35-year-old Filipina woman on probation for a drug offense. Jackie had four children born to different fathers; she said that all of her children were "ice babies."[3] Jackie's long history of serious drug addiction was originally connected to her unhappy and often abusive family life. Jackie experienced emotional, sexual, and physical abuse as a child as well as an adult. Jackie experienced significant emotional abuse early on, from both her real mother and her hanai[4] mother:

> I remember in the 3rd grade, we had a contest and the contest was called build your future, and it was out of whatever you could possibly think of, you know, some people used the ice cream, popsicle sticks. Well for me I used legos, and, uhm, I built the future. I built a huge thing, I had to put it in a huge paper box. So, I came in second place and the first three places their awards got to be displayed in the library for a month. So I remember coming home a month later with my prize, he [Dad] was very proud, my hanai mom wasn't. I had placed the project onto the kitchen table. She saw that red ribbon, she, without a second of a doubt she grabbed the broom and she smashed it. And she just yelled at me and told me second place was not allowed in this house.

---

[3]*Ice* is slang for methamphetamine in Hawaii.

[4]*Hanai* refers to a practice of informal adoption practices in Hawaii.

She also experienced regular physical abuse as a child at the hands of her hanai mother. This abuse continued for Jackie into adulthood. She entered several physically abusive relationships with men. One of these men stabbed her eight times on Christmas Day. Here is what Jackie had to say about that relationship and the impact of the abuse:

> If you notice this scar on the right side of my face, Christmas night. . . . I was stabbed eight times by my ex-boyfriend, the father of my second child. Uhm, we were well in our disease [drug addiction], but see I stayed in these relationships cause like I mentioned earlier I was stuck. Was afraid of being alone. I had the low self-esteem. No confidence. No self-worth.

Jackie was largely estranged from her family due to years of emotional, physical, and sexual abuse. As such, she did not want to go to her family of origin to escape these abusive relationships. Indeed, her hanai mother did not allow her to stay at home on the rare occasions that Jackie did try to go back— even with noticeable signs of physical abuse.

Finally, Jackie discusses the issue of sexual abuse in her childhood, noting that she grew up in a family where a lot of sexual molestation occurred. She was the victim of sexual abuse at least twice as a child. She was first sexually molested at the age of 8. Here is the reaction from her hanai mother upon reporting the sexual abuse:

> I got slapped right across the face. They told me I deserved it, because I was wearing shorts. They called me puka, which is slut. I was eight years old. So by the time that I was raped in the seventh grade, I never told anybody cause I thought it was my fault [she was raped by strangers on the way home from a school event].

Jackie began using drugs at the age of 13 and continued into adulthood. Her drug use was initially connected to her family life and the issues of abuse therein. Like many female offenders, the substance abuse continued due to lasting and untreated trauma.

This research demonstrates the difficulty that prevalent histories of abuse, coupled with the lack of trauma-related treatment, pose for female offenders. While the LSI-R does capture some measure of mental illness and certainly substance use, the context and gravity of both, particularly trauma and depression, will simply remain hidden behind the drug use. Zoe's quote makes this clear:

They're trying to run from something. They're trying to run from domestic violence, or the pain, or the shame, or anger or whatever of past experiences, molestation, or whatever they've been through. They don't do drugs just because. They actually really wanna be good mothers, but something, you know, else is holding them back. So, you know, instead of targeting and saying everyone's a cookie mold level two or three, you know, what do they really need. And you know, the prison stopped the trauma classes after 15 or 16 weeks saying that it was too much of a risk [but changed the name and continued for a period].

The women's problems isn't the f***ing addiction, it's what's behind the addiction. And if you're using one tool for screening people, in a cookie mold, and that screening is set for men [it's a problem]. Most of the women that are doing time right now are repeat offenders, most of the women are stuck in the revolving doors or recidivism. They are not targeting what they need. If you had a screening tool that targeted exactly what it was, . . . and the target is trauma. If you're not addressing their trauma then you expect them to be back.

Health and Children

The women in this study were about twice as likely to have current health problems as were men (61.5% and 38.9%, respectively), and almost two-thirds (61.5%) of the women were taking medications compared to 27.8% of the men. These health problems, which were quite serious for some of the women (e.g., breast cancer, hepatitis C) were likely to impact their ability to address other issues, namely trauma and substance abuse. The LSI-R may overclassify these women (e.g., higher assessed risk) due to contextually hidden circumstances that include the receipt of social assistance, mental health and substance use treatment, and a lack of employment. At the very least, the added contribution of health problems compounds the demands already placed on these women.

Child care and related responsibilities affect females differently than males. According to the latest national results, roughly one half of all inmates have at least one child under the age of 18. For women, the number is higher; almost two-thirds (65.3%) have at least one child under the age of 18 compared to 54.7% of the male inmates (Mumola, 2000). For this sample of offenders, 69.2% of the females had children compared to 44.4% of the men. A third of these women had their first child under the age of 18, compared to none of the men. Finally, Child and Protective Services (CPS) were more likely to have been involved in separating the mother from her children (66.7%) than for the males (37.5%).

SUPERVISION AND REINTEGRATION

For many women, trauma, abuse, drugs, and treatment cannot be considered separate from one another. Female offenders' victimization histories should be an important part of a holistic approach to case-based classification for effective correctional intervention. The predominance of victimization in this population often connects with multiple psychological/psychiatric problems, which are then compounded by ineffectual coping. This alone underscores the importance of offering intervention in this area. The LSI-R and similar tools simply do not capture this victimization since it is not measured at all. It is important to reiterate that supervision strategies follow these seemingly gender-neutral assessment strategies and thus drive case management.

Female offenders do face barriers to reintegration that are both gendered and gender neutral. The interviews with female and male offenders on community supervision in Honolulu document some of these stated differences. Both men and women were asked to identify the top five things they needed to keep them crime and drug free in the community (Davidson, 2007). The top five for the men were staying away from bad or nonsober friends, faith, work, staying occupied, and having a good girlfriend. For women, the top five were adequate work, kids/family reunification, treatment, faith, and sober friends.

While many of the factors that predict recidivism for male offenders do hold true for women, there are some salient differences, and it is often the context of female offending (Hannah-Moffat, 2009; Reisig et al., 2006) that matters. Blanchette and Taylor (2009, p. 60) note, "Research on reintegration suggests that family separation and community isolation, poor quality of life conditions, mental illness, and lack of secure, stable, legal employment are all critical factors in addressing the reintegration needs of women." The lack of consideration for the role of patriarchy and other gendered factors in the assessment and supervision of female offenders could seriously disadvantage them and result in negative and unintended consequences.

Aforementioned, particularly salient for female offenders is the prevalence and impact of abuse in their lives. Unfortunately, almost half (46.5%) of female inmates report previous physical abuse, compared to 13.4% of the men, and 39% had been sexually abused, compared to 5.8% of the men (Harlow, 1999). These types of disparities are also present in the larger community correctional offender populations, including those who end up on probation. A full 40.4% of female probationers experienced some type of abuse prior to their sentence, compared to only 9.3% of the men (Harlow, 1999).

This abuse has been linked with a number of factors, most notably trauma and mental health problems (Bloom et al., 2003; Hubbard & Matthews, 2008; Van Voorhis et al., 2008). Female offenders also face disproportionate difficulties with child care needs (Bloom et al., 2003; Hollin & Palmer, 2006; Holtfreter & Cupp, 2007; Van Voorhis et al., 2008); low social capital, including lack of education and employment skills (Holtfreter & Cupp, 2007; Reisig et al., 2006); problems with intimate relationships (Van Voorhis et al., 2008); and self-esteem and self-efficacy (Hubbard & Matthews, 2008; Van Voorhis et al., 2008). These factors should be considered in the effective treatment of female offenders in the community.

Conditions of release are in many ways determined by these newer-generation risk and need instruments that headline NIC's model of effective correctional intervention. Parolees are subject to conditions, partially based on these assessments, which are thought to reduce their likelihood of reoffending. These requirements may include geographic and social restrictions, living arrangements (i.e., halfway houses), and treatment and other programming (Turnbull & Hannah-Moffat, 2009). Since the language and stated spirit of these newer evidence-based practices center on both risk management and rehabilitation (Turnbull & Hannah-Moffat, 2009), it is important that we turn toward gender-responsive practices when supervising offenders in the community.

MOVING FORWARD: GENDER-EQUITABLE SUPERVISION FOR FEMALE OFFENDERS IN THE COMMUNITY

Practices that involve the community supervision of women on either probation or parole must incorporate a gendered approach to such supervision. Gender-responsive practices and programs are ones that understand, recognize, and act upon the unique circumstances that bring many girls and women into the criminal justice system. Many women under community supervision have different needs, needs centered on housing, employment, health care, social assistance, reuniting with children and families, and dealing with their addictions (Turnbull & Hannah-Moffat, 2009). Female offending and risks and needs must be considered in the context of their gendered lives (Turnbull & Hannah-Moffat, 2009). Focus needs to also include women's relationships (Heilbrun et al., 2008b).

Female offenders tend to be especially susceptible to relapse or recidivism early in their community supervision (Heilbrun et al., 2008b), and community correctional practitioners should thus be supportive and comprehensive from the beginning. The pathways to female offending, as mentioned previously, need to be considered as women reintegrate and/or remain under supervision in their communities.

One of the top needs for female offenders under community supervision is substance-abuse treatment (Davidson & Chesney-Lind, 2009) and it necessitates special attention. We cannot simply view women's substance-use problems in a vacuum. Rather, substance abuse for women, as compared to men, is often correlated with other important factors (Blanchette & Taylor, 2009) and should thus not be considered as a standalone criminogenic need factor. Abuse histories are key to understanding women's substance use. There has been some controversy over whether and to what extent women's victimization (as girls and later as women) matters in terms of recidivism. Yet it has been argued that female offenders' histories of victimization should at least be considered and integrated into their supervision and treatment plans (Blanchette & Taylor, 2009; Reisig et al., 2006; Van Voorhis et al., 2008).

Yet less than half of women re-entering the community from prison have this need met (Schram et al., 2006). This is indeed unfortunate. Huebner and colleagues (2010) found that women who were assessed as drug dependent were more likely (three times as likely) to violate or otherwise fail on parole. Further, roughly one-third of the women Huebner and colleagues followed over an 8-year period and who recidivated were assessed as being addicted to substances at the time of release from prison. As Huebner and colleagues (2010) note, too, substance abuse is also connected in important yet negative ways to employment, relationships with their children, and other social support networks for female offenders.

Since many female offenders are current or past victims of domestic violence, there needs to be a corresponding focus on the woman's offending status as well as her history of and potential for domestic violence victimization (Neal, 2007). This means that officers who supervise female offenders on either probation or parole need to be informed of the nature and extent of this victimization and incorporate items—such as safety plans—into supervision strategies (Neal, 2007).

Female parolees who have stable housing and employment are less likely to recidivate and return to prison while on parole (Schram et al., 2006). Women tend to also report greater instances of homelessness prior to the onset of their community supervision (Davidson, 2007) and are more likely than men to return to their children, regain custody, and become the primary care-taker (Schram et al., 2006). Thus, this need is highly important to the individual women and to the overall health of their families. Stable environments are important to the women and their children, and women who are substance abusers and have lower levels of education are more likely to recidivate, which in turn has further injurious effects of the children (Huebner et al., 2010). The focus on male offenders has rendered these types of problems and programs to address them either invisible or nonimportant.

Unfortunately, violations of probation and/or parole are a leading cause of female offender entry into prison, as they often result in a revocation of community supervision (Turnbull & Hannah-Moffat, 2009). While the current move toward evidence-based practices and the specific use of risk and need instruments can be helpful to women, it can also be harmful and counterproductive (Davidson & Chesney-Lind, 2009). Women could end up overclassified and oversupervised if their risks and needs are assessed out of context. Alternatively, they could receive inadequate treatment (or none at all) if their specific needs are not considered. These conditions could lead to greater, as opposed to the goal of lower, recidivism.

While it is a truism at this point that female offender victimization is linked to their substance use, some argue that the root cause of the substance abuse does not matter in terms of recidivism and evidence-based practices. Yet a gendered approach calls for treatment delivery that treats both the current addiction and the factors that led to the addiction and, ultimately, offending (Fortuin, 2007; Huebner et al., 2010; Schram et al., 2006). Luckily, there are a few promising examples to draw from.

PROMISING EXAMPLES FOR MOVING FORWARD

There are some model programs that jurisdictions could learn from—ones that embrace gender-responsive principles. These types of programs, when coupled with a gender-responsive approach to supervision, can reduce recidivism. Maine's Transition, Reunification and Reentry program provides evidence that an integrated, holistic, and gender-responsive approach can make a difference in female offender recidivism. Women reentering society through Maine's reentry program demonstrate recidivism rates of around 17% (Fortuin, 2007), much lower than national averages. This lower rate is attributed to the gender-responsive training of the staff and treatment of women in a trauma-informed manner. Indeed, Fortuin (2007, p. 34) notes that the program "addresses the major concerns of reentry, including housing, employment, education, family reunification and empowerment, birth control, and continuity of care for mental health, physical health, and substance abuse." The manner in which these factors are often interconnected is accounted for by staff who aid women in coordinating their multiple responsibilities, which often involve child care and work schedules. This approach thus recognizes the importance of addressing women's pathways to crime as well as their current situations.

Like the NIC model suggests, the Maine program utilizes an assessment tool prior to programming. The tool focuses on strengths rather than weaknesses (i.e., criminogenic risks and needs) and, subsequently, case management around these strengths (Fortuin, 2007). This assessment instrument utilizes domains that are relevant to gendered reentry and needs. These domains include economic stability and responsibility (including financial, employment, and child support); housing/living situation, including family and marital considerations; transportation; education and training; legal; safety and crisis planning; physical and mental health; substance abuse; leisure/recreation/community, natural supports, and peer association; personality and behavior treatment; family and natural supports; and attitudes and orientations. The results are utilized to help women build competencies and strengths in all areas relevant to their situations (Fortuin, 2007), thus considering the gendered context of their offending.

A study of female parolees who were given gender-specific interventions also highlights the benefit of thinking about effective community supervision in gendered terms. Researchers in New Jersey followed 176 women who completed a gender-specific program upon release from prison. These women were compared to a group of 241 women who did not receive such services. The gender-specific treatment program lasted from 60 to 90 days, was highly structured, and dealt with trauma, parent–child reunification, housing, employment, domestic violence, substance abuse, and mental/physical health (Heilbrun et al., 2008b). The women engaged in groups that utilized both cognitive behavioral therapy and rational emotive behavior therapy. Women in the control group were released to the communities from with they came without the benefit of this structured program.

Both groups were tracked for 6 months. The outcome measure was rearrest (not including technical violations of parole). The group that received the gender-specific services performed better than the control group. The latter had a significantly higher average number of rearrests (12.4%) compared to 6.3% of the treatment group (Heilbrun et al., 2008b).

Bui and Morash's (2010) study of 20 successful female parolees identifies promising strategies for engendering desistance from crime (tracked for 21 months postprison). While many of these women noted negative preprison networks, particularly with abusive partners or strained familial relationships, they nonetheless were likely to report positive postprison networks. The prison experience contributed in two important respects. First, time in prison allowed for a break from, and often an end to, these negative relationships. Secondly, in-prison opportunities for new relationships were taken advantage of, particularly through treatment and faith-based organizations. These in-prison networks often traveled with the women upon release to the community. Particularly salient seemed to be the faith-based networks. These networks, both family and other, allowed women access to tangible resources, such as shelter, money, and clothing, as well as intangible ones such as referrals to jobs, emotional support, and encouragement. This study reinforces the notion of positive relationships with individuals or groups that further connect women with needed resources (e.g., housing, financial, emotional, or other).

The women interviewed in Bui and Morash's study noted the importance of parole supervision. The women noted that while parole agents did refer them to programs and services in the community, they rarely found this helpful. Yet they noted that when officers treated them fairly and with understanding, they nonetheless felt supported. The following quote is useful: "For these women, good relationship meant that the officers were not mean to them, treated them fairly and reasonably, and did not cause them trouble by imposing difficult conditions. Supportive relationship meant that the officers were flexible and addressed their needs, for example by giving permission to leave town, or rescheduling their report days when necessary" (Bui & Morash, 2010, p. 15). Female offenders often do have greater competing demands, largely related to child care, and it seems as if the interviews with the women support the need for a more gendered understanding of these competing demands.

The Bui and Morash study gives further credibility to understanding the needs of the female offender under community supervision and doing more, both in prison and in the community, to help her meet these needs. The training of probation and parole officers to help assist in the building of positive relationship networks appears to be a promising approach to encouraging desistance from crime. And, while probation often does not involve a prison term (at least up front), there is reason to believe that the same strategies might be useful for probationers as well, albeit the break from negative relationships that prison time provides would necessarily be absent.

In light of evidence presented here and elsewhere, it seems that the most promising approach to effective correctional management for female offenders is to move toward a decidedly gender-centered approach to effective offender intervention. Criminologists, especially feminist criminologists, have repeatedly called for research, policy, and practice that starts with females first (Blanchette & Taylor, 2009) and methods of practice that do not simply continue the "add gender and stir" approach to female offender intervention.

This includes revamping our risk/need assessment instruments and overall gendered approach to community supervision. We need to craft instruments from the ground up, beginning with a gendered lens from creation through validation and ultimate use (Blanchette & Brown, 2006; Hannah-Moffat, 2009; Van Voorhis et al., 2008). If we did this, we would likely end up with instruments that look different than the current gender-neutral ones (Holtfreter & Cupp, 2007; Van Voorhis et al., 2008). The emergence of so-called fourth generation instruments, which incorporate strengths and protective factors, seem more appropriate for female offenders, especially given their lower risk relative to men (Blanchette & Brown, 2006).

Supervision strategies and treatment options should also be gender specific. The current NIC model is not a bad one, it is simply one that does not recognize the important role of gender in the lives, offending, and subsequent supervision of female offenders. We have enough knowledge to do better for our growing female offender population; a gender-responsive approach to effective correctional management is an essential step. This begins with an acknowledgment and recognition of the context of and pathways to offending for women. Unlike their male counterparts, female offenders often have competing demands that include their substance use/abuse issues, mental illness, histories of abuse, intimate partner violence, and limited work histories (Morash, 2009). As Morash (2009) states, "The needs that must be addressed are not confined to just those that predict recidivism; services and programming are expended on women with and without a high risk for recidivism" (p. 178). The system needs to recognize the disproportionate histories of abuse faced by female offenders while not overly controlling them for factors that are or were beyond their control.

EIGHT

CONCLUSION

———————•·◆·•———————

These are the things I think about at night: 1) will i ever be a nor-
mal person again 2) will I ever stop doing drugs 3) do i really
Forgive my Father 4) will i ever love a man 5) will I always be gay
6) Do i betrayed my mother and my sister 7) will i ever stop pushing
people away From me who care for me 8) will i ever stop prostituting
9) do I really love myself or can i 10) will i ever stop comming to
jail 11) will i ever stop being a criminal & robbing 12) will i ever
be me again

—Letter from Trina, a prostitute, in Riker's Island
prison for drug possession and loitering (LeBlanc, 1995)

I just want to go back home to my grandma and grandpa.
Please, please make that happen. I really hope your going to
be my angel and make me go back home. I know this is only a
letter but if I express it in words its going to be hard I'm going
to start crying and you won't understand me. All I ask is for
ONE MORE CHANCE!? to improve. Just one. Thank you for
your time.

—Letter from Angel, 16-year-old girl detained
in Honolulu, to judge before sentencing (Pasko, 2006)

T ucked outside of Fresno, California, is the nation's largest prison for women (LeBlanc, 1996, p. 35). Opened in 1990, the Central California Women's Facility (CCWF) sits among flat fields planted with nut trees and growing vegetables near a small, rural town called Chowchilla. CCWF is also arguably the world's largest women's prison, and yet many in Fresno do not know it is there (Owen, 1998).

In 2007, CCWF, with a design capacity of 2,000, housed 3,918 women (96% over capacity; Department of Corrections and Rehabilitation, 2007). As a result of persistent problems with overcrowding at all its women's facilities, California built a new women's prison of even greater capacity (2,200)— across the street from CCWF. Called Valley State Prison, this near-mirror-image of CCWF is the nation's second-largest prison for women, and, as of 2010, was functioning at 75% over capacity (LeBlanc, 1996; Office of the Inspector General, 2010).

This book has attempted to describe the circumstances that would bring a young woman to the California prison system or any of the crowded, newly built detention centers, jails, or women's prisons that now dot the country. That a woman, especially a "good" woman, might find her way into one of these institutions is, for most Americans, unthinkable. One hopes that, after reading this book, this comfortable assumption has been challenged.

This book has argued that girls' troubles create and set the stage for girls' and, ultimately, women's crime. Girls' pathways into crime, even into violence, are affected by the gendered nature of their environments and particularly their experiences as marginalized girls in communities wracked by poverty. The increase in girls' participation in gangs has, as we have seen, roots in the violence the girls in these communities suffer. Sadly, though, the gang that promised safety and a sense of belonging provides no such haven. Instead, the gang often becomes a new site for girls' exploitation while facilitating their further involvement in violence and crime.

Not all the girls who are arrested, however, are low-income girls of color. As we have seen, sexual abuse of children, unlike physical abuse, knows no class or racial boundaries, and almost all the girls in the juvenile justice system share this terrible and all-too-often secret scar. The links between childhood victimization (both physical and sexual) and efforts undertaken by girls to escape abuse by running away are clear. However, we as a society continue to criminalize these girls' survival strategies despite nearly three decades of efforts to deinstitutionalize status offenders, including runaways.

Judicial and parental resistance to deinstitutionalization initiatives invites comparison between the situations of the runaway girls today and the situation of runaway wives at the beginning of the last century, when adult women suffered "civil death" after marriage. As a result of having an almost complete absence of legal rights, a woman's property became her husband's. She had to ask her husband for permission to travel to visit her family or friends, and divorce was virtually impossible to secure. If a woman ran away from a brutal husband, not even her own family could legally harbor her (Sinclair, 1956). Abuses of this sort of power fueled the long march to guarantee adult women civil rights during the first wave of feminism. Unfortunately, the civil rights of young people are still severely circumscribed, making the arrest of girls, some of whom are seeking to escape the same problems, not only possible but normal.

More recently, the juvenile justice system has seen yet another pattern emerge—that of arresting girls (many of whom are arguing with their parents, often their mothers) with assault. This practice essentially morphs what was once a status offense into a violent crime, which has had disastrous consequences for the girls so labeled, pushing many girls not only further into the system but also swelling the ranks of the nation's troubled and undermonitored detention centers. And this pattern is particularly marked in the treatment of girls of color, predominantly African American girls. This pattern is largely explained by the fact that the juvenile justice system has increasingly evolved into a two-track system—one for white girls and another for girls of color. White girls are swelling the ranks in private "facilities" and hospitals or placed in social welfare settings where their rights are suspended while they are "helped" and "cured."

As sinister as these patterns are for white girls, the situation for girls of color is much worse. Here, African American girls, Hispanic girls, and Native American girls find themselves in public detention centers and training schools for offenses far less serious than those committed by boys. Additionally, they spend more time in these facilities than do their white counterparts. Finally, the conditions in these facilities are not properly monitored, resulting in a long list of scandals, often involving excessive idleness, sexual abuse, and brutality. This racialized pattern of juvenile justice runs parallel to the still prevalent sexism that has haunted the court since its outset and casts even more doubt as to whether American girls can find justice in such a system.

The role of race and violence in adult women's crime is similarly transparent if one looks at the background of "unruly" women offenders. As we have seen, the women who are filling U.S. prisons share with their counterparts in the juvenile justice system terrible histories of sexual and physical abuse. In their lives, we see that the violence that characterized their girlhoods has followed them into adulthood. In a terrible irony, revictimization, often in the forms of sexual assault and domestic violence, is a common theme in the lives of the adult woman who are arrested, jailed, and imprisoned.

There is no mystery, then, why adult women use drugs. Unlike their patterns of use as girls, when drug use might have been recreational, their involvement with drugs as adults is a mix of self-medication and economic survival (in the form of petty drug sales). The drugs used to push out the pain have become, themselves, huge problems for adult women in a society that has declared a war on drugs. For women in communities devastated by poverty, this war has dramatically increased the penalties associated with what has evolved as both a coping strategy and a way to support themselves and their children. Far from the stereotypical drug kingpin, many low-level drug dealers and drug couriers are women attempting to make ends meet in communities where legitimate jobs are scarce to nonexistent and where even prostitution markets have collapsed.

Well into the new millennium, the United States has maintained the highest female incarceration rate in the world (see Carlen & Worrall, 2004). The tenfold increase of the women's prison population since 1970 is an inadvertent but clear consequence of a society determined to crack down on crime, particularly on drug crimes. Haunted by increasing media images of amoral drug dealers and demonized strangers bent on vicious violence, the typical American is often quite surprised to discover that so many young women, many of whom are mothers, are being jailed because of the public's fears.

What else could we do? This book has identified a number of choices. Clearly, we could choose to decarcerate adult women as we decarcerated girls (particularly white girls) over the past three decades. The resulting release of adult women, like the earlier decarceration of girls, would be very unlikely to cause a surge in women's crime (particularly given the crimes for which women are serving time). Many, if not most, of the women being warehoused in U.S. prisons are in need of drug treatment and employment training. Those few who have been convicted of violent offenses have often killed an intimate (not infrequently someone who abused them) and are hardly likely to repeat the offense.

Reuniting women with their communities and their children is, at minimum, likely to save taxpayer money even if no additional treatment dollars are spent on programs to assist them (and their children) with their housing, employment, child care, and health needs. Because so many of the women sent to prison are guilty of no new crimes, dramatic decreases in prison populations could be achieved simply by policy changes aimed at reducing recommitment to prison for violations of probation and parole rules.

A society that, at one point in our history, had a vision of equality and social justice for all its citizens can surely better spend the great sums of money it is now costing us to incarcerate women offenders on improving their situations and the situations of their children. Recall that more than 70% of the women in prison have children (Bureau of Justice Statistics, 1999). For many of these children, their mother's incarceration signals a major trauma because their fathers rarely care for them. As a result, nearly three quarters of the children of female inmates are placed with relatives other than the natural father or in foster care, compared to only 10% of the children of male inmates (Donziger, 1996, p. 152). Because of the trauma associated with having a mother in prison, it makes sense that their children are far more likely than other children to end up in prison themselves (pp. 152–153).

Finally, as we think about the possibility of dramatically scaling back our reliance on imprisonment as a response to adult female offending, we might begin to consider such a response in the case of male offending. Why? The answer is simple. Currently, nearly one out of seven African American men age 25 to 29 is incarcerated, and overall, the incarceration rate for black men is more than five times that of white men and three times that of Hispanic men (who have a 29% chance of going to prison sometime during their lives; Sentencing Project, 2011).

This book has focused on the consequences of the imprisonment binge for girls and women. Ending this book is impossible, however, without noting that this pattern has also signaled a dramatic increase in the imprisonment of the brothers, fathers, and sons of these women. As noted earlier in this book, *crime* has become a code word for race in the United States. As a result, correctional supervision, especially detention and imprisonment, seems increasingly to have replaced other historic systems of racial control (slavery, Jim Crow laws, ghettoization) as a way of keeping women and men of color in their "place" (Schiraldi, Kuyper, & Hewitt, 1996). This clearly has consequences for the girls and boys, women and men who are born nonwhite in a country with a lamentable history of racism. One scholar, commenting on this trend, observed, "'prison' is being re-lexified to become a code word for a terrible place where blacks reside" (Wideman, as cited in Schiraldi et al., 1996, p. 5).

The spiraling increase in the imprisonment of adult women is one of the most dramatic measures of this trend, but increases in the male prison population are also of great concern, particularly as they differentially affect ethnic communities in the United States. The cost to all of us for indulging in such unquestioning racism is only beginning to appear to the general public. The bill that the United States is currently paying for imprisonment is staggering. Currently, there are more than 1.6 million sentenced prisoners in the United States. With an average daily operational expense of $30 per inmate, the cost of incarceration in the United States is now more than $48 billion and climbing (see Bureau of Justice Statistics, 2010c; Mauer, 1994). A conservative estimate is that each new prison cell costs about $100,000 to build and about $22,000 per bed to operate (Donziger, 1996, p. 49). As a direct result of the building boom in corrections, corrections budgets are by far a huge segment of state budgets, while state expenditures for lower and higher education as well as Medicaid continue to be challenged and decreased (see Donziger, p. 48). This means that money that once went to support low-income women and their children in the community and to provide them with educational opportunities is being cut back dramatically at the same time that money to arrest, detain, and incarcerate women on the economic margins is being increased.

Senator Jim Webb (D-VA), who is leading a national commission to look into the problem, notes prophetically, "America imprisons 756 inmates for every 100,000 residents, a rate nearly five times the world's average. About one in every 31 adults in this country is in jail or on supervised release. Either we are the most evil people in the world or we are doing something terribly wrong" (Webb, 2009, p. 1).

If we are to respond to the challenge of girls' and women's crime, we must seek solutions that are based on the real causes of women's offenses, not on myths fostered by misinformation. We must understand how gender and race shape and eliminate choices for girls, how they injure (intentionally or not), and how they ultimately create very different futures for youths who are born female in a country that promises equality yet all too frequently falls short of that dream. We must also confront the fact that the United States has the highest rates of child poverty in the industrialized world (Donziger, 1996, p. 215),[1]

---

[1]About 46% of African American children and 39% of Hispanic children are born in poverty, compared to 16% of white children and 2% of children in Sweden. This last figure is particularly important because Sweden has a higher proportion of out-of-wedlock births than the United States (Donziger, 1996, p. 215).

and we must understand the ways in which this economic marginalization has directly affected girls and their mothers. Only with these understandings finally in mind can we imagine real solutions to the terrible problems of violence and crime in women's lives.

Again, as recent dramatic decreases in women's imprisonment in states such as California and New York demonstrate, we can do things differently. Moreover, in the case of California, it was the voters themselves who led the way. As state budgets face enormous deficits caused by the nation's economic woes, there is an even greater opportunity to get the public to understand that we must seek solutions to the nation's drug problems that do not involve the enormous human and economic cost associated with mass imprisonment (Duke, 2009; Mauer & Chesney-Lind, 2002).

We have seen how even the most perplexing of behaviors—girls' and women's violence—can be understood (but not excused) by the contexts that produced it. By listening to the voices of these girls and women and hearing their stories, we can also imagine other contexts and choices that, if provided, would allow them to do different things, to hope for a better future, and to be the people they are capable of becoming. Finally, we must understand that as we provide them with a brighter future, we guarantee a better future for ourselves as well.

REFERENCES

ABC News. (2006, March 11). *Why girls are getting more violent: Violence is on the rise among high school girls.*

Acoca, L. (1999). Investing in girls: A 21st century challenge. *Juvenile Justice, 6*(1), 3–13.

Acoca, L., & Dedel, K. (1998). *No place to hide: Understanding and meeting the needs of girls in the California juvenile justice system.* San Francisco: National Council on Crime and Delinquency.

Adams-Tucker, C. (1982). Proximate effects of sexual abuse in childhood. *American Journal of Psychiatry, 193,* 1252–1256.

Adler, F. (1975a). The rise of the female crook. *Psychology Today, 9,* 42–46, 112–114.

Adler, F. (1975b). *Sisters in crime.* New York: McGraw-Hill.

Adolescent Female Subcommittee. (1994). *Needs assessment and recommendations for adolescent females in Minnesota.* St. Paul: Minnesota Department of Corrections.

Ageton, S. S. (1983). The dynamics of female delinquency, 1976–1980. *Criminology, 21,* 555–584.

Alder, C. (1986, December). "Unemployed women have got it heaps worse": Exploring the implications of female youth unemployment. *Australian and New Zealand Society of Criminology, 19,* 210–224.

Alder, C. (1995). *Delinquency prevention with young women.* Paper presented at the Delinquency Prevention Conference, Terrigal, Australia.

Alexander, R. (1995). *The "girl problem": Female sexual delinquency in New York, 1900–1930.* Ithaca, NY: Cornell University Press.

Amaro, H. (1995). Love, sex, and power: Considering women's realities in HIV prevention. *American Psychologist, 50,* 437–447.

Amaro, H., & Agular, M. (1994). *"Programa mama: Mom's project." A Hispanic/Latino family approach to substance abuse prevention.* Washington, DC: Department of Health and Human Services, Center for Substance Abuse Prevention, Mental Health Services Administration.

American Association of University Women. (1992). *How schools are shortchanging girls.* Washington, DC: American Association of University Women Educational Foundation.

American Bar Association and the National Bar Association. (2001). *Justice by gender: The lack of appropriate prevention, diversion and treatment alternatives for girls in the justice system.* Washington, DC: Author.

American Correctional Association. (1990). *The female offender: What does the future hold?* Washington, DC: St. Mary's.

Anderson, S. (1994). *Comparison of male and female admissions one year prior to implementation of structured sanctions.* Salem, OR: Oregon Department of Corrections.

Andrews, D. A., & Bonta, J. (2000). *The Level of Service Inventory-Revised: User's manual.* Ottawa, ON, Canada: Multi-Health Systems.

Andrews, R. H., & Cohn, A. H. (1974). Ungovernability: The unjustifiable jurisdiction. *Yale Law Journal, 83,* 1383–1409.

Armstrong, L. (1994). Who stole incest? *On the Issues, 3,* 30–32.

Arnold, R. (1995). The processes of victimization and criminalization of black women. In B. R. Price & N. Sokoloff (Eds.), *The criminal justice system and women* (pp. 136–146). New York: McGraw-Hill.

Austin, J., Bloom, B., & Donahue, T. (1992). *Female offenders in the community: An analysis of innovative strategies and programs.* Washington, DC: National Institute of Corrections, National Council on Crime and Delinquency.

Austin, J., Dedel Johnson, K., & Gregoriou, M. (2000). *Juveniles in adult prisons and jails: A national assessment.* Washington, DC: Bureau of Justice Assistance.

Balis, A. (2007). Female prisoners and the case for gender-specific treatment and reentry programs. In R. Greifinger (Ed.), *Public health behind bars: From prisons to communities* (pp. 320–332). New York: Springer.

Barnett, B. M. (1993). Invisible Southern black women leaders in the civil rights movement: The triple constraints of gender, race, and class. *Gender and Society, 7,* 162–182.

Barry, K. (1996). Deconstructing deconstructionism (or whatever happened to feminist studies). In D. Bell & R. Klein (Eds.), *Radically speaking: Feminism reclaimed* (pp. 188–192). Melbourne, Australia: Spinifex.

Bartollas, C. (1993). Little girls grown up: The perils of institutionalization. In C. Culliver (Ed.), *Female criminality: The state of the art* (pp. 469–482). New York: Garland.

Baskin, D., & Sommers, I. (1993). Females' initiation into violent street crime. *Justice Quarterly, 10,* 559–581.

Baskin, D., Sommers, I., & Fagan, J. (1993). The political economy of female violent street crime. *Fordham Urban Law Journal, 20*(3), 401–417.

Baum, D. (1996). *Smoke and mirrors: The war on drugs and the politics of failure.* Boston: Little, Brown.

Becker, H. S. (1963). *Outsiders.* New York: Free Press.

Beddoe, D. (1979). *Welsh convict women.* Barry, Wales: Stewart Williams.

Belknap, J. (2007). *The invisible woman: Gender, crime, and justice.* Belmont, CA: Wadsworth.

Belknap, J., & Holsinger, K. (2006). The gendered nature of risk factors for delinquency. *Feminist Criminology, 1,* 48–71.

Belknap, J., Holsinger, K., & Dunn, M. (1997). Understanding incarcerated girls: The results of a focus group study. *Prison Journal, 77*(4), 381–404.

Bell, I. P. (1970). The double standard: Age. *Transaction, 8,* 75–80.

Bergen, H., Martin, G., Richardson, A., Allison, S., & Roeger, L. (2004). Sexual abuse, antisocial behaviour and substance use: Gender differences in young community adolescents. *Australian and New Zealand Journal of Psychiatry, 38,* 34–41.

Bishop, D., & Frazier, C. (1992). Gender bias in the juvenile justice system: Implications of the JJDP Act. *Journal of Criminal Law and Criminology, 82,* 1162–1186.

Blanchette, K., & Brown, S. (2006). *The assessment and treatment of women offenders: An integrative approach.* Hoboken, NJ: John Wiley & Sons.

Blanchette, K., & Taylor, K. N. (2009). Reintegration of female offenders: Perspectives on "what works." *Corrections Today, 71*(6), 60–63.

Blasky, M. (2010). Ten members of all-female gang arrested on robbery, burglary charges. *Las Vegas Review Journal,* Aug 25. Retrieved February 22, 2011, at http://www.lvrj.com/news/ten-members-of-all-female-gang-arrested-on-robbery--burglary-robberies-101517974.html

Block, J. (1984). *Sex role identity and ego development.* San Francisco: Jossey-Bass.

Bloom, B., Chesney-Lind, M., & Owen, B. (1994). *Women in prison in California: Hidden victims of the war on drugs.* San Francisco: Center on Juvenile and Criminal Justice.

Bloom, B., Owen, B., & Covington, S. (2003). *Gender-responsive strategies: Research, practice, and guiding principles for women offenders.* Washington, DC: U.S. Department of Justice, National Institute of Corrections.

Bloom, B., & Steinhart, D. (1993). *Why punish the children?* San Francisco: National Council on Crime and Delinquency.

Blumstein, A., Cohen, J., Martin, S. E., & Tonry, M. H. (Eds.). (1983). *Research on sentencing: The search for reform* (Vols. 1–2). Washington, DC: National Academy Press.

Bonta, J. (1996). Risk-needs assessment and treatment. In A. T. Harland (Ed.), *Choosing correctional options that work: Defining the demand and evaluating the supply* (pp. 18–32). Thousand Oaks, CA: Sage Publications.

Boritch, H., & Hagan, J. (1990). A century of crime in Toronto: Gender, class and patterns of social control, 1859–1955. *Criminology, 28,* 567–599.

Bowker, L. (1978). *Women, crime and the criminal justice system.* Lexington, MA: Lexington Books.

Bowker, L., & Klein, M. (1983). The etiology of female juvenile delinquency and gang membership: A test of psychological and social structural explanations. *Adolescence, 13,* 739–751.

Boyer, D. (2008). *Who pays the price? An assessment of youth involvement in prostitution in Seattle.* Seattle, WA: Human Services Department.

Brown, M., & Bloom, B. (2009). Reentry and renegotiating motherhood maternal identity and success on parole. *Crime and Delinquency, 55*(2), 313–336.

Brown, W. K. (1977). Black female gangs in Philadelphia. *International Journal of Offender Therapy and Comparative Criminology, 21,* 221–228.

Browne, A., & Finkelhor, D. (1986). Impact of child sexual abuse: A review of research. *Psychological Bulletin, 99,* 66–77.

Bui, H. N., & Morash, M. (2010). The impact of network relationships, prison experiences, and internal transformation on women's success after prison release. *Journal of Offender Rehabilitation, 49*(1), 1–22.

Bullock, K., & Tilley, N. (2002). Shootings, gangs and violent incidents in Manchester: Developing a crime reduction strategy. *Crime Reduction Research Series Paper 13.* London: Home Office.

Bureau of Justice Statistics. (1988). *Profile of state prison inmates, 1986.* Washington, DC: U.S. Department of Justice.

Bureau of Justice Statistics. (1989). *Criminal victimization in the United States.* Washington, DC: U.S. Department of Justice.

Bureau of Justice Statistics. (1999). *Women offenders.* Washington, DC: U.S. Department of Justice.

Bureau of Justice Statistics. (2001). *Prison and jail inmates at midyear 2001.* Washington, DC: U.S. Department of Justice.

Bureau of Justice Statistics. (2002a). *Prisoners in 2001.* Washington, DC: U.S. Department of Justice.

Bureau of Justice Statistics. (2010a). *Prisoners in 2009.* Washington, DC: U.S. Department of Justice.

Bureau of Justice Statistics. (2010b). *Prison and jail inmates at midyear 2009.* Washington, DC: U.S. Department of Justice.

Bureau of Justice Statistics. (2010c). *Correctional populations in the United States, 2009.* Washington, DC: U.S. Department of Justice.

Burkhart, K. (1973). *Women in prison.* New York: Doubleday.

Bush-Baskette, S. R. (1999). The war on drugs: A war against women? In S. Cook & S. Davies (Eds.), *Harsh punishment* (pp. 211–229). Boston: Northeastern University Press.

Buzawa, E. S., & Hotaling, G. T. (2006). Impact of relationship status, gender, and minor status in the police response to domestic assaults. *Victims and Offenders 1*(4), 323–360.

Bynum, V. E. (1992). *Unruly women.* Chapel Hill: University of North Carolina Press.

Cain, M. (Ed.). (1989). *Growing up good: Policing the behavior of girls in Europe.* Newbury Park, CA: Sage.

Calahan, M. (1986). *Historical corrections statistics in the United States, 1850–1984.* Washington, DC: Bureau of Justice Statistics.

Cameron, M. B. (1953). *Department store shoplifting.* Unpublished doctoral dissertation, Indiana University.

Campagna, D. S., & Poffenberger, D. L. (1988). *The sexual trafficking in children.* Dover, MA: Auburn House.

Campbell, A. (1981). *Girl delinquents.* New York: St. Martin's.

Campbell, A. (1984). *The girls in the gang.* Oxford, UK: Basil Blackwell.

Campbell, A. (1990). Female participation in gangs. In R. Huff (Ed.), *Gangs in America* (pp. 163–182). Newbury Park, CA: Sage.

Canter, R. J. (1982a). Family correlates of male and female delinquency. *Criminology, 20,* 149–167.

Canter, R. J. (1982b). Sex differences in self-report delinquency. *Criminology, 20,* 373–393.

Carlen, P., & Worrall, A. (2004). *Analyzing women's imprisonment.* Cullompton, UK: Willan Publishers.

Carmen, E., Crane, B., Dunnicliff, M., Holochuck, S., Prescott, L., Rieker, P., et al. (1996, January 25). *Massachusetts Department of Mental Health task force on the restraint and seclusion of persons who have been physically or sexually abused. Report and recommendations.* Boston: Massachusetts Department of Mental Health.

Carter, T. (1979). Juvenile court dispositions: A comparison of status and non-status offenders. *Criminology, 17,* 341–359.

Catalano, S., Smith, E., Snyder, H., & Rand, M. (2009). *Female victims of violence.* Washington, DC: Bureau of Justice Statistics.

CBS. (1992, August 6). Girls in the hood [Television series episode]. In *Street stories.*

Center for Policy Studies. (1991). *Violence against women as bias motivated hate crime.* Washington, DC: Center for Women Policy Studies.

Center for the Study of the States. (1993, November). State-local employment continues to grow. Albany, NY: *Rockefeller Institute of Government, 15,* 2.

Cepeda, A., & Valdez, A. (2003). Substance use, and crime risk behaviors among young Mexican American gang-associated females: Sexual relations, partying. *Journal of Adolescent Research, 18,* 90–106.

Chain gang death. (1996, May 17). *Birmingham News,* p. 8A.

Chapman, J. R. (1980). *Economic realities and the female offender.* Lexington, MA: Lexington Books.

Chavkin, W. (1990). Drug addiction and pregnancy: Policy crossroads. *American Journal of Public Health, 80,* 483–487.

Chesney-Lind, M. (1971). *Female juvenile delinquency in Hawaii.* Unpublished master's thesis, University of Hawaii at Manoa.

Chesney-Lind, M. (1973). Judicial enforcement of the female sex role. *Issues in Criminology, 8,* 51–71.

Chesney-Lind, M. (1986). Women and crime: The female offender. *Signs, 12,* 78–96.

Chesney-Lind, M. (1987). Female offenders: Paternalism reexamined. In L. Crites & W. Hepperele (Eds.), *Women, the courts, and equality* (pp. 114–140). Newbury Park, CA: Sage.

Chesney-Lind, M. (1993). Girls, gangs and violence: Reinventing the liberated female crook. *Humanity and Society, 17,* 321–344.

Chesney-Lind, M. (2002a). Imprisoning women: The unintended victims of mass imprisonment. In M. Mauer & M. Chesney-Lind (Eds.), *Invisible punishment: The collateral consequences of mass imprisonment* (pp. 79–94). New York: The New Press.

Chesney-Lind, M. (2002b). The unintended victims of mass incarceration. In M. Chesney-Lind & M. Mauer (Eds.), *Invisible punishment: The collateral consequences of mass imprisonment* (pp. 79–94). New York: New Press.

Chesney-Lind, M., & Belknap, J. (2002, May). *Gender, delinquency, and juvenile justice: What about girls?* Paper presented at Aggression, Antisocial Behavior and Violence Among Girls: A Development Perspective: A Conference, Duke University, Durham, North Carolina.

Chesney-Lind, M., & Hagedorn, J. (1999). *Female gangs in America: Essays on girls, gangs, and gender.* Chicago: Lakeview Press.

Chesney-Lind, M., & Irwin, K. (2008). *Beyond bad girls: Gender, violence and hype.* New York: Routledge.

Chesney-Lind, M., & Paramore, V. (1998, November). *Are girls getting more violent? Exploring juvenile robbery trends.* Paper presented at the annual meeting of the American Society of Criminology, Washington, DC.

Chesney-Lind, M., & Pollock-Byrne, J. (1995). Women's prisons: Equality with a vengeance. In J. Pollock-Byrne & A. Merlo (Eds.), *Women, law, and social control* (pp. 155–175). Boston: Allyn & Bacon.

Chesney-Lind, M., Rockhill, A., Marker, N., & Reyes, H. (1994). Gangs and delinquency: Exploring police estimates of gang membership. *Crime, Law and Social Change, 21,* 201–228.

Chesney-Lind, M., & Rodriguez, N. (1983). Women under lock and key. *Prison Journal, 63,* 47–65.

Chesney-Lind, M., & Shelden, R. G. (2004). *Girls, delinquency, and the juvenile justice system* (2nd ed.). Pacific Grove, CA: Brooks/Cole.

Children's Defense Fund and Girls Inc. (2002). *The Juvenile Justice and Delinquency Prevention Act: Fact book.* New York: Author.

Christian, J., & Thomas, S. (2009). Examining the intersections of race, gender, and mass incarceration. *Journal of Ethnicity in Criminal Justice, 7*(1), 69–84.

Clarke, S. H., & Koch, G. C. (1980). Juvenile court: Therapy and crime control, and do lawyers make a difference? *Law and Society Review, 14,* 263–308.

Cloward, R. A., & Ohlin, L. E. (1960). *Delinquency and opportunity.* New York: Free Press.

Cobbina, J. E. (2009). *From prison to home: Women's pathways in and out of crime.* Washington, DC: National Institute of Justice.

Cobbina, J. E. (2010). Reintegration success and failure: Factors impacting reintegration among incarcerated and formerly incarcerated women. *Journal of Offender Rehabilitation, 49*(3), 210–232.

Cohen, A. K. (1955). *Delinquency in boys: The culture of the gang.* New York: Free Press.

Cohen, L. E., & Kluegel, J. R. (1979). Selecting delinquents for adjudication. *Journal of Research on Crime and Delinquency, 16,* 143–163.

Cohn, Y. (1970). Criteria for the probation officer's recommendation to the juvenile court. In P. G. Garbedian & D. C. Gibbons (Eds.), *Becoming delinquent* (pp. 262–275). Chicago: Aldine.

Coles, F. (1991, February). *Women, alcohol, and automobiles: A deadly cocktail.* Paper presented at the Western Society of Criminology Meetings, Berkeley, CA.

Conly, C. (1998). *The Women Prison's Association: Supporting women offenders and their families.* Washington, DC: National Institute of Justice.

Connell, R. W. (1987). *Gender and power.* Stanford, CA: Stanford University Press.

Corrado, R., Odgers, C., & Cohen, I. (2000, April). The incarceration of female young offenders: Protection for whom? *Canadian Journal of Criminology,* 189–207.

Costello, J. C., & Worthington, N. L. (1981). Incarcerating status offenders: Attempts to circumvent the Juvenile Justice and Delinquency Prevention Act. *Harvard Civil Rights—Civil Liberties Law Review, 16,* 41–81.

Craig, G. (1995, April 8). Videotaped frisks anger women inmates. *Rochester Democrat and Chronicle,* pp. 1A, 8A.

Craig, G. (1996, March 23). Advocates say nude filming shows need for new laws. *Rochester Democrat and Chronicle,* pp. A1, A6.

Crime and Justice Institute. (2004). *Implementing evidence-based principles in community corrections: The principles of effective intervention.* Washington, DC: National Institute of Corrections, U.S. Department of Justice.

Crites, L. (1976). *The female offender.* Lexington, MA: Lexington Books.

Crittenden, D. (1990, January 25). You've come a long way, Moll. *Wall Street Journal,* p. A14.

CTV Staff. (2006). Number of female gang members on the rise: Police. *Toronto Star,* May 17. Retrieved February 15, 2011, at http://www.ctv.ca/CTVNews/Canada/20060517/girls_gangs_060517/

Curriden, M. (1993, September 20). Prison scandal in Georgia: Guards traded favors for sex. *National Law Journal,* 8.

Curry, G. D. (1995, November). *Responding to female gang involvement.* Paper presented at the American Society of Criminology Meetings, Boston.

Curry, G. D., Fox, R. J., Ball, R. A., & Stone, D. (1992). *National assessment of law enforcement anti-gang information resources: Final report.* Washington, DC: National Institute of Justice.

Curtin, M. (2002). Lesbian and bisexual girls in the juvenile justice system. *Child and Adolescent Social Work Journal, 19,* 285–301.

Daly, K. (1989). Gender and varieties of white-collar crime. *Criminology, 27,* 769–793.

Daly, K. (1994). *Gender, crime, and punishment.* New Haven, CT: Yale University Press.

Daly, K., & Chesney-Lind, M. (1988). Feminism and criminology. *Justice Quarterly, 5,* 497–538.

Datesman, S., & Scarpitti, F. (1977). Unequal protection for males and females in the juvenile court. In T. N. Ferdinand (Ed.), *Juvenile delinquency: Little brother grows up* (pp. 59–77). Beverly Hills, CA: Sage.

Davidson, J. T. (2007). *Risky business: What standard assessments mean for female offenders.* Doctoral Dissertation, University of Hawaii, Manoa.

Davidson, J. T. (2009). Discounting women: Context matters in risk and need assessment. *Critical Criminology, 17,* 221–245.

Davidson, J. T., & Chesney-Lind, M. (2009). Discounting women: Context matters in risk and need assessment. *Critical Criminology, 17*(4), 321–345.

Davidson, J. T., Pasko, L., & Chesney-Lind, M. (2011). "She's way too good to lose": An evaluation of Honolulu's Girls Court. *Women and Criminal Justice, 21*(4), 308–327.

Davis, S. (2007). Gender ideology construction from adolescence to young adulthood. *Social Science Research, 36*(3), 1021–1041.

DeHart, D. (2009). *Polyvictimization among girls in the juvenile justice system: Manifestations and associations with delinquency.* Washington, DC: National Institute of Justice.

DeJong, A. R., Hervada, A. R., & Emmett, G. A. (1983). Epidemiologic variations in childhood sexual abuse. *Child Abuse and Neglect, 7,* 155–162.

Dembo, J. S., Sue, C. C., Borden, P., & Manning, D. (1995, August). *Gender differences in service needs among youths entering a juvenile assessment center: A replication study.* Paper presented at the annual meeting of the Society of Social Problems, Washington, DC.

Dembo, R., Williams, L., & Schmeidler, J. (1993). Gender differences in mental health service needs among youths entering a juvenile detention center. *Journal of Prison and Jail Health, 12,* 73–101.

Department of Corrections and Rehabilitation. (2010). *California prisoners and parolees, 2009.* Sacramento, CA: Author.

Department of Justice. (2005). Conditions of the Hawaii Youth Correctional Facility. Washington, DC: Author. Retrieved at http://www.usdoj.gov/crt/split/documents/hawaii_youth_findlet_8-4-05.pdf

Deschenes, E., & Esbensen, F. (1999). Violence among girls: Does gang membership make a difference? In M. Chesney-Lind & J. Hagedorn (Eds.), *Female gangs in America.* Chicago: Lake View Press.

Deschenes, E. P., Owen, B., & Crow, J. (2006). *Recidivism among female prisoners: Secondary analysis of the 1994 BJS Recidivism Data Set.* Washington, DC: U.S. Department of Justice, Bureau of Justice Statistics.

Dingeman, R. (2004). Ex-guard guilty in sex assault. *Honolulu Advertiser.* Posted April 30, 2004, on http://the.honoluluadvertiser.com/article/2004/apr/30/in/in14a.html

Dohrn, B. (2004). All Ellas: Girls locked up. *Feminist Studies, 30,* 302–324.

Donziger, S. (Ed.). (1996). *The real war on crime.* New York: HarperPerennial.

Dorais, M., & Corriveau, P. (2009) *Gangs and girls: Understanding prostitution.* Montreal: McGill-Queen's University Press.

Duke, S. B. (2009). Mass imprisonment, crime rates, and the drug war: A penological and humanitarian disgrace, *9 CONN. PUB. INT. L.J. 17,* 17.

Dungworth, T. (1977). Discretion in the juvenile justice system. In T. N. Ferdinand (Ed.), *Juvenile delinquency: Little brother grows up* (pp. 19–44). Beverly Hills, CA: Sage.

Eaton, M. (1986). *Justice for women?* Milton Keynes, UK: Open University Press.

Eghigian, M., & Kirby, K. (2006). Girls in gangs: On the rise in America. *Corrections Today, 68*(2), 48–51.

Eligon, J. (2011). Juvenile justice counselor is guilty of sexually assaulting two girls. New York Times, January 22. Online version, http://www.nytimes.com/2011/01/22/nyregion/22simmons.html

Elis, L., MacKenzie, D., & Simpson, S. (1992, October). *Women and shock incarceration.* Paper presented at the Focus group meeting, Department of Criminology, College Park, MD: University of Maryland.

English, K. (1993). Self-reported crimes rates of women prisoners. *Journal of Quantitative Criminology, 9,* 357–382.

Enos, S. (2001). *Mothering from the inside: Parenting in a women's prison.* New York: State University of New York Press.

Esbensen, F., Deschenes, E. P., & Winfree, L. T., Jr. (1999). Differences between gang girls and gang boys: Results from a multi-site survey. *Youth and Society, 31,* 27–53.

Esbensen, F. A., & Huizinga, D. (1993). Gangs, drugs, and delinquency in a survey of youth. *Criminology, 31,* 565–589.

Fagan, A., Van Horn, M. L., Hawkins, D. J., & Arthur, M. W. (2007). Gender similarities and differences in the association between risk and protective factors and self-reported serious delinquency. *Prevention Science, 8,* 115–124.

Faludi, S. (1991). *Backlash: The undeclared war against women.* New York: Crown.

Fantz, A. (2008). Sex abuse, violence alleged at teen jails across the U.S. CNN.com/crime. Retrieved from http://www.cnn.com/2008/CRIME/04/04/juvenile.jails/

Federal Bureau of Investigation. (1973). *Crime in the United States—1972.* Washington, DC: U.S. Department of Justice.

Federal Bureau of Investigation. (1976). *Crime in the United States—1975.* Washington, DC: U.S. Department of Justice.

Federal Bureau of Investigation. (1980). *Crime in the United States—1979: Uniform crime reports.* Washington, DC: U.S. Department of Justice.

Federal Bureau of Investigation. (1995). *Crime in the United States—1994.* Washington, DC: U.S. Department of Justice.

Federal Bureau of Investigation. (1998). *Crime in the United States—1997.* Washington, DC: U.S. Department of Justice.

Federal Bureau of Investigation. (2006). *Crime in the United States—2005.* Washington, DC: U.S. Department of Justice.

Federal Bureau of Investigation. (2010a). *Crime in the United States—2009.* Washington, DC: U.S. Department of Justice.

Federal Bureau of Investigation. (2010b). *2009 uniform crime reports.* Washington, DC: Author.

Feeley, M., & Little, D. L. (1991). The vanishing female: The decline of women in the criminal process. *Law and Society Review, 256,* 719–758.

Feinman, C. (1980). *Women in the criminal justice system.* New York: Praeger.

Feld, B. (2009). Girls in the juvenile system. In M. Zahn (Ed.), *The delinquent girl* (pp. 225–265). Philadelphia: Temple University Press.

Female Offender Resource Center. (1977). *Little sisters and the law.* Washington, DC: American Bar Association.

Fessenden, F. (2000, April 9). They threaten, seethe, and unhinge, then kill in quantity. *New York Times,* sec. 1, p. 1.

Figueira-McDonough, J. (1985). Are girls different? Gender discrepancies between delinquent behavior and control. *Child Welfare, 64,* 273–289.

Figueira-McDonough, J., & Selo, E. (1980). A reformulation of the "equal opportunity" explanation of female delinquency. *Crime and Delinquency, 26,* 333–343.

Finkelhor, D. (1982). Sexual abuse: A sociological perspective. *Child Abuse and Neglect, 6,* 95–102.

Finkelhor, D., & Baron, L. (1986). Risk factors for child sexual abuse. *Journal of Interpersonal Violence, 1,* 43–71.

Fishman, L. T. (1995). The Vice Queens: An ethnographic study of black female gang behavior. In M. Klein, C. Maxson, & J. Miller (Eds.), *The modern gang reader* (pp. 83–92). Los Angeles: Roxbury.

Flowers, R. B. (1987). *Women and criminality.* Westport, CT: Greenwood.

Flowers, R. B. (2001). *Runaway kids and teenage prostitution.* London: Greenwood.

Foley, C. (1974, October 20). Increase of women in crime and violence. *Honolulu Sunday Star-Bulletin and Advertiser,* p. 1.

Fortuin, B. (2007). Maine's female offenders and reentering—and succeeding. *Corrections Today Magazine, 69*(2), 34–37.

Foster, H., & Hagan, J. (2009). The mass incarceration of parents in America: Issues of race/ethnicity, collateral damage to children, and prisoner reentry. *The Annals of the American Academy of Political and Social Science, 623,* 179–194.

Franklin, R. (1996, April 26). Ala. to expand chain gangs—adding women. *USA Today,* p. 3A.

Freedman, E. (1981). *Their sisters' keepers.* Ann Arbor: University of Michigan Press.

Frost, N., Green, J., & Pranis, K. (2006). *Hard hit: The growth in women's imprisonment, 1977–2004.* New York: Institute on Women and Criminal Justice.

Funk, S. J. (1999). Risk assessment for juveniles on probation: A focus on gender. *Criminal Justice and Behavior, 26,* 44–68.

Gaarder, E., & Belknap, J. (2004). Little women: Girls in adult prisons. *Women & Criminal Justice 15*(2), 51–80.

Gelsthorpe, L. (1989). *Sexism and the female offender: An organizational analysis.* Aldershot, UK: Gower.

General Accounting Office. (1978). *Removing status offenders from secure facilities: Federal leadership and guidance are needed.* Washington, DC: Author.

Gibbons, D. (1983). *Delinquent behavior.* Englewood Cliffs, NJ: Prentice Hall.

Gibbons, D., & Griswold, M. J. (1957). Sex differences among juvenile court referrals. *Sociology and Social Research, 42,* 106–110.

Gibbs, B. (June 19, 2001). *Number of girls in gangs increasing.* Retrieved from http://abclocal.go.com/wtvd/features/061901_CF_girlsgangs.html

Gilfus, M. (1992). From victims to survivors to offenders: Women's routes of entry into street crime. *Women and Criminal Justice, 4*(1), 63–89.

Giordano, P., Cernkovich, S., & Pugh, M. (1978). Girls, guys and gangs: The changing social context of female delinquency. *Journal of Criminal Law and Criminology, 69,* 126–132.

Girls Incorporated. (1996). *Prevention and parity: Girls in juvenile justice.* Indianapolis, IN: Girls Incorporated National Resource Center.

Girshick, L. (1999). *No safe haven: Stories of women in prison.* Boston: Northeastern University Press.

Glaze, L. E., & Bonczar, T. P. (2007). *Probation and parole in the United States, 2006.* Washington, DC: U.S. Department of Justice, Bureau of Justice Statistics.

Glaze, L. E., & Bonczar, T. P. (2010). *Probation and parole in the United States, 2009.* Washington, DC: U.S. Department of Justice. NCJ 231674.

Glaze, L. E., & Maruschak, L. M. (2008). Parents in prison and their minor children. *Bureau of Justice Statistics Special Report.* Washington, DC: Bureau of Justice Statistics.

Gora, J. (1982). *The new female criminal: Empirical reality or social myth.* New York: Praeger.

Green, P. (Ed.). (1996). *Drug couriers: A new perspective.* London: Quartet.

Greene, Peters, & Associates. (1998). *Guiding principles for promising female programming: An inventory of best practices.* Nashville, TN: Office of Juvenile Justice and Delinquency Prevention.

Greene, J., & Pranis, K. (2007). *Gang wars—the failure of enforcement tactics and the need for effective public safety strategies.* Washington DC: The Justice Policy Institute. Web edition, http://www.justicestrategies.org/sites/default/files/Gang_Wars_Full_Report_2007.pdf

Hagan, J., Gillis, A. R., & Simpson, J. (1985). The class structure of gender and delinquency: Toward a power-control theory of common delinquent behavior. *American Journal of Sociology, 90,* 1151–1178.

Hagan, J., Simpson, J., & Gillis, A. R. (1987). Class in the household: A power-control theory of gender and delinquency. *American Journal of Sociology, 92,* 788–816.

Hanawalt, L. B. (1982). Women before the law: Females as felons and prey in 14th-century England. In D. K. Weisberg (Ed.), *Women and the law* (pp. 165–196). Cambridge, MA: Schenkman.

Hancock, L. (1981). The myth that females are treated more leniently than males in the juvenile justice system. *Australian and New Zealand Journal of Sociology, 16,* 4–14.

Haney, L. (2010). *Offending women: Power, punishment, and the regulation of desire.* Berkeley, CA: University of California Press.

Hannah-Moffat, K. (2009). Gridlock or mutability: Reconsidering "gender" and risk assessment. *Criminology & Public Policy, 8,* 209–219.

Hannah-Moffat, K., & Shaw, M. (2003). The meaning of "risk" in women's prisons: A critique. In B. Bloom (Ed.), *Gendered justice: Addressing female offenders* (pp. 45–68). Durham, NC: Carolina Academic Press.

Hanson, K. (1964). *Rebels in the streets: The story of New York's girl gangs.* Englewood Cliffs, NJ: Prentice Hall.

Harcourt, B. E. (2007). *Against prediction: Profiling, policing, and punishing in an actuarial age.* Chicago: University of Chicago Press.

Harer, M. D., & Langan, N. P. (2001). Gender differences in predictors of prison violence: Assessing the predictive validity of a risk classification system. *Crime & Delinquency, 47,* 513–536.

Harlow, C. W. (1999). *Prior abuse reported by inmates and probationers.* Washington, DC: U.S. Department of Justice.

Hartjen, C., & Priyadarsini, S. (2003). Gender, peers and delinquency: A study of boys and girls in rural France. *Youth and Society, 34*(4), 387–414.

Hartney, C. (2006). *Youth under 18 in the adult criminal justice system.* Oakland, CA: NCCD.

Harris, A. (2004). *All about the girl: Culture, power, and identity.* New York: Routledge.

Harris, M. G. (1988). *Cholas: Latino girls and gangs.* New York: AMS Press.

Hartman, M. S. (1977). *Victorian murderesses.* New York: Schocken.

Heilbrun, K., DeMatteo, D., Fretz, R., Erickson, J., Yasuhara, K., & Anumba, N. (2008a). How "specific" are gender-specific rehabilitation needs? *Criminal Justice and Behavior, 35,* 1382–1397.

Hennessey, M., Ford, J., Mahoney, K., Ko, S., & Siegfried, C. (2004). *Trauma among girls in the juvenile justice system.* Los Angeles, CA: National Child Traumatic Stress Network.

Herman, J. L. (1981). *Father-daughter incest.* Cambridge, MA: Harvard University Press.

Hesse-Biber, S. N. (2007). *The cult of thinness* (2nd ed.). New York: Oxford.

Hirschi, T. (1969). *Causes of delinquency.* Berkeley: University of California Press.

Hoard, Walter B. (1973). *Anthology: Quotations and sayings of people of color* (p. 36). San Francisco, CA: R & E Associates.

Hochschild, A. (1989). *The second shift.* New York: Viking.

Hollin, C. R., & Palmer, E. J. (2006). Criminogenic need and women offenders: A critique of the literature. *Legal and Criminological Psychology, 11,* 179–195.

Holsinger, K., Belknap, J., & Sutherland, J. (1999). *Assessing the gender specific program and service needs for adolescent females in the juvenile justice system.* Columbus, OH: Office of Criminal Justice Services.

Holtfreter, K., & Cupp, R. (2007). Gender and risk assessment: The empirical status of the LSI-R for Women. *Journal of Contemporary Criminal Justice, 23,* 363–382.

Holtfreter, K., Reisig, M. D., & Morash, M. (2004). Poverty, state capital, and recidivism among women offenders. *Criminology & Public Policy 3*(2), 185–208.

Howard, B. (1996, July/August). Juvenile Justice Act's mandates: Stay or go? *Youth Today,* 22.

Hubbard, D. J., & Matthews, B. (2008). Reconciling the differences between the "gender-responsive" and the "what works" literature to improve services for girls. *Crime & Delinquency, 54,* 225–258.

Huebner, B. M., DeJong, C., & Cobbina, J. (2010). Women coming home: Long-term patterns of recidivism. *Justice Quarterly, 27*(2), 225–254.

Hulen, T. (1996, April 28). Governor's stand on women in chains: Insult or chivalry. *Birmingham News,* pp. 1A, 2A.

Huling, T. (1995, November). *African American women and the war on drugs.* Paper presented at the annual meeting of the American Society of Criminology, Boston.

Huling, T. (1996). Prisoners of war: Women drug couriers in the United States. In P. Green (Ed.), *Drug couriers: A new perspective* (pp. 46–60). London: Quartet.

Human Rights Watch. (1993). *The Human Rights Watch global report on prisons.* New York: Author.

Human Rights Watch, Children's Rights Project. (1995). *Children in confinement in Louisiana.* New York: Human Rights Watch.

Human Rights Watch, Children's Rights Project. (1996). *Children in confinement in the state of Georgia.* New York: Human Rights Watch.

Human Rights Watch, Children's Rights Project. (1997). *Children in confinement in Colorado.* New York: Human Rights Watch.

Human Rights Watch & American Civil Liberties Union. (2006). *Custody and control: Conditions of confinement in New York's juvenile prisons for girls.* New York: Authors.

Hunt, G., & Joe-Laidler, K. (2001). Situations of violence in the lives of girl gang members. *Health Care for Women International, 22,* 363–384.

Ianni, F. A. J. (1989). *The search for structure: A report on American youth today.* New York: Free Press.

Irvine, A. (2010). We've had three of them: Addressing the invisibility of lesbian, gay, bisexual, and gender non-conforming youth in the juvenile justice system. *Columbia Journal of Gender and Law, 19*(3), 675–702.

Jankowski, M. S. (1991). *Islands in the streets: Gangs and American urban society.* Berkeley: University of California Press.

Joe, K., & Chesney-Lind, M. (1995). Just every mother's angel: An analysis of gender and ethnic variations in youth gang membership. *Gender and Society, 9,* 408–430.

Johnson, D. R., & Scheuble, L. K. (1991). Gender bias in the disposition of juvenile court referrals: The effects of time and location. *Criminology, 29*(4), 677–699.

Jones, A. (1980). *Women who kill.* New York: Fawcett.

Jones, N. (2009). *Between good and ghetto: African American girls and inner city violence.* Newark, NJ: Rutgers University Press.

Junger-Tas, J., Marshall, I., Enzmann, D., Killias, M., Skeketee, M., & Gruszczynska, B. (2009). *Juvenile delinquency in Europe and beyond.* New York: Springer.

Kahler, K. (1992, May 17). Hand that rocks the cradle is taking up violent crime. *Sunday Star-Ledger,* p. 3A.

Kamler, B. (1999). *Constructing gender and difference: Critical perspectives on early childhood.* Cresskill, NJ: Hampton Press.

Katz, P. A. (1979). The development of female identity. In C. B. Kopp (Ed.), *Becoming female: Perspectives on development* (pp. 3–27). New York: Plenum.

Kim, E. (1996, August 16). Sheriff says he'll have chain gangs for women. *Tuscaloosa News,* p. 1A.

Kirp, D., Yudof, M., & Franks, M. S. (1986). *Gender justice.* Chicago: University of Chicago Press.

Klein, D., & Kress, J. (1976, Spring/Summer). Any woman's blues: A critical overview of women, crime and the criminal justice system. *Crime and Social Justice, 5,* 34–48.

Klemesrud, J. (1978, January 16). Women terrorists, sisters in crime. *Honolulu Star Bulletin,* p. C1.

Knupfer, A. (2001). *Reform and resistance: Gender, delinquency, and America's first juvenile court.* New York: Routledge.

Koop, C. E. (1989, May 22). *Violence against women: A global problem.* Address by the Surgeon General of the U.S. Public Health Service at a conference of the Pan American Health Organization, Washington, DC.

Kratcoski, P. C. (1974). Delinquent boys and girls. *Child Welfare, 5,* 16–21.

Krisberg, B., Schwartz, I. M., Fishman, G., Eisikovits, Z., & Guttman, E. (1986). *The incarceration of minority youth.* Minneapolis, MN: Hubert Humphrey Institute of Public Affairs.

Kumar, S. (2010). *The caged birds sing: A report by the girls on Unit A at Waxter.* Washington, DC: ACLU.

Kunzel, R. (1993). *Fallen women and problem girls: Unmarried mothers and the professionalization of social work, 1890–1945.* New Haven, CT: Yale University Press.

LaFromboise, T. D., & Howard-Pitney, B. (1995). Suicidal behavior in American Indian female adolescents. In S. Canetto & D. Lester (Eds.), *Woman and suicidal behavior* (pp. 157–173). New York: Springer.

Laidler, K., & Hunt, G. (2001). Accomplishing femininity among the girls in the gang. *British Journal of Criminology, 41*(4), 656–678.

Lamb, S., & Brown, L. M. (2006). *Packaging girlhood: Rescuing our daughters from marketers' schemes.* New York: St. Martin's Press.

Langan, P. A. (1991, March 29). America's soaring prison population. *Science, 251,* 1569.

Larence, E. (2010). *Juvenile justice: Technical assistance and better defined evaluation plans will help girls' delinquency programs.* Testimony before the Subcommittee on Crime, Terrorism, and Homeland Security, Committee on the Judiciary, House of Representatives. U.S. Government Accountability Office.

Lauderback, D., Hansen, J., & Waldorf, D. (1992). Sisters are doin' it for themselves: A black female gang in San Francisco. *Gang Journal, 1,* 57–72.

Lauderdale, M., & Burman, M. (2009). Contemporary patterns of female gangs in correctional settings. *Journal of Human Behavior in the Social Environment, 19*(3), 258–280.

LeBlanc, A. (1995). Trina and Trina. *Literary Journalism, 2,* 213–233.

LeBlanc, A. (1996, June 2). A woman behind bars is not a dangerous man. *New York Times Magazine,* 34–40.

Lee, F. R. (1991, November 25). For gold earrings and protection, more girls take the road to violence. *New York Times,* pp. A1, B7.

Leslie, C., Biddle, N., Rosenberg, D., & Wayne, J. (1993, August 2). Girls will be girls. *Newsweek,* 44.

Lewis, N. (1992, December 23). Delinquent girls achieving a violent equality in DC. *Washington Post,* pp. A1, A14.

Lindquist, J. (1988). *Misdemeanor crime.* Newbury Park, CA: Sage.

Lipsey, M. (1992). Juvenile delinquency treatment: A meta-analytic inquiry in the variability of effects. In T. A. Cook, H. Cooper, D. S. Cordray, H. Hartmann, L. V. Hedges, R. J. Light, et al. (Eds.), *Meta-analysis for explanation: A casebook* (pp. 83–126). New York: Russell Sage.

Lopez, S. (1993, July 8). Fifth guard arrested on sex charge. *Albuquerque Journal,* pp. A1, A2.

Lopez, V., Chesney-Lind, M., & Foley, J. (2011). Power, control, and dating violence among Latina girls. Forthcoming in *Violence Against Women.*

Los Angeles Times Service. (1975, August 7). L.A. police chief blames libbers. *Honolulu Advertiser,* pp. B4.

MacKinnon, C. (1987). *Feminism unmodified: Discourses on life and law.* London: Harvard University Press.

Majd, K., Marksamer, J., & Reyes, C. (2009). *Hidden injustice: Lesbian, gay, bisexual, and transgender youth in juvenile courts.* San Francisco, CA: Autumn Press.

Males, M. (1994, March/April). Bashing youth: Media myths about teenagers. *Extra,* 8–11.

Mallicoat, S. (2007). Gendered justice: Attributional differences between males and females in the juvenile courts. *Feminist Criminology, 2,* 4–30.

Manchak, S. M., Skeem, J. L., Douglas, K. S., & Siranosian, M. (2009). Does gender moderate the predictive utility of the Level of Service Inventory Revised (LSI-R) for serious violent offenders? *Criminal Justice and Behavior, 36,* 425–442.

Mann, C. (1979). The differential treatment between runaway boys and girls in juvenile court. *Juvenile and Family Court Journal, 30,* 37–48.

Mann, C. (1984). *Female crime and delinquency.* Tuscaloosa: University of Alabama Press.

Maquire, K., & Pastore, A. L. (Eds.). (1994). *Sourcebook of criminal justice statistics—1993.* Washington, DC: U.S. Department of Justice.

Martin, L., Hearst, M., & Widome, R. (2010). Meaningful differences: Comparison of adult women who first traded sex as a juvenile versus as an adult. *Violence Against Women, 16*(11), 1252–1269.

Martin, M. (2002, April 21). Changing population behind bars: Major drop in women in state prisons. *San Francisco Chronicle.* Online version, found at http://www .sfgate.com/cgi-bin/article.cgi?f=/c/a/2002/04/21/MN233500.DTL

Maruschak, L. (2001). *HIV in prisons and jails, 1999.* Washington, DC: Bureau of Justice Statistics.

Maruschak, L. (2002). *HIV in prisons, 2000.* Washington, DC: Bureau of Justice Statistics.

Mauer, M. (1994, September). *Americans behind bars: The international use of incarceration, 1992–1993.* Washington, DC: The Sentencing Project.

Mauer, M. (1999). *The crisis of the young African American male and the criminal justice system.* Washington, DC: Sentencing Project.

Mauer, M. (2006). *Race to incarcerate.* New York: New Press.

Mauer, M., & Chesney-Lind, M. (2002). *Invisible punishment: The collateral consequences of mass imprisonment.* New York: New Press.

Mauer, M., & Huling, T. (1995). *Young black Americans and the criminal justice system: Five years later.* Washington, DC: Sentencing Project.

Mayer, J. (1994, July). *Girls in the Maryland juvenile justice system: Findings of the Female Population Taskforce.* Paper presented at the Gender Specific Services Training, Minneapolis, MN.

McClellan, D. S. (1994). Disparity in the discipline of male and female inmates in Texas prisons. *Women and Criminal Justice, 5*(2), 71–97.

McCormack, A., Janus, M., & Burgess, A. W. (1986). Runaway youths and sexual victimization: Gender differences in an adolescent runaway population. *Child Abuse and Neglect, 10,* 387–395.

McDermott, M. J., & Blackstone, S. J. (1994). *White slavery plays of the 1910's: Fear of victimization and the social control of sexuality.* Paper presented at the annual meeting of the American Society of Criminology, Miami, FL.

McRobbie, A., & Garber, J. (1975). Girls and subcultures. In S. Hall & T. Jefferson (Eds.), *Resistance through rituals: Youth subculture in post-war Britain* (pp. 209–222). New York: Holmes and Meier.

Meiselman, K. (1978). *Incest.* San Francisco: Jossey-Bass.

Merton, R. K. (1938). Social structure and anomie. *American Sociological Review, 3,* 672–682.

Messerschmidt, J. (1987). Feminism, criminology, and the rise of the female sex delinquent, 1880–1930. *Contemporary Crises, 11,* 243–263.

Meyer, M. (1992, November 9). Coercing sex behind bars: Hawaii's prison scandal. *Newsweek,* 23–25.

Miller, E. (1986). *Street woman.* Philadelphia: Temple University Press.

Miller, J. (1994). Race, gender and juvenile justice: An examination of disposition decision-making for delinquent girls. In M. D. Schwartz & D. Milovanovic (Eds.), *The intersection of race, gender and class in criminology* (pp. 219–246). New York: Garland.

Miller, J. (2001). *One of the guys: Girls, gangs, and gender.* New York: Oxford University Press.

Miller, J. (2002). Young women in street gangs: Risk factors, delinquency, and victimization risk. In W. Reed & S. Decker (Eds.), *Responding to gangs: Evaluation and research* (pp. 68–105). Washington, DC: National Institute of Justice.

Miller, J. (2008). *Getting played: African American girls, urban inequality, and gendered violence.* New York: NYU Press.

Miller, W. B. (1958). Lower class culture as a generating milieu of gang delinquency. *Journal of Social Issues, 14,* 5–19.

Miller, W. B. (1975). *Violence by youth gangs and youth groups as a crime problem in major American cities.* Washington, DC: Government Printing Office.

Miller, W. B. (1980). The Molls. In S. K. Datesman & F. R. Scarpitti (Eds.), *Women, crime, and justice* (pp. 238–248). New York: Oxford University Press.

Minton, T. D. (2010). *Jail inmates at mid-year, statistical tables.* Washington, DC: Bureau of Justice Statistics, U.S. Department of Justice. NCJ 230122.

Mitchell, K. J., Finkelhor, D., & Wolak, J. (2009). Conceptualizing juvenile prostitution as child maltreatment: Findings from the National Juvenile Prostitution Study. *Child Maltreatment, 15*(1), 18–36.

Moloney, M., Hunt, G., Joe-Laidler, K., & MacKenzie, K. (2011). Mother (in the) hood: Gang girls' negotiation of new identities. *Journal of Youth Studies, 14*(1), 1–19.

Moone, J. (1993a). *Children in custody: Private facilities.* Washington, DC: Office of Juvenile Justice and Delinquency Prevention.

Moone, J. (1993b). *Children in custody: Public facilities.* Washington, DC: Office of Juvenile Justice and Delinquency Prevention.

Moore, J. (1991). *Going down to the barrio: Homeboys and homegirls in change.* Philadelphia: Temple University Press.

Moore, J., & Hagedorn, J. (1995). What happens to the girls in the gang? In R. C. Huff (Ed.), *Gangs in America* (2nd. ed., pp. 205–220). Thousand Oaks, CA: Sage.

Moore, J., & Hagedorn, J. (2001). *Female gangs: A focus on research.* Washington, DC: Office of Justice Programs.

Moore, J., Vigil, D., & Levy, J. (1995). Huisas of the street: Chicana gang members. *Latino Studies Journal, 6*(1), 27–48.

Morash, M. (2009). A great debate over using the Level of Service Inventory-Revised (LSI-R) with women offenders. *Criminology and Public Policy, 8,* 173–181.

Morash, M. (2010). *Women on probation & parole: A feminist critique of community programs and services.* Boston: Northeastern University Press.

Morash, M., & Bynum, T. (1996). *Findings from the national study of innovative and promising programs for women offenders.* East Lansing: Michigan State University, School of Criminal Justice.

Morgan, E. (2000). Women on death row. In R. Muraskin (Ed.), *It's a crime: Women and justice* (pp. 269–283). Upper Saddle River, NJ: Prentice Hall.

Morris, A. (1987). *Women, crime and criminal justice.* New York: Basil Blackwell.

Morrissey, B. (2003). *When women kill: Questions of agency and subjectivity.* New Brunswick, NJ: Routledge.

Motivans, M. (2008). *Federal justice statistics, 2005.* Rockville, MD: Urban Institute.

Motivans, M. (2010). *Federal justice statistics, 2007.* Rockville, MD: Urban Institute.

Mumola, C. (2000). Incarcerated parents and their children. *Bureau of Justice Statistics Special Report.* Washington, DC: Bureau of Justice Statistics.

Naffine, N. (1987). *Female crime: The construction of women in criminology.* Sydney, Australia: Allen and Unwin.

Naffine, N. (1989). Toward justice for girls. *Women and Criminal Justice, 1,* 3–19.

NAPW. (2011). *Medical and public health statements on the prosecution and punishment of pregnant women.* New York: National Advocates for Pregnant Women.

National Gang Center (2009). National Gang Survey Analysis. http://www.national gangcenter.gov/Survey-Analysis/Defining-Gangs

National Institute of Justice. (1998). *Women offenders: Programming needs and promising approaches.* Washington, DC: Author.

National Symposium on Female Offenders. (2000). *Conference proceedings: Treat the women, save the children.* Kauai, HI: Author.

NBC. (1993, March 29). *NBC nightly news.* [Television broadcast]. Diana Koricke in East Los Angeles.

Neal, C. (2007). Women who are victims of domestic violence: Supervision strategies for community corrections professionals. *Corrections Today Magazine, 69*(4), 38–41, 43.

Nelson, L. D. (1977, October 23). Women make gains in shady world, too. *Honolulu Sunday Star-Bulletin and Advertiser,* p. G-8.

Ness, C. (2010). *Why girls fight: Female youth violence in the inner city.* New York: NYU Press.

Nichols, S., & Good. T. (2004). *America's teenagers—Myths and realities.* New York: Routledge.

Noble, A. (1988). *Criminalize or medicalize: Social and political definitions of the problem of substance use during pregnancy.* Sacramento, CA: Department of Health Services, Maternal and Child Health Branch.

Odem, M. E., & Schlossman, S. (1991). Guardians of virtue: The juvenile court and female delinquency in early 20th century Los Angeles. *Crime and Delinquency, 37,* 186–203.

Office of the Inspector General, State of California. (2010). *Valley State Prison for Women, Warden Tina Hornbeak one-year audit.* Sacramento, CA: Author.

Office of Juvenile Justice and Delinquency Prevention. (1992). *Arrests of youth 1990.* Washington, DC: Author.

Office of Juvenile Justice and Delinquency Prevention. (1998). *Guiding principles for promising female programming.* Washington, DC: Author.

Office of Juvenile Justice and Delinquency Prevention. (2001). *OJJDP statistical briefing book.* Retrieved from http://www.ojjdp.ncjrs.org/ojstabb/qa178.html

Olson, D. E., Alderden, M., & Lurigio, A. J. (2003). Men are from Mars, women are from Venus, but what role does gender play in probation recidivism? *Journal of the Justice Research and Statistics Association, 5,* 33–54.

Orenstein, P. (1994). *School girls.* Garden City, NY: Doubleday.

Ostner, I. (1986). Die Entdeckung der Mädchen. Neue Perspecktiven für die. *Kolner-Zeitschrift für Soziologie und Sozialpsychologie, 38,* 352–371.

O'Toole, L., & Schiffman, J. (1997). *Gender violence: Interdisciplinary perspectives.* New York: New York University Press.

Owen, B. (1998). *In the mix: Struggle and survival in a women's prison.* New York: State University of New York.

Pasko, L. (1997). *From sin to syndrome: The medicalization of juvenile sex offense.* Unpublished master's thesis, University of Nevada, Reno, December 2007.

Pasko, L. (2006). *The gendered nature of juvenile justice and delinquency in Hawaii.* Unpublished dissertation. University of Hawaii at Manoa, August 2006.

Pasko, L. (2008). The wayward girl revisited: Understanding the gendered nature of juvenile justice and delinquency. *Sociology Compass, 2*(2), 1–16.

Pasko, L. (2010a). Damaged daughters: The history of girls' sexuality and the juvenile justice system. *Journal of Criminal Law and Criminology, 100*(3), 1099–1130.

Pasko, L. (2010b). Setting the record "straight": Girls, sexuality, and the juvenile correctional system. *Social Justice, 37*(1), 7–26.

Pasko, L., & Chesney-Lind, M. (2010). Under lock and key: Trauma, marginalization, and girls' juvenile justice involvement. *Justice Research and Policy, 12*(2), 25–49.

Pasko, L., & Chesney-Lind, M. (2011). Girls' violence and juvenile justice: A critical examination. In W. DeKeseredy, & M. Dragiewicz, *Handbook of critical criminology.* New York: Routledge.

Pasko L., & Dwight, D. (2010). *Understanding and responding to the female juvenile offender in Colorado.* Denver, CO: Division of Criminal Justice.

Patrick, D. L. (1995, March 27). Letter to Gov. John Engler, Re: Crane and Scott Correctional Centers.

Peterson, D., Miller, J., & Esbensen, F. A. (2001). The impact of sex composition on gang member attitudes and behavior. *Criminology, 39,* 411–440.

Phelps, R. J., McIntosh, M., Jesudason, V., Warner, P., & Pohlkamp, J. (1982). *Wisconsin female juvenile offender study project summary report.* Madison: Wisconsin Council on Juvenile Justice, Youth Policy and Law Center.

Platt, A. M. (1969). *The childsavers.* Chicago: University of Chicago Press.

Poe, E., & Butts, J. A. (1995). *Female offenders in the juvenile justice system.* Pittsburgh, PA: National Center for Juvenile Justice.

Poe-Yamagata, E., & Butts, J. A. (1996). *Female offenders in the juvenile justice system.* Washington, DC: U.S. Department of Justice.

Pollock-Byrne, J. (1990). *Women, prison, and crime.* Pacific Grove, CA: Brooks/Cole.

Pope, C., & Feyerherm, W. H. (1982). Gender bias in juvenile court dispositions. *Social Service Research, 6,* 1–17.

Portillos, E., & Zatz, M. S. (1995, November). *Not to die for: Positive and negative aspects of Chicano youth gangs.* Paper presented at the meeting of the American Society of Criminology, Boston.

Province of British Columbia. (1978). *Youth services in juvenile justice.* Victoria, BC: Information Services, Corrections Branch.

Public Law 102-586. (November 4, 1992). Juvenile justice and delinquency prevention, fiscal years 1993, 1994, 1995, 1996. 106 Stat. 4982 (1992)

Puzzanchera, C., Adams, B., & Stahl, A. (2010). *Juvenile court statistics 2006–2007.* Washington, DC: National Center for Juvenile Justice.

Puzzanchera, C., & Kang, W. (2010). Easy access to juvenile court statistics: 1985–2007. Online. Available: http://ojjdp.ncjrs.gov/ojstatbb/ezajcs/.

Quicker, J. C. (1983). *Homegirls: Characterizing Chicano gangs.* San Pedro, CA: International University Press.

Raeder, M. (1993). *Gender and sentencing: Single moms, battered women and other sex-based anomalies in the gender free world of the federal sentencing guidelines.* Unpublished manuscript.

Rafter, N. H. (1990). *Partial justice: Women, prisons and social control.* New Brunswick, NJ: Transaction Books.

Rand, M. (2009). *Criminal victimization, 2008, Bureau of Justice Statistics Bulletin.* Washington DC: Bureau of Justice Statistics.

Rans, L. (1975). *Women's arrest statistics. (The women offender report).* Washington, DC: American Bar Association, Female Offender Resource Center.

Ravoira, L. (2008). *New National Center for Girls and Young Women to launch this week.* Oakland, CA: National Center on Crime and Delinquency.

Ray, D. (2002). *Official letter sent to Claudia McMullin.* American Bar Association. March 20.

Read, P. (2009, July 28). "Operation Bloodette" nets 43 members of female-led drug ring. *New Jersey Star Ledger.* Retrieved February 10, 2011, at http://www.nj.com/news/index.ssf/2009/07/operation_bloodette_nets_43_me

Reisig, M. D., Holtfreter, K., & Morash, M. (2006). Assessing recidivism across female pathways to crime. *Justice Quarterly, 23,* 384–405.

Reitsma-Street, M. (1993). Canadian youth court charges and dispositions for females before and after implementation of the Young Offenders Act. *Canadian Journal of Criminology, 35,* 437–458.

Rennison, C. M. (2001). *Intimate and partner violence and age of victim.* Washington, DC: Bureau of Justice Statistics.

Renzetti, C., & Curran, D. J. (1995). *Women, men, and society.* Boston: Allyn & Bacon.

Rice, R. (1963, October 19). A reporter at large: The Persian Queens. *New Yorker,* 153–187.

Richie, B. (1996). *Compelled to crime: The gender entrapment of battered black women.* New York: Routledge.

Richie, B. (2000). Exploring the links between violence against women and women's involvement in illegal activity. In B. Richie, K. Tsenin, & C. Widom (Eds.), *Research on women and girls in the criminal justice system* (pp. 1–13). Washington, DC: National Institute of Justice.

Roberts, D. (2002). *Shattered bonds: The color of child welfare.* New York: Basic Civitas Books.

Roberts, S. (1971, June 13). Crime rate of women up sharply over men's. *New York Times,* pp. 1, 72.

Robinson, R. (1990). *Violations of girlhood: A qualitative study of female delinquents and children in need of services in Massachusetts.* Unpublished doctoral dissertation, Brandeis University, Waltham, MA.

Rogers, K. (1972, Winter). "For her own protection . . .": Conditions of incarceration for female juvenile offenders in the state of Connecticut. *Law and Society Review,* 223–246.

Roiphe, K. (1993). *The morning after.* Boston: Little, Brown.

Romer, D., Jamieson, K., & Aday, S. (2003). Television news and the cultivation of fear. *Journal of Communication, 53*(1), 88–104.

Rossi, A. (1973). *The feminist papers: From Adams to Beauvoir.* New York: Columbia University Press.

Rowe, D. C., Vazsonyi, A. T., & Flannery, D. J. (1995). Sex differences in crime: Do means and within-sex variation have similar causes? *Journal of Research in Crime and Delinquency, 31*(1), 84–100.

Sabol, W. J., & Couture, H. (2008). *Prison inmates at midyear 2007,* Washington, DC: U.S. Department of Justice, Bureau of Justice Statistics.

Sabol, W. J., & Minton, T. D. (2008). *Jail inmates at midyear 2007,* Washington, DC: U.S. Department of Justice, Bureau of Justice Statistics.

Salisbury, E., & Van Voorhis, P. (2009). Gendered pathways: A quantitative investigation of women probationers' paths to recidivism. *Criminal Justice and Behavior, 36*(6), 541–566.

Santiago, D. (1992, February 23). Random victims of vengeance show teen crime: Troubled girls, troubling violence. *Philadelphia Inquirer,* p. A1.

Schiraldi, V., Kuyper, S., & Hewitt, S. (1996). *Young African Americans and the criminal justice system in California: Five years later.* San Francisco: Center on Juvenile and Criminal Justice.

Schlossman, S., & Wallach, S. (1978). The crime of precocious sexuality: Female juvenile delinquency in the Progressive Era. *Harvard Educational Review, 48,* 65–94.

Schram, P. J., Koons-Witt, B. A., Williams III, F. P., & McShane, M. D. (2006). Supervision strategies and approaches for female parolees: Examining the link between unmet needs and parolee outcome. *Crime & Delinquency, 52,* 450–471.

Schur, E. (1984). *Labeling women deviant.* New York: Random House.

Schwartz, I. M. (1989). *(In)Justice for juveniles: Rethinking the best interests of the child.* Lexington, MA: Lexington Books.

Schwartz, I. M., Jackson-Beeck, M., & Anderson, R. (1984). The "hidden" system of juvenile control. *Crime and Delinquency, 30,* 371–385.

Schwartz, I. M., & Orlando, F. (1991). *Programming for young women in the juvenile justice system.* Ann Arbor: University of Michigan, Center for the Study of Youth Policy.

Schwartz, I. M., Steketee, M., & Schneider, V. (1990). Federal juvenile justice policy and the incarceration of girls. *Crime and Delinquency, 36,* 503–520.

Sentencing Project. (2007). *Women in the criminal justice system.* Washington, DC: Author.

Sentencing Project. (2011). *Mass incarceration in America.* Washington, DC: American Prospect.

Sewenely, A. (1993, January 6). Sex abuse charges rock women's prison. *Detroit News,* pp. B1, B7.

Shacklady-Smith, L. (1978). Sexist assumptions and female delinquency. In C. Smart & B. Smart (Eds.), *Women and social control* (pp. 74–86). London: Routledge & Kegan Paul.

Shaffner, L. (2006). *Girls in trouble with the law.* New Brunswick: Rutgers.

Sharp, C., Aldridge, J., & Medina, J. (2006). Delinquent youth groups and offending behaviour. Home Office Online Report 14/06. http://www.homeoffice.gov.uk/rds/pdfs06/rdsolr1406.pdf

Shaw, C. R. (1930). *The jack-roller.* Chicago: University of Chicago Press.

Shaw, C. R. (1938). *Brothers in crime.* Chicago: University of Chicago Press.

Shaw, C. R., & McKay, H. D. (1942). *Juvenile delinquency in urban areas.* Chicago: University of Chicago Press.

Shelden, R. (1981). Sex discrimination in the juvenile justice system: Memphis, Tennessee, 1900–1971. In M. Q. Warren (Ed.), *Comparing male and female offenders* (pp. 55–72). Beverly Hills, CA: Sage.

Shelden, R. G., Snodgrass, T., & Snodgrass, P. (1993). Comparing gang and non-gang offenders: Some tentative findings. *Gang Journal, 1,* 73–85.

Sherman, F. (2002, August/September). Promoting justice in an unjust system: Part two. *Women, Girls & Criminal Justice, 3,* 65–80.

Shorter, A. D., Schaffner, L., Shick, S., & Frappier, N. S. (1996). *Out of sight, out of mind: The plight of girls in the San Francisco juvenile justice system.* San Francisco: Center for Juvenile and Criminal Justice.

Sickmund, M. (2000). *Offenders in juvenile court, 1997.* Washington, DC: Office of Juvenile Justice and Delinquency Prevention.

Sickmund, M., Sladky, T.J., Kang, W., & Puzzanchera, C. (2008). Easy access to the Census of Juveniles in Residential Placement. Available: http://ojjdp.ncjrs.gov/ojstatbb/ezacjrp/

Simon, R. (1975). *Women and crime.* Lexington, MA: Lexington Books.

Simon, R. J., & Landis, J. (1991). *The crimes women commit, the punishments they receive.* Lexington, MA: Lexington Books.

Simons, R. L., Miller, M. G., & Aigner, S. M. (1980). Contemporary theories of deviance and female delinquency: An empirical test. *Journal of Research in Crime and Delinquency, 17,* 42–57.

Sinclair, A. (1956). *The better half.* New York: Harper & Row.

Singer, L. R. (1973). Women and the correctional process. *American Criminal Law Review, 11,* 295–308.

Smart, C. (1976). *Women, crime and criminology: A feminist critique.* London: Routledge & Kegan Paul.

Smith, D., & Paternoster, R. (1987). The gender gap in theories of deviance: Issues and evidence. *Journal of Research in Crime and Delinquency, 24,* 140–172.

Smith, D. E. (1992). Whistling women: Reflections on rage and rationality. In W. K. Carroll, L. Christiansen-Ruffman, R. F. Currie, & D. Harrison (Eds.), *Fragile truths: 25 years of sociology and anthropology in Canada* (pp. 207–226). Ottawa, Canada: Carleton University Press.

Smith, D. K., Leve, L. D., & Chamberlain, P. (2006). Adolescent girls' offending and health-risking sexual behavior: The predictive role of trauma. *Child Maltreatment, 11,* 346–353.

Smith, E. L., & Farole, D. J., Jr. (2009). *Profile of intimate partner violence cases in large urban counties.* Washington, DC: Bureau of Justice Statistics.

Smith, P., Cullen, F. T., & Latessa, E. J. (2009). Can 14,737 women be wrong? A meta-analysis of the LSI-R and recidivism for female offenders. *Criminology & Public Policy, 8,* 183–208.

Snell, T. L., & Morton, D. C. (1994). *Women in prison. (Special report).* Washington, DC: Bureau of Justice Statistics.

Snyder, H. N., & Sickmund, M. (2006). *Juvenile offenders and victims: 2006 national report.* Report. Washington, DC: U.S. Department of Justice, Office of Justice Programs, Office of Juvenile Justice and Delinquency.

Sommers, I., & Baskin, D. (1992). Sex, race, age, and violent offending. *Violence and Its Victims, 7*(3), 191–201.

Sommers, I., & Baskin, D. (1993). The situational context of violent female offending. *Crime and Delinquency, 30,* 136–162.

Sprague, J. (2005). *Feminist methodologies for critical researchers: Bridging differences.* Walnut Creek, CA: AltaMira Press.

Sprott, J., & Doob, A. (2009). *Justice for girls? Stability and change in the youth justice systems of the United States and Canada.* Chicago: University of Chicago Press.

Stark, E., Flitcraft, A., Zuckerman, D., Grey, A., Robison, J., & Frazier, W. (1981). *Wife abuse in the medical setting: An introduction for health personnel.* Domestic Violence Monograph Services, No. 7. Rockville, MD: National Clearinghouse on Domestic Violence.

Steffensmeier, D., & Allan, E. (1995). Criminal behavior: Gender and age. In J. Sheley (Ed.), *Criminology: A contemporary handbook* (pp. 83–114) Florence, KY: Wadsworth.

Steffensmeier, D., & Schwartz, J. (2009). Trends in girls' delinquency and the gender gap: Statistical assessment of diverse sources. In M. Zahn (Ed.), *The delinquent girl* (pp. 50–83). Philadelphia: Temple University Press.

Steffensmeier, D., Schwartz, J., Zhong, H., & Ackerman, J. (2005). An assessment of recent trends in girls' violence using diverse longitudinal sources: Is the gender gap closing? *Criminology 43*(2), 355–406.

Steffensmeier, D. J. (1980). Sex differences in patterns of adult crime, 1965–1977. *Social Forces, 58,* 1080–1108.

Steffensmeier, D. J., & Steffensmeier, R. H. (1980). Trends in female delinquency: An examination of arrest, juvenile court, self-report, and field data. *Criminology, 18,* 62–85.

Stein, B. (1996, July). Life in prison: Sexual abuse. *The Progressive*, pp. 23–24.

Stephan, J. (2008). *Census of state and federal correctional facilities.* Washington, DC: Bureau of Justice Statistics.

Straus, M. A., Gelles, R. J., & Steinmetz, S. (1980). *Behind closed doors: Violence in the American family.* Garden City, NY: Doubleday.

Street-Porter, J. (2008). Sugar and spice . . . Why have our little girls turned sour? *London's Independent,* Aug 3. London, UK. Retrieved February 10, 2011, at http://www.independent.co.uk/opinion/columnists/janet-street-porter/editorat large-sugar-and-spice-why-have-our-little-girls-turned-sour-883767.html

Streib, V. (2010). *Death penalty for female offenders, January 1, 1973, to October 31, 2010.* Ada, OH: Ohio Northern University. Retrieved at http://www.deathpenalty info.org/documents/femaledeathrow.pdf

Streib, V. (2011). *Death penalties for female offenders.* Ada, OH: Ohio Northern University.

Sutherland, E. (1978). Differential association. In B. Krisberg & J. Austin (Eds.), *Children of Ismael: Critical perspectives on juvenile justice* (pp. 128–131). Palo Alto, CA: Mayfield.

Sutherland, E., & Cressey, D. (1978). *Criminology* (10th ed.). Philadelphia: Lippincott.

Swanson, D. (2007). Sex abuse alleged at 2nd youth jail—agency denies cover-up after guard accused of luring girls with drugs. *Dallas Morning News,* March 2. Retrieved February 1, 2011, at http://www.highbeam.com/doc/1G1-159996128.html

Szerlag, H. (1996, February). Teen's death probed at YSI Iowa center. *Youth Today,* 42, 48.

Tappan, P. (1947). *Delinquent girls in court.* New York: Columbia University Press.

Task Force on Juvenile Female Offenders. (1991). *Young women in Virginia's juvenile justice system: Where do they belong?* Richmond, VA: Department of Youth and Family Services.

Taylor, C. (1990). *Dangerous society.* East Lansing: Michigan State University Press.

Taylor, C. (1993). *Girls, gangs, women and drugs.* East Lansing: Michigan State University Press.

Teilmann, K. S., & Landry, P. H., Jr. (1981). Gender bias in juvenile justice. *Journal of Research in Crime and Delinquency, 18,* 47–80.

Thorne, B. (1993). *Gender play: Girls and boys in school.* New Brunswick, NJ: Rutgers University Press.

Thrasher, F. M. (1927). *The gang.* Chicago: University of Chicago Press.

Toby, J. (1957). Social disorganization and stake in conformity: Complementary factors in predatory behavior of hoodlums. *Journal of Criminal Law, Criminology and Police Science, 48,* 12–17.

Tracy, P. E., Wolfgang, M. E., & Figlio, R. M. (1985). *Delinquency careers in two birth cohorts.* Washington, DC: U.S. Department of Justice.

Truman, J. (2011). Criminal victimization, 2010. *Bureau of Justice Statistics Bulletin.* Washington DC: Bureau of Justice Statistics.

Truman, J. L., & Rand, M. R. (2010). Criminal victimization, 2009. *Bureau of Justice Statistics Bulletin.* Washington DC: Bureau of Justice Statistics.

Turnbull, S., & Hannah-Moffat, K. (2009). Under these conditions: Gender, parole and the governance of reintegration. *British Journal of Criminology 49,* 532–551.

U.S. Department of Justice, Office of Justice Programs. (1989). *Children in custody, 1975–1985.* Washington, DC: Author.

U.S. House of Representatives. (1992). *Hearings on the reauthorization of the Juvenile Justice and Delinquency Prevention Act of 1974: Hearings before the Subcommittee on Human Resources of the Committee on Education and Labor.* 102nd Congress, Serial No. 102–125. Washington, DC: Government Printing Office.

U.S. House of Representatives, Subcommittee on Human Resources of the Committee on Education and Labor. (1980). *Juvenile justice amendments of 1980.* Washington, DC: Government Printing Office.

U.S. Sentencing Commission. (2010). *2009 datafiles.* Washington, DC: Author.

U.S. Statutes at Large. Ninety-Sixth Congress, 2nd sess. (1981). *Public Law 96-509— December 1981.* Washington, DC: Government Printing Office.

Valentine Foundation and Women's Way. (1990). *A conversation about girls.* (Pamphlet). Bryn Mawr, PA: Valentine Foundation.

Van Voorhis, P. (2005). *Gender responsive assessments.* Presentation given in Honolulu, Hawaii, at the Department of Public Safety on July 11, 2005.

Van Voorhis, P., Salisbury, E., Wright, E., & Bauman, A. (2008). *Achieving accurate pictures of risk and identifying gender responsive needs: Two new assessments for women offenders.* Washington, DC: U.S. Department of Justice, National Institute of Corrections.

Vedder, C. B., & Somerville, D. B. (1970). *The delinquent girl.* Springfield, IL: Charles C Thomas.

Veysey, B. M., & Hamilton, Z. (2007). Girls will be girls: Gender differences in predictors of success for diverted youth with mental health and substance abuse disorders. *Journal of Contemporary Criminal Justice, 23,* 341–362.

Vigil, D. (1995). Barrio gangs: Street life and identity in Southern California. In M. W. Klein, C. L. Maxson, & J. Miller (Eds.), *The modern gang reader* (pp. 125–131). Los Angeles: Roxbury.

Walters, S. T., Clark, M. D., Gingerich, R., & Meltzer, M. L. (2007). *A guide for probation and parole: Motivating offenders to change.* Washington, DC: U.S. Department of Justice, Office of Justice Programs, National Institute of Corrections.

Watson, T. (1992, November 16). Ga. indictments charge abuse of female inmates. *USA Today,* pp. A3.

Webb, Jim. (March, 2009). Why we must fix our prisons. *Parade Magazine.* http://www.parade.com/news/2009/03/why-we-must-fix-our-prisons.html

Weis, J. G. (1976). Liberation and crime: The invention of the new female criminal. *Crime and Social Justice, 6,* 17.

Weithorn, L. A. (1988). Mental hospitalization of troublesome youth: An analysis of skyrocketing admission rates. *Stanford Law Review, 40,* 773–838.

Weller, R. (1996, July 11). Teens returned to parents after claiming abuse by camp counselors. *Associated Press,* pp. 1–2.

Wells-Parker, E., Pang, M. G., Anderson, B. J., McMillen, D. L., & Miller, D. I. (1991). Female DUI offenders. *Journal of Studies in Alcohol, 52,* 142–147.

West, H. C. (2010). *Prison inmates at mid-year—statistical tables.* Washington, DC: Bureau of Justice Statistics, U.S. Department of Justice. NCJ 230113.

West, H. C., & Sabol, S. J. (2010). *Prisoners in 2009.* Washington, DC: Bureau of Justice Statistics, U.S. Department of Justice.

White, B. (2003). American Civil Liberties Union report on the Hawaii Youth Correctional Facility. Retrieved from http://www.acluhawaii.org/pages/news/030826youth correction.html

Widom, C. S. (1988). *Child abuse, neglect, and violent criminal behavior.* Unpublished manuscript.

Widom, C. S. (2000). Childhood victimization and the derailment of girls and women to the criminal justice system. In B. Richie, K. Tsenin, & C. Widom (Eds.), *Research on women and girls in the criminal justice system* (pp. 27–36). Washington, DC: National Institute of Justice.

Widom, C. S., & Kuhns, J. B. (1996). Childhood victimization and subsequent risk for promiscuity, prostitution, and teenage pregnancy: A prospective study. *American Journal of Public Health, 86,* 1607–1610.

Williams, K., Curry, G. D., & Cohen, M. I. (2002). Gang prevention programs for female adolescents: An evaluation. In W. L. Reed & S. H. Decker (Eds.), *Responding to gangs: Evaluation and research* (pp. 225–263). Washington, DC: U. S. Department of Justice, National Institute of Justice.

Wilson, H. W., & Widom, C. S. (2010). The role of youth problem behaviors in the path from child abuse and neglect to prostitution: A prospective examination. *Journal of Research on Adolescence, 20,* 210–236.

Wilt, S., & Olson, S. (1996). Prevalence of domestic violence in the United States. *Journal of the American Medical Women's Association, 51*(3), 77–83.

Winick, C., & Kinsie, P. M. (1971). *The lively commerce: Prostitution in the United States.* New York: New American Library.

Wolf, N. (1993). *Fire with fire.* New York: Random House.

Young, M., & Gainsborough, J. (2000). *Prosecuting juveniles in adult court.* Washington, DC: The Sentencing Project.

Youth Risk Behavior Surveillance System (YRBSS). (2010). *The 2009 youth risk behavior survey summary and results.* Atlanta, GA: Centers for Disease Control. Available online at www.cdc.gov.

Zahn, M. (2009). *The delinquent girl.* Philadelphia: Temple University Press.

Zahn, M., Hawkins, S., Chiancone, J., & Whitworth, A. (2008). *Girls study group— Charting the way to delinquency prevention for girls.* Washington, DC: Office of Juvenile Justice and Delinquency Prevention.

Zatz, M. S. (1985). Los Cholos: Legal processing of Chicano gang members. *Social Problems, 33,* 13–30.

Zietz, D. (1981). *Women who embezzle or defraud: A study of convicted felons.* New York: Praeger.

INDEX

ABOUT THE AUTHORS

Meda Chesney-Lind, Ph.D., is Professor of Women's Studies at the University of Hawaii at Manoa. Nationally recognized for her work on women and crime, and the author of seven books, she has just finished two books on trends in girls' violence titled *Beyond Bad Girls: Gender, Violence and Hype,* written with Katherine Irwin, and *Fighting for Girls,* co-edited with Nikki Jones. *Fighting for Girls* recently won an award from the National Council on Crime and Delinquency for "focusing America's attention on the complex problems of the criminal and juvenile justice systems." She received the Bruce Smith, Sr. Award "for outstanding contributions to Criminal Justice" from the Academy of Criminal Justice Sciences in April 2001. She was named a fellow of the American Society of Criminology in 1996 and has also received the Herbert Block Award for service to the society and the profession from the American Society of Criminology. She has also received the Donald Cressey Award from the National Council on Crime and Delinquency for "outstanding contributions to the field of criminology," the Founders Award of the Western Society of Criminology for "significant improvement of the quality of justice," and the University of Hawaii Board of Regents' Medal for Excellence in Research.

Finally, Chesney-Lind has recently joined a group studying trends in youth gangs organized by the National Institute of Justice, and she was among the scholars working with the Office of Juvenile Justice and Delinquency Prevention's Girls Study Group. In Hawaii, she has worked with the Family Court, First Circuit, advising them on the recently formed Girls Court as well as helping improve the situation of girls in detention with the recent JDAI initiative.

Lisa Pasko, Ph.D., is Assistant Professor in the Department of Sociology and Criminology at the University of Denver. She received her Ph.D. from the University of Hawaii at Manoa, and her primary research and teaching interests include criminology, the female offender, delinquency and the juvenile justice system, sexualities, and punishment. Her dissertation examined juvenile delinquency and justice in Hawaii, with particular attention on the differential impacts institutional policies and decision making have on boys and girls. She recently finished a Colorado Division of Criminal Justice–funded grant titled "In and Out of the System: Understanding and Addressing the Female Juvenile Offender in Colorado." Dr. Pasko's latest research examines correctional attitudes about girls, their sexual behavior, reproductive decision making, and sexual identity issues. As a public sociologist, she is also a board member for the Colorado Coalition for Girls and is performing an ongoing evaluation of InterCept, a girl offender intervention program in Colorado Springs, Colorado. In addition to being co-author of *The Female Offender,* she has also authored several articles, book chapters, and technical reports that focus on girls' experiences inside and outside the correctional system.